❦ MY ❦
INDIANA

MY INDIANA

by Irving Leibowitz

PRENTICE-HALL, INC.
Englewood Cliffs, N.J.

My Indiana, by Irving Leibowitz

© 1964 by Prentice-Hall, Inc.
Library of Congress Catalog Card Number: 63–18598.
T–60848

PRENTICE-HALL INTERNATIONAL, INC., *London*
PRENTICE-HALL OF AUSTRALIA, PTY., LTD., *Sydney*
PRENTICE-HALL OF CANADA, LTD., *Toronto*
PRENTICE-HALL FRANCE, S.A.R.L., *Paris*
PRENTICE-HALL OF INDIA (PRIVATE) LTD., *New Delhi*
PRENTICE-HALL OF JAPAN, INC., *Tokyo*
PRENTICE-HALL DE MEXICO, S.A., *Mexico City*

Printed in the United States of America

This book is dedicated with affection to Asa J. Smith, the gentleman from Indiana at his best.

Asa was born in Wabash, Indiana, on January 20, 1894. His father, a doctor, was a Methodist. His mother was a Quaker.

In 1915, he was graduated from DePauw University and, in 1917, from the Indiana University Law School.

Asa was a conservative Republican, a lawyer, a writer, a politician, a historian and one of the proudest members of the United States Marine Corps, in which he was a private during World War I and a lieutenant colonel in World War II.

—He was secretary to United States Senator Harry S. New, 1919–1921.

—He was a member of the Indiana House of Representatives, 1923.

—He was United States Commissioner for Southern Indiana, 1947–1950.

—He was chief deputy prosecutor of Marion County, 1954–1958.

—He was the one who obtained Madge Oberholtzer's dying declaration that helped convict Ku Klux Klan grand dragon D. C. Stephenson.

—He was the principal trial deputy, under Prosecutor John Tinder, who helped expose the state highway scandals and helped convict powerful politicians in his own party.

Asa fought the good fight.

BACK HOME AGAIN
IN INDIANA

*I am convinced the old call is still here; and when
I return I have a feeling that out here on the farms,
driving the cows in the morning and at evening, in
the small towns and hanging around the old water-
gaps along the creeks, are boys just like we used to
be, to whom the most vital thing in life is this call
and longing—to be free.*

—THEODORE DREISER

EVANSVILLE, OCT. 19 (UPI) An Indiana University professor charged today that Hoosiers are so interested in sports, politics and social affairs, local recognition and materialistic success
that they generally fail to become national leaders.

Stephen S. Visher, professor emeritus of geography, told the
Indiana Academy of Science, that Indiana has failed to produce
its share of the national leaders due to apathy among Hoosiers
toward scholarly achievement.

Visher said there have been no Indiana natives to become
President of the United States and none to become president of
leading scientific or legal groups.

"Many of our more capable people have left the state," he
said.

Visher said there is an "excessive interest in sports, politics
and social affairs.

"What counts most with most Hoosiers is local recognition or materialistic success," he said.

This book is not an exposé. It is an interpretation. Indiana has been deplored and denounced, diagnosed and dissected, described and deified. But not understood.

Indiana is a state where flag-waving patriotism is a way of life—where every day is the Fourth of July. And it is a state where many of the people honestly and sincerely regard the federal government in Washington—whether under President John F. Kennedy or President Dwight D. Eisenhower—as not to be trusted.

You write a book not necessarily to entertain or inform, but mainly because you can't help it. This is my Indiana.

Indiana is cynical precinct politics and exciting high school basketball, the Ku Klux Klan and the easygoing, good life of James Whitcomb Riley and Booth Tarkington, Bill Vukovich roaring around the oval track at the Speedway and farmers hanging around the town square on Saturday, and a dash of Gene Debs' socialism.

I came from the sidewalks of New York City. Where do I come off writing a book about Indiana? I have *chutzpah*. It is almost impossible to translate *chutzpah* from Yiddish to English. It means more than gall, more than brass. For example, if a boy murdered his mother and father and then threw himself on the mercy of the court because he was an orphan, it could be said he had *chutzpah*.

Outside of *chutzpah*, I have no extraordinary qualifications or credentials to make me an authority on Indiana. As a newspaperman, I have had a front row seat (and an inside look). I sang with Bill Jenner, trudged through Brown County woods, followed Henry Schricker's white hat on the campaign trail, crossed pens with publisher Eugene Pulliam, recharged my intellectual batteries on the Indiana University campus, fought the John Birch Society (which got its start in Indianapolis), boozed with Jep Cadou, Sr., dean of

Indiana newspapermen, and fell in love with the whole state.

I have taken an irreverent delight in covering my beat, which extends from Lake Michigan to the Ohio River.

When I was dispatched to cover a football game at South Bend, I wrote this precede on my story: "In the interest of fairness and objectivity, *The Times* has assigned to cover the Notre Dame–Southern Methodist game Irving Leibowitz."

Republican Homer Capehart was a good vote-getter, but for eighteen years he also had phenomenal luck in defeating the best-known politicians the Democrats would run against him. Capehart's luck became a joke even to seasoned politicians. "Capehart is so lucky," I once wrote, "that if motherhood was the issue, he would get pregnant."

The first time I covered the State Legislature in 1949 gave me some insight into the Southern flavor of Indiana, particularly in the rural areas. This General Assembly distinguished itself by ending segregation in public schools and with an assortment of lesser bills, including one which would require farmers to keep their goats fenced in. When the session was over, I asked one of the powerful rural lawmakers what he thought were the accomplishments of the Legislature. He replied, "We penned up the goats and let out the niggers."

His Holiness, Pope John XXIII, was elected shortly after the alumni of Notre Dame had publicly and privately complained about the poor coaching record of Terry Brennan, which culminated in his dismissal just before Christmas. "There is no truth to the report," I wrote, "that the Notre Dame alumni association has given Pope John one year to make good."

In some ways, Indiana is no different than other states. Griff Niblack of the *Indianapolis News* told the story of an Indiana high school boy who went with a tour group to Washington, visited the Lincoln Memorial, climbed the Washington Monument, saw Congress in session and drank in an array of historic sights. When he was asked by his mother what he enjoyed most, he answered, "The pillow fights."

This is my Indiana, and my people. Here are the big cities and tiny towns, the farms and forests, the mills and mines. Best of all, here are the Hoosiers, the good and the bad, the kind and the wicked—a special kind of people, rich in humor and proud of their home country.

A Hoosier may forsake his state, but he remains a Hoosier to the day he dies—and never ceases to brag about it.

What are their traditions, biological stock, environments? How do they make a living, govern themselves, handle the problems of power, prestige and politics? How do they work, play and educate children?

What makes Hoosiers different?

CONTENTS

❧ MY ❧

INDIANA

one

BILL JENNER:
SYMBOL OF INDIANA

I am happy to return to the life of a private citizen. No people anywhere in our country care more for home and family, for private life and our local communities than the people of Indiana. We have something of the feeling that our local communities are the hub of the universe, which was so strong among Americans in colonial and pioneer days.
—BILL JENNER (farewell speech in Senate, August 21, 1958)

How CAN Indiana produce a Wendell Willkie and a Gene Debs and then elect to the United States Senate a William E. Jenner?

Willkie and Debs lit up the skies everywhere and warmed men's hearts. But Jenner was Indiana's shooting star. No one ever represented the thinking and feeling and heart of Hoosierland with more fidelity than Bill Jenner. He is arrogantly proud of his state, suspicious of strangers and fearful of new ideas. This provincial and patriotic attitude—"more Hoosier than thou," Robert Benchley once said—is patently peculiar to Hoosierland.

"We want Willkie! We want Willkie!" the Willkie cult chanted in 1940 at the Republican national convention in Philadelphia. "One World," he preached. Before Dwight D. Eisenhower ever cast his first ballot, before he even knew he was a Republican, Willkie had reshaped the image of the Republican Party from isolationist to internationalist. He took the Grand Old Party down the middle of the road, for which his fellow Hoosier Republicans never forgave him.

"Debs! Debs! Debs!" the immigrant railroaders and coal-miners used to cry. Eugene Victor Debs battled and went to jail for them. In the 1890's, he was the social conscience of the nation. He wrote: "While there is a lower class I am in it; While there is a criminal element I am of it; While there is a soul in prison I am not free." He was a Socialist.

People everywhere, except Indiana, showered affection, love and respect on Willkie and Debs. The overwhelming majority of Hoosiers was opposed to their policies and principles. Willkie and Debs never represented Indiana. But Bill Jenner did.

William Ezra Jenner was—and is—pure Indiana. To understand the state, it is worth taking a longer, more careful look at him.

Why pick Jenner, who no longer is in the United States Senate? Why not Congressman Charles Halleck, who was President Eisenhower's good right arm on Capitol Hill?

Halleck's dalliance with Eastern Republicans takes him out of the typical Indiana class. Jenner is the Indiana symbol. And what a symbol! He pounds the desk. He cusses. He dramatizes. He shouts. He whispers. He can be warm and gregarious. He can be ice cold. He can turn his emotions on and off.

Jenner has been described variously as a southern Indiana hillbilly, a demagogue, a wild and woolly vigilante, a witch-hunter, a grand inquisitor and a fascist firebrand.

His political associates picture him as one of the last of the great patriots, a courageous and militant battler for

American sovereignty, the preservation of the U.S. Constitution and the uprooting of the Soviet fifth column.

He is both loved and hated as passionately as if he were still in the United States Senate, which he voluntarily quit to come back home to Indiana to raise his only son, Billy, as a Hoosier. What makes Jenner tick would make an engrossing study for any psychiatrist, writer or student of political history.

It is a standing joke that when traveling he carries more medicine in his suitcase than clothes. He is an incurable hypochondriac. His wife Janet simply cannot get sick because once she does, he gets the same thing—"only worse." Janet tells friends the only time she was able to "suffer alone and in peace" was when she gave birth to Billy.

"Bill didn't know how to cope with that," she says.

When you question Jenner about this he shrugs his shoulders and says, "It runs in the family. I used to hear my daddy and mom complain from the minute they got up in the morning."

According to his Indiana friends, Jenner is loyal, extremely thoughtful, kind and generous. According to his enemies, Jenner is a "hater."

Lisle Wallace, grain merchant of Sheridan, Indiana, and an old political pro who once managed Robert A. Taft's campaign for President in Indiana, puts it this way: "If you're his friend, Jenner'll lead you through hell. If you're his enemy, he'll push you through hell."

Hugh Gray, fishing pal, confidant and adviser to Jenner, says, "Bill never forgets a friend—or an enemy."

At Republican rallies, receptions, parties and conventions, Jenner once was the undisputed king of applause. Today, though no longer in public life, he still gets a bigger ovation from Indiana Republicans than any politician, except Senator Barry Goldwater, champion of the right wing.

In 1956, at the Republican state convention in Indianapolis, Jenner's bitter factional foe was Governor George N.

Craig. The Craig machine had charge of decorations, bunting and seating. Huge, blown-up pictures of President Eisenhower, Governor Craig and Senator Capehart looked down on delegates in the State Fairgrounds Coliseum, but there was not one single poster of Senator Jenner.

Yet, when Jenner's chum and protégé Harold Handley won the nomination for Governor and the balloting was over, the delegates, weary and tired from an exciting full day of voting in hot and humid weather, whooped and hollered, "We want Jenner!"

Flushed with victory after four years of bickering with Governor Craig, Jenner marched dramatically from his inconspicuous box to the rostrum, his face wreathed in one big crease of a smile.

"This," he said, "is the end of a perfect day." The ovation that followed was one of the most exciting, and sentimental, in the long and turbulent history of Indiana's political conventions.

How does Jenner react to such adulation?

He eats it up. This is when the "ham" in him comes out. He's liable to embrace, hug or kiss the nearest person. He'll throw both hands up into the air over his head in the shape of a giant "V" and shout, "God love you."

In 1952, when Eisenhower was campaigning in Indianapolis, he stood on the same platform with Jenner in the Butler University fieldhouse. They received a tumultuous reception. Tom Stokes and other Washington correspondents were aghast, they said, at the undisguised act of Senator Jenner clasping Eisenhower's hand high in the air in the traditional political salute. Some of the newspapermen wrote about "the ugly display" of coattail riding by Jenner. Jenner says the newspaper photographers in front were pleading and yelling, "Hold up his hand, Jenner."

What Stokes and the others couldn't understand apparently was that Jenner was doing what comes naturally to a politician acknowledging a warm reception. It is a wonder the effervescent Jenner didn't do cartwheels across the stage.

With the death of Senator Joseph McCarthy of Wisconsin, his close friend, Jenner automatically inherited some of McCarthy's pals and all of his enemies.

In one important respect Jenner differed from McCarthy. All the time McCarthy was probing Communists, his fellow Senators rarely went along. It was usually a one-man investigation. On the other hand, every committee report on subversion submitted by Jenner, as chairman, was unanimously adopted. Jenner's subcommittee report, "Interlocking Subversion in Government," almost sold as well as the Kinsey Report in Washington and was a monumental work of spotlighting Communist influence in our own government. He named the men and women who pledged allegiance to the Soviet Union.

Even Jenner's critics took notice. The *Richmond Times-Dispatch* editorialized:

> Senator Jenner is not one of our favorite statesmen (it was he who termed the career of General George C. Marshall 'a living lie'), but it must be conceded that the report he and his Senate subcommittee have unanimously made on the subject of Interlocking Subversion in Government Departments is one of the most startling documents of the decade. . . . All in all, the Jenner subcommittee has done an effective and important piece of research.

Jenner's enemies say he is brutal. When President Eisenhower had a heart attack before his second election, a colleague asked Jenner in the Senate cloakroom what would happen to Republican chances if the President died.

"If necessary, we'll stuff him and run him and still win," Jenner said, jokingly.

To understand Bill Jenner, who comes from the hills of southern Indiana (Marengo, population 800), you've got to know him as a baby, boy, collegian and businessman.

Jenner was born July 21, 1908 to L. L. Woody and Jane McDonald Jenner in a two-room "smokehouse" shack close to the tracks of the Southern Railroad. He was a sickly infant and nearly died a couple of days later. His father was a country fellow who later ran a general store where you could buy feed, food or a Ford. It is still operated today by the oldest son, Donald (Donnie) Jenner. A third and youngest son, Loren, is in charge of a hatchery at Shelbyville.

"Bill was a little puny as a kid, but just a regular fella like the rest of the kids," says Donnie. "He got into the same trouble the other kids did."

Jenner doesn't know where he got his flair for dramatics, but he recalls that a woman he called "Auntie" back in Marengo taught him elocution lessons—"where to place the emphasis." He also remembers performing as an actor and singer in the deep Marengo Cave, a regional attraction that was illuminated by carbon lights. He received $1.50 for each ten-hour day. His specialty was singing "When I'm Big Like My Daddy" and reciting "Barefoot Boy."

Although Jenner and his Scotland-born and Indiana-reared wife, a stunning sight in taffy-colored hair, shunned the glittering social whirl when he was in the Senate, they did occasionally step out to parties and dinners with intimate friends. At one affair given by the late Senator Styles Bridges of New Hampshire, "the Marengo kid" went to town. He got out in the middle of the floor and did a classy Charleston with Ruth Montgomery, a Hoosier who is a top Washington correspondent for Hearst newspapers. When the orchestra struck up "Back Home Again in Indiana," Bill got up again and sang a solo.

Jenner's favorite relaxation is with an intimate circle of hometown friends who call themselves "the mutual admiration society." A rule of each party is that everyone present must perform at least once—sing, dance, tell a story or recite a poem. Jenner is always the center of attraction, always the star.

At Indiana University, Jenner was fascinated by politics, dramatics and singing, in about that order. He got good grades, but was considered "lazy." Once, his father paid a surprise visit to the Bloomington campus. He went to the classroom on twentieth century drama, where young Jenner was supposed to be, but Bill wasn't there. Woody Jenner finally found his son upstairs in his room at the Delta Tau Delta fraternity house—sleeping.

He threw him out of bed, hit him a couple of licks on the head, booted him on the backside and pushed him down the stairs, hollering, "You bum. You're not going to sleep when I pay money for you to go to school."

"Dad, don't embarrass me in front of all my friends," Bill pleaded.

The more young Jenner protested, the angrier his father became. "Dad was an emotional fella," Jenner recalls.

This was an occasional, but not typical happening in the Jenner household. Bill revered his father. As a youngster he sat around a potbellied stove in the Jenner general store and listened to his father, Republican chairman of Crawford County, spin tales of the Republican heroes of yesterday—men like Speaker Joe Cannon, Senator Albert J. Beveridge and Senator Sunny Jim Watson. Woody Jenner was forever teaching Bill. Just before he died in 1950 he was playing cards in a rustic cabin Bill owns with Hugh Gray on the east bank of the White River near Shoals. Woody borrowed forty dollars from his son. After the game, Bill reminded his father about the loan.

"Let that be a lesson," his father said. "Never lend money to a gambling man."

In the depths of the Depression, Jenner received his law degree and was admitted to the Indiana bar. He couldn't get a job, but his father wouldn't let him come back to work in the store.

"I sent you to college," Woody Jenner admonished him. "Don't you come back to these poor hills."

When the late Indiana Supreme Court Justice Frank Gilkison was elected a Circuit Court judge, Jenner took over his law office—two tiny rooms over a grocery store and a barbershop alongside the B & O railroad tracks in Shoals, Indiana. The rent was six dollars a month.

At about this time one farmer became so enraged with another that he shot him right between the eyes with a Spanish revolver. Jenner got the case. The colorful jury trial, involving heated accusations on both sides, provided a perfect setting for the now-famous Jenner histrionics.

Bill made a legal plea of self-defense (although eye-witnesses said the victim was driving a team of horses at the time). The principal argument advanced by barrister Jenner was that the victim was a rotten character who "needed killing." Apparently the all-farmer jury agreed. They acquitted the defendant in a matter of minutes.

The judge was furious. "This is the first time I ever heard of a legal killing," he fumed.

In 1934, in a Model A Ford that cost $125, Bill campaigned for State Senator in Lawrence, Martin and Orange counties—the craggy hill country of southern Indiana. He was elected, and has never since been defeated in a general election.

Jenner's plunge into politics didn't cause a ripple in the State Legislature in Indianapolis. At the insistence of his father, he went to see Harry Fenton for advice on how to act in the Senate. Fenton, a political genius, was secretary of the Republican Central Committee, and considered "the most conservative Republican in Indiana."

Fenton was unimpressed with Jenner. "Son, I know your type. You're another one of those young smart-aleck know-it-alls. You sit your ass down in the Senate and don't say a damn word for thirty days."

Jenner didn't open his mouth. Once he dozed off and fell out of his chair. He would have kept silent for the entire sixty-one-day session, except that one day the presiding officer in the Senate, Lieutenant Governor Clifford M. Townsend,

addressed a statewide women's meeting at the Athletic Club.
His topic was the Senate and he gave a humorous word picture of all the Senators. Jenner, he saved for last.

"I can't tell you a thing about Jenner," Townsend told
the ladies, "he's been asleep for thirty days."

The quote was printed in the Democratic newspaper the
Indiana Sentinel and widely distributed around the state.
Jenner was mortified. When he went home for the weekend
his neighbors laughed at him. "That's a helluva way to represent us, Jenner," they said. "What are we payin' ya fer, to
sleep?"

Bright and early Monday morning, Jenner was waiting
for Fenton to come to work at Republican headquarters. He
was blazing. When Fenton entered, Jenner threw a copy of
the *Indiana Sentinel* at him and cried, "That's what I get
for listening to you. You made a buffoon out of me."

Fenton calmed him down. "I hear you make a pretty
fair country speech," he said. "Don't do it today or tomorrow,
but you wait for a good opportunity and take the floor on a
point of personal privilege and then you let 'er rip."

Jenner didn't have long to wait. Jacob Weiss, the Democratic Senate leader, wasn't content to have one of his bills
pass. He picked it up, waved it while he turned to the galleries and pompously boasted, "This is just another promise
of the Democratic platform being fulfilled for the people."

Jenner was on his feet. "Mr. President! Mr. President!"
he screamed.

Lieutenant Governor Townsend couldn't believe his
eyes. Finally he said, "The chair recognizes the wide-awake
Senator from Orange, Martin and Lawrence counties."

Jenner poured it on. All his pent-up rage and humilia-
tion came flooding out in a torrent of abuse at the Democrats.
He blasted them for what they promised and what they
delivered. Today, Jenner still calls it the best speech he
ever made. It was widely reported. From that emotional out-

burst on, Jenner was marked for greater service by the Republican high command. Fenton, who lost his own son, practically adopted him.

In 1937 and 1939, Jenner served as Republican minority leader of the State Senate. In 1941, when the Republicans captured control of the State Senate, he was elected President Pro Tempore.

After the outbreak of World War II, Jenner resigned from the State Senate and volunteered for the Army Air Force. While still overseas, he was nominated and then elected to the United States Senate to serve the unexpired term of the late Senator Frederick Van Nuys.

In later campaigns, Jenner was an indefatigable worker. Like his Senatorial colleague, Homer Capehart, Jenner would do most anything to attract a crowd—sing, dance, act or ride an elephant down Main Street, as he once did in Danville, Indiana. Even his most bitter factional foes concede he is one of the shrewdest strategists in a convention or a general election. He is a team player who places loyalty and discipline above other traits.

"He likes to carry the ball," a close friend said. "But he'll carry the water, too. The important thing to Bill is that he wins."

Jenner came up in politics when the Ku Klux Klan influence was dying. Nevertheless, political foes have accused him of sympathy with the Klan or friendship with men who were Kluxers. There is no question that Jenner knew politicians who were Kluxers. There was scarcely a figure in the Republican Party who wasn't in the Klan in the 1920's.

Jenner went to the funeral of Robert Lyons, onetime Klan treasurer. He sat in the front row, deliberately. He said he wouldn't turn his back on a friend. (Lyons had engineered the maneuver to make Jenner the Senator for the unexpired term of Van Nuys.)

Jenner was a boy when the Klan was in its heyday. He was growing up at a time when the Indiana Klan was not alone in making righteous war on Bolsheviks, Catholics, Jews, Negroes, pacifists, evolutionists, foreigners and others considered "immoral." It was the Hoosier way. Although thousands of Poles, Hungarians, Italians and Czechs had come to work in the steel mills and coal fields, Catholics, Jews and foreigners were oddities in many parts of Indiana.

The isolation and boredom of small towns made them fertile ground for suspicion and bigotry. Jenner was exposed to all the traditions of intolerance.

He rang the rafters with blood-and-thunder political speeches in the Billy Sunday style. He damned the Bolsheviks. In Congress, opposing the Marshall Plan, he cried that we were pouring American money down the rat holes of Europe. He "wrapped" himself in the American flag and charged that mysterious people in high places were undermining and subverting the country.

All the time, Jenner was saying out loud what the people were whispering in the hills of southern Indiana—in Marengo, Paoli and Shoals. Jenner said it with tears streaming down his face, with his voice breaking. He said it with indignation and ridicule. He said it with thunder in his voice and lightning in his eyes. He peppered his words with earthy and colorful (sometimes purple) prose.

I used to wonder how he managed to work himself up, to make himself angry enough to bring real tears. He told me, "I always build a straw man and then I tear hell out of him."

This is not to evaluate whether Jenner was right or wrong. Later historians will do that. Jenner was earnest, sincere and believed in what he was doing. What he said was pure Hoosier. He is more a "made in Indiana" product than the Indiana limestone that is blasted out of the rock quarries of Bedford, his present hometown.

But whatever his prejudices, Jenner is no Kluxer, no bigot.

When Indiana high schools would not allow Negro

schools to participate in the state basketball tournament, Jenner helped push through the State Senate a bill opening the tourney to all public and parochial schools, regardless of race or religion. State Senator Robert Lee Brokenburr, son of a slave, who rose to become an alternate delegate to the United Nations, is one of the most respected Negro civic leaders in Indiana. He credits Jenner with helping to break down the Jim Crow barriers in Indiana sports.

Nor can any politician in Indiana forget the tremendous battle Jenner waged and won, over the powerful protest of publisher-politician Eugene Pulliam, to get Cale J. Holder, a Catholic, appointed a federal judge.

It seems to me that Jenner always was trying to prove, to himself and the world, that what he stands for represents a real and permanent value. He doesn't believe, as former Defense Secretary Charles Wilson was quoted as saying, that what is good for General Motors is necessarily good for the United States. Jenner has his own yardstick on complicated foreign and domestic policy: "Is it good for Billy?"

Jenner believes that if it is good for his only child, William Edward, it will be good for the millions of other Billys in America.

Just where does Jenner stand politically today? He is about as far to the right as you can get and still stay inside the Republican Party. Jenner summed up his political feelings in his farewell message to the Senate:

> You know how it (the Republican Party) was taken over by Paul Hoffman and his kind, the modern Republicans, and the men in the shadows behind them. . . . You know how the Democratic Party was transformed from a party accepting Franklin Roosevelt's temporary reforms, but still committed to the Constitution, into a party managed by Harry Hopkins, Dean Acheson, Walter Reuther and the men in the shadows behind them.
>
> . . . a government with too much money to spend destroys the society it governs, in two ways. A spending govern-

ment corrupts the weak with the current equivalent of bread and circuses. Today we call them Federal aid and summit conferences. More important, a spending program must destroy the strong.

I say the American people are being pushed in the direction of catastrophic inflation by wild-eyed Socialists, ambitious intellectuals, power-seeking demagogues and hidden Communists.

Some of Bill Jenner's best friends, as the saying goes, are Democrats—conservative Southern Democrats who share his philosophic views. Jenner is flattered by right-wingers who want to run him for President on extreme third-party platforms. He has shied away from all splinter parties. His intuitive political sense tells him that they do not have the broad base to succeed.

From time to time, Jenner has been on intimate terms— politically and socially—with Richard Nixon. Yet, when John F. Kennedy defeated Nixon for the Presidency by an eyelash, Jenner said privately, "The only difference between Kennedy and Nixon is that it would take Nixon eight years to take us down the same road to socialism that it takes Kennedy four years to do. Nothing can stop us now. Jumpin' Jez-sus H. Christ, we're headed for socialism."

Jenner evaluates Nixon as "an astute politician, no better or no worse than the average politician . . . an opportunist with no courage."

About Goldwater, Jenner says, "I'd rather see him President than any other man I know." President Eisenhower never was an idol to Jenner.

"He (Eisenhower) had the greatest opportunity to reverse the trend of government spending and utterly failed," Jenner says. "Ike was popular, but he could never transfer his popularity to the party. He left his party in a weakened position. He didn't understand politics. He didn't care about politics and he didn't work for the party. He was made by Wall Street and the international bankers."

Jenner, now out of politics (for good, he says), speaks
darkly of the future. He doesn't think there is a man in the
Republican or the Democratic parties who can save the country today.

"We're broke," Jenner says. "We're bankrupt. There's
no stopping. No reversing now. You could have Jesus Christ
himself as President and you couldn't change it. Ever since
(Franklin D.) Roosevelt, we've been accelerating toward centralization of government, one world, socialism.

"It won't be men who'll change it. It'll take a calamity,
a disaster, fiscal collapse, something worse than the Hoover
Depression. They talk about Social Security. How much
Social Security will you have after a fiscal collapse? Out of
the ashes of ruin, a man might come along who would help
us. If we're lucky, it'll be a man like Goldwater. It could be
a man like Walter Reuther. What would we do then?"

It is uncertain at this point whether Jenner ever will
make a comeback in Indiana politics. He is well established
in a profitable law office and has little regard for the Hoosiers
running the Republican Party today. The feeling is mutual.
Yet there are some Republicans who are concerned that in a
normally Republican state, in 1963, Indiana had a Democratic Governor (Matthew Welsh) and two Democratic Senators (Vance Hartke and Birch Bayh.)

"At this stage of the game," said former Republican
State Chairman Robert Matthews, "the Republican Party
needs Bill Jenner more than he needs it."

There are those who contend that Democrat Henry F.
Schricker, and not Bill Jenner, is the real symbol of Indiana.
It is possible that the quiet and soft-spoken Schricker might
be the "gentleman from Indiana" at his best.

He doesn't arouse strong emotions in anybody's breast,
as Jenner does. Hoosiers either admire Jenner or hate him.
They generally like Schricker.

A Democrat close to Governor Welsh insisted that I was

wrong in picking Jenner over Schricker as the Indiana symbol. He painted a convincing picture.

Schricker, he said, was "nice people, corny, basically honest and everybody knows it . . . he gives a strong feeling of standing on his own feet and doesn't want to try anything for the first time. He has a distrust of change. Hoosiers just don't get as excited and concerned about things as Jenner. They're calm, like Schricker. You get the idea that Schricker won't set the world on fire but in his own way he's pretty slick."

William Madigan, former Statehouse correspondent for the Associated Press, used to call him "Slippery Hank" because (1) it was difficult to pin him down, (2) he kept everyone guessing about where he stood and (3) he could change his mind often. The Democrats called him "The White Hat." They used his white hat as the party's emblem of purity.

Schricker was born in North Judson, Indiana, August 30, 1883. He took a home-study legal course, passed the bar, practiced law, was a small-town banker at twenty-three, and later became editor of a good weekly newspaper, the *Starke County Democrat*. He likes to remind people that his parents were poor immigrants from the old country (Germany).

Schricker plays the part of a country fellow to perfection. He probably has eaten more chicken dinners and attended more church socials and fish fries than any politician in Indiana. He is proud of membership in his hometown volunteer fire department and his work with the Boy Scouts.

He made a name for himself all over Indiana when he was State Senator and later Lieutenant Governor. "If Henry says it's good, I'm fer it," was a typical comment in the Legislature.

In Indiana, a Governor cannot succeed himself. Yet Schricker twice was honored with the highest office in the state. In 1940 his personal popularity put him into the Governorship. No other Democrat went to the Statehouse with him, as Republicans swept every other state office. In 1948, Schricker led the Democrats back into the Statehouse while President Harry S Truman lost the state.

Twice Schricker ran for U.S. Senator and lost. It is almost as if Hoosiers trusted his judgment and honesty to run the state, but wanted a much more outspoken conservative in Washington. The Republicans who defeated him for Senator were Bill Jenner and Homer Capehart.

The interesting dilemma over which is the Indiana symbol, Jenner or Schricker, is that both men are basically conservative.

An Eisenhower Republican who has had political run-ins with both Schricker and Jenner summed up the argument this way: "We all like to think of Schricker as the Indiana symbol, but Jenner really is."

two

THE CITIES

Indiana is a state of towns and not a state of cities.

—IRVIN S. COBB

TERRE HAUTE (population 72,500) is a town that never really grew up. It just got old and dirty. The *Saturday Evening Post* called it "Indiana's Delinquent City." Indianapolis newspapers which, from time to time, have exposed its brothels and gambling joints, called it "sin town."

The city's four-time Mayor, Democrat Ralph C. Tucker, looks, acts, talks and dresses like a sporty Broadway character out of Damon Runyon. When he ran for Governor in 1952 he traveled up and down the state trying to bury the issue of Terre Haute's notorious reputation. "Ask the ministers of Terre Haute," he cried. In assessing the shellacking Republican George N. Craig dealt Tucker (with help from Dwight D. Eisenhower), one political observer suggested, "Maybe they *did* ask the ministers."

In 1904, Terre Haute was going places. It had breweries, distilleries, industries, coal to stoke the furnaces—and the Wabash River. People called Terre Haute "the Pittsburgh of the West." Its merchants clothed, fed and supplied Hoosiers in the whole Wabash Valley. (One clothing store advertised: "You won't feel sheepish in Wolf's clothing.")

In 1919, lusty Terre Haute stopped growing. Between 1920 and 1950, when other Indiana cities and towns were bursting at the seams, Terre Haute lost population. Terre Haute was the victim of (1) Prohibition, which shut down its breweries and distilleries, (2) bitter and intense strikes in the coal mines, which crippled production and left lasting wounds between management and labor and (3) lack of municipal and civic leadership.

Something good in the way of plans to uplift the city has been offered the taxpayers on many occasions since the city went into decline after World War I. As one merchant said, "The people just don't care."

As a result, the Wabash still overflows its banks and floods parts of the town. Prostitution and gambling operate today. In 1960, U.S. Treasury agents raided a gambling center in Terre Haute, untouched by local cops, which had been raking in bets from as far away as Canada, Texas, New York and Las Vegas. Industry still thinks twice about locating in town, although there has been some small spurt in new business. Except for a few new store fronts, downtown Terre Haute still looks like a Hollywood set for a horror film—depressing.

Disaster struck hard at Terre Haute in 1963. An explosion at the Home Packing Company on January 13 killed seventeen and injured more than fifty persons. Within a month, two more mysterious explosions injured others and caused considerable damage. Firemen pointed suspicious fingers at leaking gas. Hardly over the shock, townspeople were sarcastically muttering, "Boomtown, U.S.A.," when a downtown fire March 20 destroyed six buildings and damaged others on Wabash Avenue, between Sixth and Seventh streets. Out of the devastation, it is said, could come the physical, if not spiritual, reawakening of Terre Haute.

The town's leading citizen, who gets the credit or the blame for everything that goes on in Terre Haute, is Anton

The riverboat *John W. Hubbard* as it steams down the Ohio River on Indiana-Kentucky border.

Downtown Indianapolis 1857.

Downtown Indianapolis today.

(Tony) Hulman, Jr. Tony and his family own the biggest chunk of downtown. In addition, the Hulman family owns or controls: two newspapers (the morning *Star* and evening *Tribune*, which report the news but offer little leadership), the only TV station, the Terre Haute House, a leading hotel; Clabber Girl baking powder; as well as the biggest bank, the leading plumbing-supply company, a soft-drink manufacturing firm, the gas company, a truck line, the first and biggest shopping center and the largest and choicest suburban subdivision. Then there is Hulman & Co., parent company for wholesale grocers, furniture and hardware merchants.

This is the same Tony Hulman who owns and operates the Indianapolis Speedway race track, the Hulman building in Evansville, the gas company in Richmond and the Hulman building in Dayton, Ohio.

"If Tony would only pay as much attention to Terre Haute as he does the Indianapolis Speedway," one civic leader said, "this wouldn't be a half bad place to live."

Half the town, it seems, blames Hulman for not doing something for the town and the other half says he is sticking his nose into too many of Terre Haute's affairs. Tony is a shy, gentle man who recoils at controversy.

Terre Haute was the home of Eugene V. Debs, who for half a century preached the economic brotherhood of man. It also boasts of such other famous sons and daughters as sculptor Janet Scudder, novelist Theodore Dreiser (*An American Tragedy*) and his brother, songwriter Paul Dresser ("On the Banks of the Wabash").

Three institutions of higher learning are situated in or near the city: the splendid, scholarly Rose Polytechnic Institute, which distinguished itself in 1961 by not winning a football game, St. Mary-of-the-Woods for Catholic girls and state-owned Indiana State College.

Before we leave town, I should like to report that the correct pronunciation of "Terre Haute" is *Ter-ra Hote,* as in "note." Not *Ter Ho.* Not *Ter Hut.* In the *Indianapolis Star,* Joe Adams composed a weather "naute" about Terre Haute.

> *I took off for old Terre Haute*
> *With my rubbers and trusty raincaute.*
> *But the downpour of rain*
> *Made it cruelly plain*
> *What I needed was really a baute.*

MADISON (population 10,097) is the loveliest town in Indiana, calm and quiet and nestled in the green and grassy hills that circle it along the gravelly bank that sweeps down to the beautiful Ohio River.

Here, Jenny Lind, the Swedish nightingale, sang in a hog-packing house on April 11, 1851 in a concert promoted, as only he could, by P. T. Barnum, the circus impresario.

Here, tempestuous Frank Sinatra made the movie *Some Came Running* in the late 1950's (to the horror of townsfolk unaccustomed to Hollywood behavior).

Here, Captain Charles Lewis Shrewsbury, who made a fortune in river shipping and James Franklin Doughty Lanier, who made an even greater fortune in banking and railroading, had spent some $50,000 apiece to build two magnificent homes, both designed by Francis Costigan, the classical Frank Lloyd Wright of his day.

Many other fine southern-style homes were built among the elm trees along the river front, on First and Second streets, when steamboats ploughed the Ohio River and in saloons men gambled for high stakes and couples danced.

During World War II, Madison was picked by the Office of War Information as a "typical American town." Movies were made in thirty-two languages and distributed around the world to give GIs overseas a glimpse of what they were fighting for and the rest of the world a peek at a charming town.

"Where once it symbolized a rural, more parochial America," the *National Observer* reported in 1962, "it now represents with remarkable fidelity, the many small towns of America which have grown and matured since World War II."

You can bet that when a transplanted Hoosier in Chicago or New York is sobbing in his beer about "Back Home Again in Indiana," as he often does, he's not weeping for Anderson, Terre Haute, Whiting or Hammond. He's yearning for Madison, or some place like it—on a bank of the Ohio River, the Wabash River or even, let's face it, Wildcat Creek.

EVANSVILLE (population 141,543) was a dying river town in 1956 when Vance Hartke became "the boy mayor" at age thirty-six. Down at the foot of Main Street, old, empty warehouses stared through dirty windows at a deserted waterfront, and a young sheriff named Frank McDonald was learning how to foreclose mortgages on businesses and homes.

Thousands of people were out of work. Servel had shut its doors on 12,000 jobs; International Harvester had closed its branch on more thousands of jobs and Chrysler, closing its Bridge Body works and Plymouth assembly plants, had moved to a new plant in St. Louis. Things got so bad the city was forced to face up to its problems to survive. Even so, Evansville was not prepared for the shock of seeing itself as it was portrayed in an impartial survey by Fantus Factory Locating Service of Chicago.

The only thing great about Evansville, Fantus reported, was its "inferiority complex."

There was much more:

> Evansville people resent authority. Evansville people resent anyone in power, whether it be union power, government power, business power or social power. . . .
> Evansville is racked by pessimism, gloom, inability to work in unified fashion; one group stymies another simply

because of personal differences. The city as a whole is unable to accomplish anything.

An incredible thing happened. The whole town went to work on its own salvation. Sweeping across all political, business, labor, civic, religious and fraternal lines—and in stratified Evansville these lines were like the Berlin Wall—the movement found enthusiasm in just about every leader in town: editors, bankers, businessmen, labor officials, educators, industrialists, even politicians. All united under the do-good optimistic banner of "Evansville's Future, Inc." And just to keep the old feuds out of it, the organization selected as its first president the unbiased, intelligent Dr. Melvin Hyde, president of the city's respected (and only booming product) Evansville College.

Industries were lured to town. When the waterfront was cleaned up, a new motel moved there. New highways and expressways sped traffic through and around town. Shopping centers opened—and flourished. Downtown was spruced up.

Old industries expanded. Metrecal, the diet drink, is supposed to make you thin. It made its owner, Mead Johnson & Co., fat. It made the town grateful for a successful product in lean times.

Today, hardworking Evansville, tucked in the pocket of Indiana near the junction of the Ohio and Wabash rivers, is the acknowledged capital of a tri-state area rich in oil, coal, timber, cattle and agricultural wealth—southern Indiana, southern Illinois and western Kentucky.

One thing hasn't changed: politics. In Evansville, "politics" is a dirty word. It had been the custom for men of prestige and wealth to play footsie with scheming politicians in both parties for personal profit or for the advantage of all concerned. It still is not uncommon in Evansville for Democratic politicians to privately support a Republican candidate or Republican politicians to give subrosa support to a Democrat. There have even been times when the Democratic and

Republican candidates—for Mayor, sheriff and Congress—ran as much against the politicians in their own party as they did against the opposition party. The late A. Brown Ransdall, Indiana correspondent for the *Louisville Courier-Journal,* called southern Indiana's Eighth Congressional district "the bloody eighth." Evansville was, and is, its most troublesome spot.

All the evils of bipartisan politics are still present—factional strife, politics for profit, backroom deals and double deals and, as a result, putrid public service.

If you wanted anything in Evansville in the last thirty years, the man to see was banker-publisher-politician Charles B. Enlow. People who should know say no man ever became Mayor of Evansville since the Depression without getting the nod from Enlow, chairman of the National City Bank. Evansville's longtime political Republican boss, the late Ben Bartlett, took orders from Enlow, as did Democratic politicians of lesser influence.

John K. Jennings, active in Democratic affairs for nearly half a century, operated the Independent Hay and Grain Company and the Diamond Mills Feed Company in Evansville. Jennings says Enlow had complete control of the town. "You wouldn't build anything, run for sheriff, or start a business without first talking to Enlow. I don't know where he misused his power, either. Some of the men he controlled would do things, perhaps. But Enlow always did the best for Evansville."

Enlow conducted his business on the ground floor of the National City Bank. "He had no door on his office," recalls Jennings, "you could always see who was doing business with him."

Enlow came from a small town in Ohio. He started working in the National City Bank as a cashier. How did he become, in effect, boss of the town? Jennings says, "He had acumen and a knack and an interest in everything. He was a natural for a town that size."

Enlow acquired many businesses and interests in town, including the morning *Evansville Courier,* which he later made a present to his son Robert, now also president of his father's bank. Evansville has two other papers, Scripps-Howard's *Press,* edited by Gordon Hanna, and the Sunday *Courier-Press,* edited by Robert Kirkpatrick and owned jointly by Enlow interests and Scripps-Howard. All three papers have high standards and crusade in the public's interest. Newcomers are impressed also by the good schools, parks, museums, zoo, spectacular sports program, shows and even a symphony orchestra.

The foundation was laid in 1913 when the energetic Benjamin Bosse was elected Mayor of the sleepy, conservative town. L. B. Benezet, school superintendent, recalled, "Bosse mapped out his plans and headed straight for his objectives. Sometimes he cut corners and occasionally walked across the property of others. But he got there."

Big Ben Bosse's fist hammered the table and things happened. He discarded the antique horse-drawn fire engines, built a new police station, paved more streets, erected a municipal market, gave the city a fine system of public playgrounds, tennis courts and swimming pools. He bought land and fathered two gorgeous parks, Garvin and Mesker.

Bosse's greatest gift may have been the constant encouragement he gave the public schools. He appointed some of the city's most capable citizens to the school board: Enlow, Abraham Strouse, Daniel Wertz and Harold Roosa. New buildings and improved facilities were added. Plans for two new high schools were mapped. A merit system for teachers was adopted with pay increases geared to training and ability.

If Ben Bosse was Evansville's bright spot, the town also had an ugly spot. D. C. Stephenson started his Ku Klux Klan campaign of bigotry in Evansville in the 1920's from headquarters in the Vendome Hotel. The man who later made and broke mayors and governors, infiltrated the Methodist Church and controlled the State of Indiana, ran for Congress in the 1920 primary as a wet Democrat. He lost when the

Anti-Saloon League licked him. Years later he turned up in Indianapolis as a bone-dry Republican.

No good reason exists (outside of inbred apathy, crooked politics and jealousy) for Evansville to ever again be a depressed area. It has water at its front door and coal at its back door. It could be the Ruhr Valley of America. In steamboating days the roistering waterfront presented a solid array of great brick warehouses, whorehouses and saloons. Once the town tears down all of its deserted, obsolete river buildings, as planned, it will find itself with a waterfront as choice as Pittsburgh's Golden Triangle.

Despite the suspicion they have shown toward each other from time to time, Evansville labor and management have a history of working together in times of crisis.

In 1946, Frank Ford, then editor of the *Evansville Press,* wrote: "The Chamber of Commerce board has adopted a resolution commending the Central Labor Union for civic achievement. The Central Labor Union, which was made up of all AFL unions, retaliated by taking out membership in the Chamber of Commerce."

John G. Soucie, president of the Central Labor Union, started the romance when he took a quarter-page ad out in the *Chicago Journal of Commerce* and proclaimed in a banner: "We treat you right in Evansville."

FORT WAYNE (population 161,776) was, in the 1790's, wild Indian country in the path of United States expansion, blocking civilization westward. Here the Indian tribes banded together into a huge confederacy and made their stand. Settlers were captured and tortured by Indians, many of them encouraged by the English.

President George Washington sent General Josiah Harmar to plant the American flag in the wilderness and establish a U.S. trading post. The Indians outwitted, overwhelmed and defeated Harmar's army.

Washington promptly dispatched another American

army, under General Arthur St. Clair, to do what Harmar had failed to do. When this army was routed, Washington selected his master disciplinarian, General "Mad" Anthony Wayne, to clear the territory.

Even before they met in the showdown battle, the Indians learned to respect Wayne. He drilled his soldiers scientifically. He was audacious. From tribe to tribe the Indians passed their name for the new white warrior—"the chief who never sleeps."

Respect him as they did, the Indians were nonetheless prepared for General Wayne and his troops. They had built their own Maginot Line in the forest and called it Fallen Timbers. It seemed, to them, impenetrable.

Unlike previous American commanders, who went cavalry-charging after the Indians in the heavy woods, General Wayne figured the Indians had set a trap for him. Concealed behind trees, thick bushes, undergrowth and stumps, the Indians were waiting.

General Wayne ordered his cavalry to guard the flanks and dispatched his legion of 2,000 foot soldiers in two long lines in open formation with fixed bayonets. At the long roll of the drums, the legionnaires charged, yelling like demons, right into Fallen Timbers. The astonished Indians had no chance, armed only with knife and tomahawk. The well-drilled legionnaires were upon them, cutting and thrusting with bayonets and shooting them down at close range. The Indians broke and fled, chased by the cavalry. English soldiers in a nearby military post not only refused to come to the aid of the Indians, but slammed the gates shut in their faces. Indians who survived never forgave the English.

Nearby, where St. Mary's River joins St. Joseph River to form the Maumee, General Wayne established a military post which President Washington gratefully named Fort Wayne. It became an important fur-trading post and years later developed as a commercial and industrial city.

In the summer of 1940, *Life* magazine assigned Eliot

Elisofen to photograph "the best people in town." "It was a good-natured, happy bunch," Elisofen reported of the country-club set. "All of them wanted to buy me a drink." Elisofen captured them in all their carefree, pre-war gaiety: golfing early in the morning, when the first dew was off the grass; kids splashing in the pool at noontime; college boys swinging a tennis racket and girls sunning themselves. At night, under the yellow brilliance of a full Indiana moon, he photographed white-coated boys and starry-eyed girls dancing on the club's open-air dance floor. Those were the golden days in Fort Wayne.

It is a splendid city today, perhaps the most cosmopolitan in all Indiana. There are smart supper clubs, swank saloons and more places in which to eat fine food than in Indianapolis. Natives like to take out-of-towners to the Trolley Bar or Harold Van Orman's Hotel North Crest. The town boasts a symphony, literary societies and sports galore.

It is a thriving, highly diversified industrial and railroad center in the heart of a rich farm area. It makes trucks, trailers, axles, auto parts and processes farm products, notably soybeans. More than thirty bridges span the three rivers, which come together near the heart of the city. Fort Wayne is clean, proud and generous.

Perhaps because of its rich history, there is a fierce hometown pride, with surprisingly little petty civic bickering, jealousies and cliques. People care and work together. A leading Lutheran helps with the Catholic fund drive. Religious leaders get along in helpful harmony.

The traditions, customs and character of the town are firmly imbedded. John W. Dawson, writer, lawyer and civic leader, commented on Fort Wayne society in 1838:

> . . . the punctilio which had attained from long military domination had so impressed society, the politeness which the French population had infused into it; and the unaffected hospitality which early privations had made a necessity among the citizens, gave to it (Fort Wayne) not

only a high and refined tone, but a character of generosity
which made it appreciated at home as well as distinguished
abroad.

Hotelman James Keenan (Keenan Hotel) is said to be
one of the richest men in Indiana. He made his money in
real estate and in stocks of the affluent Lincoln Life Insurance Company of Fort Wayne. Keenan finds time to sit down
with Dale McMillan of Central Soya and publisher-indus-
trialist James Fleming to discuss the Wildcat Baseball League
for 4,000 kids or the symphony drive. More than likely,
they'll be joined by Walter Menzie and Ed Auer of Lincoln
Life. Executives of the two biggest industries in town, General Electric and International Harvester, pitch in, too. The
pattern of businessmen furnishing the energy and drive for
civic affairs was set many years ago by the late Charles
Busching, onetime president of Lincoln National Bank &
Trust Co. He was the biggest banker in town and the most
active civic worker.

Fort Wayne is blessed with two good and influential
newspapers, the Democratic morning *Journal-Gazette* and
the militantly Republican evening *News-Sentinel*. They both
do an alert job of keeping the town informed, alive, active
and honest. It is a surprise when a policeman is found to be
moonlighting as a burglar.

For years Wolf and Dessauer's has been one of the smartest department stores in the Midwest. But the city, despite
its fine location, did not always prosper. As recently as the
early 1950's, Fort Wayne was losing industries. In 1958 the
Chamber of Commerce made a survey of what was wrong.

Not much had been done during the war and immediately after to keep the town booming. The result: millions
were spent on bridges and roads, downtown was given a
face-cleaning and a face-lifting.

Fort Wayne people do things. In 1953, TWA carried
three planeloads of women, all under forty, from Fort

Wayne's General Electric plant to Europe. "Once the girls decided on a trip to Europe, not even the choice of mink coats would have swayed them," said a GE supervisor. The working girls saved $1,000 apiece for the trip. They carried their lunches to work, watched their pennies, made old clothes do for a little longer. TWA reports it was the largest single group to cross the Atlantic up to that time.

SOUTH BEND (population 132,445) is a manufacturing city in north-central Indiana which regards itself as a part of Michigan. The downtown business district is called "Michiana" and the state line is only five miles away.

Townspeople say "South Bend is not Notre Dame," much the same as Indianapolis citizens say the 500 Mile Race is not Indianapolis. In South Bend, they point to famous hometown names like Studebaker and Bendix. But they worship the Knute Rockne legend and live and die each Saturday when Notre Dame plays a football game.

Two men are principally responsible for the good relations between university and town. When Rockne was coach at Notre Dame, he'd wander through town to argue football strategy at the barbershop or with local merchants. Even so, there was an aloofness, for students were confined to campus except for special occasions. A warm, handsome priest by the name of John J. Cavanaugh became president of Notre Dame in the 1940's. He relaxed the restraints on students and became almost as much a part of South Bend as he was of the university.

The heart of South Bend is drab, but along the St. Joseph River it is pretty. The West Side is inhabited by people with European backgrounds—Polish, German, Hungarian, Italian, Russian and Belgian. If you live in South Bend, there's a good chance you work at Bendix or Studebaker or one of the other large industries—Oliver Corporation, South Bend Range, O'Brien Corporation, Ball Band plant of U.S. Rubber, South Bend Lathe or Sibley Machine & Foundry.

There is no slum district. South Bend is a city of clean homes and well-manicured lawns. Surprisingly, for an industrial center, it has a high moral tone. Outside of a few pinball machines, it is a clean town, with graft and corruption negligible.

Much of this cleanliness can be traced directly to the late Frederick A. Miller, who was president and editor of the *South Bend Tribune,* the only daily newspaper in town. Miller's paper usually supports Republicans, but the Democrats always get a fair shake in the news columns. Miller would hit out at corruption wherever it was. He permitted no liquor ads and his employees were not allowed to smoke cigarettes on the job. For some inexplicable reason, cigars were not banned. Paul Neville, managing editor of the *Tribune,* gave up cigarettes for cigars. Now managing editor of the *Buffalo Evening News,* Paul is back on cigarettes.

Miller was an honest and open foe of corruption and immorality, but he was no stuffed shirt. Once, at a Gridiron Show the newspapermen put on to poke fun at city and state politicians, the fastidious Miller was persuaded to slouch across the stage dressed in rags, with a cigarette dangling from his lips and a bottle of booze in his hand. He didn't say a word, but his bit part brought down the house.

Miller was proud his newspaper was one of the few in Indiana which fought the Klan. The *Tribune* is now ably handled by Harvard-educated, Miller-trained Franklin D. Shurz, who is intelligent, well-liked and attractive. He is a nephew of Mrs. Miller.

In the 1920's, despite the close proximity of the most famous Catholic university in the United States, South Bend was in the Ku Klux Klan belt. But in 1950, thanks largely to the efforts of the *Tribune* and the University of Notre Dame, it won the Brotherhood Award of the National Conference of Christians and Jews.

Miller, Father Cavanaugh and Coach Rockne had perhaps the biggest impact on the town. But one South Bend resident was a force not only in the town but in the world. He is Paul S. Hoffman, former president of Studebaker and the man who directed the Marshall Plan program, which put Europe on its feet.

Two South Bend politicians scaled the political heights to national prominence. Schuyler Colfax was Vice President of the United States under Ulysses S. Grant. Paul M. Butler, longtime national chairman of the Democratic Party, was a courageous and effective opponent of the Eisenhower Administration. He not only fought the Dixiecrats in the Democratic Party (over segregation), but he was one of the first big political names who dared denounce Senator Joseph McCarthy's Communist-hunting tactics and the only Democrat to challenge the divinity and "great white father image" of President Dwight D. Eisenhower before the Sherman Adams–Bernard Goldfine vicuña coat episode. Butler believed not only in party politics and party principles, but also in party responsibility and party morality.

South Bend has seen good and bad times. A strong union town, there was a time, in 1956, when workers voted themselves a pay cut and saved Studebaker. It is an ideal town for doctors, they say. "The climate is so terrible how can they lose? You always have sinus."

ANDERSON (population 67,449) is not as bad as its downtown looks. It's worse.

The town is a monument to indifference. Many obsolete structures, relics of a gas boom in 1887, still stand on Main Street.

William F. Hovernale of the Chamber of Commerce is proud of the new $300,000 Young Women's Christian Association building and the new $3,250,000 Community Hospital, both raised through public subscription. He might also be proud of Anderson College and General Motors' huge Delco Remy and Guide Lamp plants. Charles E. Wilson came out of the Anderson plants to become chairman of the board of GM and later served as Secretary of Defense under President Eisenhower.

The Mounds State Park, close to Anderson, is a famous landmark. But there is not much else to be proud of.

Political hacks in both parties control the city. Gamblers with police or political connections run wide open. For years a number of brothels operated one block from the police station. Good-time Charlies from Indianapolis used to park their cars near the police station (for safekeeping?) and walk to the professional whorehouses.

Anderson has its share of fine, decent citizens. It has spent $8 million on improving its churches. But it is a town without real civic leadership.

The town's two newspapers, the evening *Bulletin* and the morning *Herald,* are both printed in the same plant but are owned by different families. They share the same business, circulation and advertising offices. Both papers are careful not to offend "the right people." One is an apologist for the Republican Party and the other is Democratic with conservative leanings. Neither prints, or tries to print, the hard news of the town. Both are dull. Neither campaigns for slum clearance or downtown rehabilitation.

The gas boom hit Anderson in 1886. Within two years, thirty-seven factories sprang up, lured by the apparently inexhaustible supply of fuel. In a decade the boom was over and the city declined. This was not the first collapse for Anderson. In 1837, a year before Anderson was incorporated as a town, a branch of the Wabash and Erie Canal was proposed to extend from Logansport to Indianapolis, passing near Anderson. Settlers flocked to town. The canal was abandoned and Anderson surrendered its incorporation.

Today, with eighty-seven plants employing 27,000 people, Anderson is experiencing another industrial boom.

Workers are living in ranch-style homes in suburban developments. The town's potential is tremendous.

One of the best-known political figures to come out of Anderson was Colonel Winfield T. Durbin, who became Governor of Indiana in 1901. The town is waiting patiently for another leader.

RICHMOND (population 44,149) is called the City of Roses, because it has thirty acres of hothouses for roses in an industry which sends roses in refrigerated trucks and by air to wholesalers all over the U.S.A. But it also produces bus bodies, precision tools, phonograph records, lawn mowers, metal casket shells and automotive parts.

Situated on U.S. 40, straddling the old national road, Richmond is not a boom-or-bust town. It has a healthy diversity of industry and rich farmland. It has lovely parks and homes, some old-fashioned historic types and many ranch-style modern ones. One Mayor, Lester E. Meadows, had printed on his stationery: "Richmond the beautiful." The town had the first junior high school in America. But it doesn't boast of being progressive.

"You might call us conservative if by conservative you mean we don't go off on a new tangent with every wind that blows," is the way Richmond's Committee of 100, a group of civic boosters, explains the philosophy of the town in an illustrated pamphlet.

The town gets that way from the newspaper it reads daily, except Saturday—the *Palladium-Item,* a strong conservative journal founded in 1831. Westbrook Pegler enthused about it and exulted in print: "Rudolph Leeds, who has owned it since 1906 is so against the United Nations, he sets the name without capitals like this—united nations or u.n."

Richmond was founded by soldiers who had been with George Rogers Clark at the capture of Fort Sackville. In

1816, the year Indiana became a state, Richmond was plotted as a town. A community of Quakers soon sprang up and a large population of Friends still exists. The Friends gave the town Earlham College, a small but distinguished liberal arts school.

It was in Richmond on October 1, 1842 that Henry Clay, the Kentucky statesman, lost the Presidency of the United States to James Polk. Clay addressed a gathering of 20,000 Whigs when a number of Quakers, led by Hiram Mendenhall, challenged him by petition to free his slaves.

Clay answered by declaring that while he regarded slavery as an evil, it was "nothing in comparison with the far greater evil which would inevitably flow from a sudden and indiscriminate emancipation." He said he owned about fifty slaves, worth about $15,000, and asked his hecklers if they would be willing, should he be induced to free them, to raise $15,000 for their benefit. As a parting shot, Clay advised Mendenhall to return home and mind his own business.

The speech was widely printed and became a great issue in the hotly contested presidential election of 1844, especially in New York. Polk captured New York by 5,000 votes. If Clay had carried New York, where there was much antislavery feeling, he would have gone to the White House.

MUNCIE (population 68,603) is a town ruled by a reigning royal family, the Ball brothers. This was the conclusion of two social studies of this typical American city by sociologists from Columbia University, Dr. Robert S. Lynd and his wife Helen. Beginning in 1924, they undertook a candid appraisal of Muncie and ten years later they retraced their steps.

"They are the town," the Lynds wrote about the five Ball brothers, Frank, George, Edmund B., William and Lucius. "Nothing goes on in Muncie industrially, financially, socially, politically, educationally and philanthropically without them."

Today, the original Ball brothers are dead. The Ball family still contributes to the Ball Memorial hospital, helps with funds at Ball State Teachers College, keeps people working at various plants in towns and rules the bank. Gone, though, is the personal Ball participation on the school board, the community-fund drive and other civic affairs.

The Ball Brothers had a factory in Buffalo, New York, manufacturing fruit jars. When natural gas was discovered in Indiana in 1886, the Balls visited a dozen communities. Muncie gave the Balls free fuel, $5,000 cash and some land to locate there. Natural gas was a major factor in glassmaking, and the Midwest market for glass jars was growing. The Balls bought land and prospered.

People began talking about Muncie as the "Birmingham of the North." The newspaper crowed:

> *Tell me not in mournful numbers*
> *That the town is full of gloom*
> *For the man's a crank who slumbers*
> *In the bursting days of boom.*

The bubble burst when the gas gave out. The Balls were the first to foresee the failure of gas. They installed control valves. They built factories at new gas fields in Texas and Kansas. They established plants in Illinois and Oklahoma. They diversified—real estate, banks, a retail store, newspapers, oil, a brewery.

Although they expanded beyond Muncie they retained their heavy influence there. The Mayor, the Chamber of Commerce, the editor, the banker, the builder, the industrialist all consulted the Balls. Their influence increased most during the Depression. On the eve of the bank holiday the newspaper announced:

BALL BROTHERS GUARANTEE
SUFFICIENT CASH TO MEET
NEEDS OF 3 MUNCIE BANKS

No one who worked for the Balls was fired. Wall Street was amazed when George A. Ball, with a Cleveland man, stepped up and bought control of 23,000 miles of railroad for about the price of two first-class locomotives—$3 million. Apparently no one else had the cash or the willingness to part with it.

By the time the Depression had ended, the Balls owned considerable property and had amassed an enormous fortune. A religious, educational and charitable foundation was formed. From this foundation the Balls gave millions to Indiana University, a hospital in Muncie, Riley Memorial Hospital for children at Indianapolis, YMCA and YWCA, the Masonic Temple and the American Legion.

Today Muncie has grown too large for single-handed control, from even such a large family. Other Muncie men are on the school board, building suburbs, improving downtown, pushing the United Fund over the top, eradicating slums, trying to persuade new industry to locate in town. Typical of the new breed is William Craig, part owner of WLBC-TV and radio and former president of the Chamber of Commerce.

More and more, though, the imported plant managers are running things in town. With the giant subsidiaries and factories came the AFL and the CIO. (Not too many years ago, Muncie plants had signs posted at entrances: "No Union Men Wanted.") Today union men are participating more, but are still without real influence in the community.

A newspaperman who grew up in Muncie and loves the people there, complains that the town looks shabby. There are some new store fronts, but no new buildings downtown. Few towns in Indiana attracted as many prostitutes and criminals as Muncie in its boom days. Many are gone, but some stayed and settled down. A stranger (or sociologist) can still find a place to gamble or get a girl if he looks hard enough.

Muncie's two newspapers, the morning *Star* and evening

Press, are controlled by Eugene C. Pulliam, publisher of the *Indianapolis Star* and *News.*

When the Lynds finished their second study of Muncie, they reported it was no longer "the typical American city," because it is becoming a college town. The influence of Ball State Teachers College over Muncie is greater than ever now.

LAFAYETTE (population 42,330) cost its founder, William Digby, $1.25 an acre in 1824, and he thought he was cheated. He sold the whole works, except for a landing dock, one year later for $240.

Today Lafayette is the home of the largest technological university in the world, Purdue; the largest aluminum extrusion mill in the world, Alcoa, and the largest manufacturer of homes in the world, National Homes.

An innocent traveler from a metropolis who thinks Lafayette is a stick-in-the-mud city industrially and culturally will get some surprises. Industry is diversified, healthy and well-balanced. The town produces auto gears, tools, sponge-rubber products, safes and locks, electrical appliances, machinery, food, feed and heating equipment. Each year Purdue brings to the campus twenty outstanding professional groups and individuals, for meetings which are open to the public. In 1962, for example, the series included the Berlin Philharmonic Orchestra, Broadway productions of *The Music Man* and *The Miracle Worker,* the San Francisco Ballet and lecturer William L. Shirer, author of the monumental *The Rise and Fall of the Third Reich.*

There is charm in Lafayette that doesn't escape the metropolitan visitor, or the big-industry recruiter hunting gems among the graduating seniors. Gone are the long commuting hours and the big-city tensions.

Lafayette is surrounded by rolling, lush hills and fertile valleys along the banks of the Wabash River, sixty miles northwest of Indianapolis and 125 miles southeast of Chicago. Within a few hours you can drive to the 500 Mile Race in Indianapolis, the Kentucky Derby in Louisville or pro football and major-league baseball games in Chicago.

Lafayette has a distinguished past, which thankfully it isn't living in. The Battle of Tippecanoe was fought seven miles north of the city on November 7, 1811. General William Henry Harrison and his small army decisively defeated the Wabash Indian tribes under the leadership of The Prophet, brother of Tecumseh.

Biggest news out of the town since Digby named it in honor of the French General Marquis de Lafayette was the immense and immediate success of the prefabricated homes produced by brothers James and George Price in 1940.

Overenthusiastic natives may tell you the first U.S. airmail started in Lafayette on August 17, 1859 when Professor John Wise took a mailbag aloft in his balloon Jupiter. The truth is the balloon, which was destined for New York City 800 miles away, landed at Crawfordsville, twenty-seven miles south of the city in the wrong direction. The mail, which included twenty-three circulars and 113 letters, finally reached New York City—by train.

By far the town's most colorful character is Roger Branigin, an eminently successful attorney, poet, wit, philanthropist and politician. Since World War II, there hasn't been an election when he hasn't been prominently mentioned for Governor or Senator on the Democratic ticket. One of his pals and boosters, Frank McHale, watched him flounder twice while the nomination for Governor went to other men. McHale, an old pro, shakes his head sadly when he thinks of the erudite Branigin's gracious manners and highly polished literary speeches: "You'd think he was running for president of the Bar Association."

One of the promising newcomers in town is the publisher of the once rigidly conservative *Lafayette Journal and Courier,* John A. (Jack) Scott, former mayor of South Bend. An Eisenhower Republican in the heart of Taftland, Scott could be the biggest force for moderation among Republicans in Indiana. He is articulate, attractive, active and anxious, and would make a splendid Governor. Because of the paper's influence, being the only major daily in a large area, Scott is bound to have an important voice in political, social and civic affairs not only in Lafayette, but in Indiana as well. He is an enigma to many. A Mason, he was graduated with honors from Notre Dame. In Indiana, where it is considered political poison to be talking sympathetically about minority groups and human relations, Scott accepted an appointment on President Dwight D. Eisenhower's Civil Rights Advisory Commission for Indiana. He was also one of the few Marine reservists to retire as a much-decorated general.

Republican Scott and Democrat Branigin are close friends. They were among the best toastmasters the Indianapolis Press Club ever hired (for free) at its Gridiron Shows to lampoon politicians.

NEW ALBANY (population 37,812) was the largest city in Indiana when Indianapolis was swampland and forest. Along the Ohio and Mississippi rivers, from Pittsburgh to New Orleans, it had a reputation as a bustling, colorful community famed commercially for the ships it built and socially for the brilliance of vacationtime life for aristocratic families from the far South.

Today, while it has factories of its own (clothing, plywood, shirts), it has become for many the bedroom community of Louisville, Kentucky, across the Ohio River. Not a few people who are obliged to work in Louisville nevertheless prefer to stay in New Albany, where the living is easy— with its 1850 and 1960 mansions, gorgeous flower gardens, progressive schools, fine civic leadership and home-town pride. Ninety-nine percent of its residents are native, mostly of French, German and Irish ancestry.

The Ohio River overflowed its banks in 1937 inundating cities and towns along the way. Many never fully recovered. New Albany, with standout leadership, not only recovered but prospered, principally because its merchants, industrialists, politicians and civic leaders showed the way— men like C. Pralle Erni (four-time mayor), Bill Worden, B. L. Curry, Walter Coyle, Gernett Inman and Dr. A. P. House.

In 1812, three brothers, Joel, Abner and Nathaniel Scribner came from New York State and bought 826 acres of land for $8,000 from Colonel John Paul of Madison, Indiana. The next year they built a double log cabin, plotted the town and advertised in Eastern newspapers the sale of lots. The *Aurora,* a paper in Philadelphia, carried this ad:

NEW ALBANY

The town, just laid out with spacious streets, public squares, market and other convenient things, is situated on the banks of the Ohio River at the crossing place from Louisville to Vincennes, about two miles below the falls, in the Indiana territory, affords a beautiful and commodious harbor. The beauty of the prospect is not surpassed by any other Western country. . . .

New Albany produced, in time, famous sons and daughters all out of proportion to its size. R. Carlyle Buley won a Pulitzer Prize in 1951 for his two-volume history *The Old Northwest.* Cardinal Joseph Elmer Ritter of St. Louis, a leader in racial integration within the Catholic Church and one of the most respected clergymen in the Midwest, was born in New Albany and spent much of his youth there. The town produced authors William Vaughn Moody (*The Great Divide* and *Faith Healer*), Forceythe Willson (*The Old Sergeant*) and Robert S. Lynd (*Middletown*) and big-league baseball players Billy Herman, Jowett Meekire, Max Macon and Eddie Moore.

An Indiana Governor (at age thirty-six), Ashbel P. Willard, and Speaker of the United States House of Representatives, Michael C. Kerr, came from New Albany, as did industrialist John B. Ford, choral music composer Joseph W. Clokey, Major General Edward M. Lewis (who breached the Hindenburg Line in World War I), theatrical stars J. Warren Kerrigan and his sister Kathleen and headliner Charles E. (Bert) Kenny of the old Keith-Orpheum vaudeville circuit.

Sherman (Shay) Minton was a New Deal U.S. Senator from New Albany who tried to pack the U.S. Supreme Court with justices more friendly to President Franklin D. Roosevelt. And when Minton himself was nominated for the U.S. Supreme Court, the Senate Judiciary Committee closely questioned his partisan role in FDR's court-packing plan.

"When I was a young man and played baseball, I was a fierce competitor and partisan," Minton said. "Years later, when I became an umpire, I was completely neutral and unbiased." He got the job.

Dan Kidney, Washington correspondent for the *Indianapolis Times* and the *Evansville Press,* used to tell what happened when Minton was stopped for speeding by a cop in Georgia.

"Yur name, please?" drawled the policeman.

"Sherman Minton."

"Sherman!" the cop glared.

"No," Minton replied, "Herman."

What Notre Dame is to South Bend and the 500 Mile Race is to Indianapolis, the famous riverboat *Robert E. Lee* once was to New Albany. It was the fastest and best-known on the Mississippi. Its only rival was the *Eclipse,* also built in New Albany.

During this period, the colorful taverns of New Albany were filled with steamboat captains who came to Indiana to superintend construction of new boats. The favorite stopping place for the captains (and the aristocratic Southern families) included Hale Tavern, the Black Horse Inn and Marsh's Goose Horn Tavern.

Since the greatest part of its commerce was with the

South, New Albany fell upon hard times at the start of the Civil War. Railroads already had come to town, reducing the town's shipbuilding and river commerce. The development, for a time, of a glass industry and other manufacturing helped restore some trade after the war. But the conflict had forever ended the reign of wealthy, leisurely Southern aristocracy. It remains, nevertheless, a good place to live and bring up children.

KOKOMO (population 47,197) has been the joke of the nation. Mention the town's name and you get hoots of derisive laughter. "I met this girl in Kokomo" is all a comedian had to say to bring down the house. It could have been worse. Suppose the good citizens had retained the complete name of the Miami Indian chief they honor—Kokomoko?

There is nothing funny about Kokomo, which is fifty miles straight north from Indianapolis up broad, affluent Meridian Street. Like most small manufacturing centers in Indiana, it gives the impression of being a larger city than it actually is.

John Bartlow Martin described Kokomo right after the boys came marching home from World War II:

> Now on this August night in 1946, the Isis Theater is offering a double feature, "Shady Lady" and "Live Wires" and a Nickel Plate freight runs right up the street beside the Hotel Frances, clanging and whistling, and some kids drive by with cutouts open, headed for the dance pavilion at Lake Manitou where a big name band is playing one night only.

In 1950, children helping to build a church recreation center in Mulfalfa Park found in the undergrowth three crosses and other paraphernalia used by the Ku Klux Klan. This inspired a brotherhood drive.

In 1922 the Klan bought twenty-five acres of Mulfalfa Park, where it dressed up in white robes and hoods, marched up and down, burned fiery crosses, terrified some people and held secret meetings.

D. C. Stephenson promoted himself to Grand Dragon of the Klan in Indiana the next year. To celebrate, he arranged at Kokomo's Mulfalfa Park on July 4, 1923 the greatest gathering of the Klan ever held in the state. By his own estimate, 200,000 Knights had assembled for the *konklave*. Stephenson, always spectacular, swooped down from the sky in a gilded airplane, stepped from it clad in resplendent robes and pledged his undying devotion and unfaltering leadership. Before he majestically departed, the hysterical crowd threw coins and jewelry at his feet.

Dow Richardson, respected editor of the *Kokomo Tribune* and the town's leading citizen, biggest booster and indefatigable civic leader, says Kokomo has changed since the Klan days.

"There isn't a sheet around," he says. "All that stuff is forgotten."

Q. What's good about Kokomo?

A. I'd have to say the quality of the people . . . the enthusiastic spirit that brought the town back from three near disastrous depressions. We have progressive schools.

Q. Downtown looks dingy and it takes an act of the Legislature to get through town during rush hour. True?

A. Like most Indiana cities, we haven't done too much with downtown. We're working on the traffic problem now, floating a bond issue to help pay for it and we're trying to fix up some store fronts.

The trouble with downtown Kokomo is the trouble with many cities across the state. A big chunk is owned by a few conservative families. But there are healthy signs. D. D. Mitchell's old-established Union Bank & Trust Company is feuding with Donald B. Smith, Sr.'s First National Bank. The people can't lose this way.

Each political party is blessed with fresh, spirited leaders. Robert S. Whitehead, city attorney, is the Democratic chief and a bright one. His counterpart is Richard Ellis, popular former State Senator, who might someday be the Republican candidate for Senator. Once a Republican stronghold, the mounting union strength has turned Kokomo into a Democratic city.

Chamber of Commerce literature calls Kokomo the city of firsts. Elwood Haynes (with Elmer Apperson assisting) invented the first commercial auto. Haynes also invented stainless steel and other Kokomo citizens introduced the pneumatic auto tire, aerial bomb, commercial canned tomatoes, auto muffler and metal life rafts.

The city has its economic ups and downs. Like other Indiana cities it brags about its native, white labor force (90 percent American born, 4 percent foreign born and 6 percent non-white). For years its factories produced goods without union help. Today the town is 85 percent unionized.

Some of Kokomo's native sons have gone on to greater glory—jockey Tod Sloan, actor Richard Bennett and Civil War general T. J. Harrison.

But Kokomo needs more men like Editor Dow Richardson. It lost the flavor of a college town when Kokomo Junior College became a sterile extension of Indiana University.

GARY (population 178,320) is in Indiana. But it's not Indiana. It's Chicago.

Belching industrial smoke of Gary blends with the gas fumes, soot, stink and dirt of East Chicago (population 57,-669) and Hammond (population 111,698) and Whiting (population 8,137). This is the Calumet region in Lake County—a dense, grimy, unending string of factory smokestacks, oil-refinery tanks, coal piles and steel mills in the northwest corner of Indiana, next door to Chicago.

You can't tell where one town ends and another begins. You'll never know when you cross from Indiana into Illinois.

You get the same merchants, the same political machines, the same racketeers, the same slums and the same streets of teeming foreigners.

Down in Indianapolis, when the State Legislature is in session, there usually is one cow county legislator each session who gets up and proposes a law deeding Lake County to Chicago. It gets a laugh.

It used to be that if you lived in Gary, you worked in the terrible heat of a steel furnace or you didn't work. Ambitious high school kids couldn't wait to graduate to leave town. There are more and varied industries in town today. But the exodus is still on. The bright youngsters want out.

Not far from the industrial haze, along the beautiful shore of Lake Michigan in northeast Gary, are the sand dunes, the poplar trees and the fancy homes, priced anywhere between $20,000 and $75,000. This could be a different world—and, in a sense, it is, for there are the homes of doctors and lawyers, merchants and corporation executives.

What's wrong with Gary? Why do Hoosiers instinctively distrust Lake County? Why can't a politician from Lake County ever be elected Governor or Senator?

Lake County is corrupt. The plunderworld wants it that way. So long as gambling, prostitution and robberies are confined to certain notorious districts of the community, decent citizens shrug and go blissfully about making a living, mowing the lawn and cooking supper.

In Gary there are six bookie joints within two blocks of City Hall. In adjoining Hammond, some of the choice horse-bet parlors are operated by the syndicate in Chicago. In East Chicago, there are gambling dens within two blocks of City Hall.

Reform movements, clean-up campaigns and antigambling crusades in Lake County are as plentiful as slot machines in Las Vegas. Billy Sunday himself couldn't have taken so many morality crusades. Yet nothing has been able to stop the tide of political corruption and collusion between public officials and racketeers, grafters, gamblers and criminals. Lake County has developed a tolerance, if not a taste, for it.

The latest reform movement started in June 1959 when a United States Senate investigation focused national attention on crime and corruption in the Calumet. Senator John L. McClellan said: "The illicit operations which appear to have flourished in Lake County since 1950 would have been impossible without the knowledge, acquiescence and cooperation of some public officials."

People like A. F. Endres, manager of Standard Oil of Whiting, got together with Professor James Savage of Valparaiso University, Albert Berdis, president of Midwest Steel Company, Frederick A. Dudderrar, general superintendent of U.S. Steel Corporation in Gary and Cornelius J. Verplank, Jr., veteran of other Lake County reform movements. With teachers, religious leaders, merchants and bankers, they formed the Northwest Indiana Crime Commission, hired ex-FBI agent Francis E. Lynch and persuaded Attorney General Robert F. Kennedy to appoint a special assistant to the U.S. Attorney.

Kennedy sent Jay Goldberg, a Harvard-trained New Yorker who had experience as a rackets prosecutor working for Frank Hogan, district attorney in New York City. It didn't take long for something to happen.

Metro Holavachka was found guilty of evading federal income taxes while prosecutor of Lake County. A federal grand jury the same day indicted Mayor George Chacharis of Gary. He was charged with neglecting to pay income taxes on $226,696 in payoffs he received from construction companies. Ten other public officials were indicted with him, including Sheriff Peter Mandich of Lake County and City Engineer Harold Zeig of Gary.

Chacharis, affectionately called "Cha Cha" by his friends, pleaded guilty and was sentenced to prison. Charges against the others were dropped.

There were other cases. A policy-wheel operator admitted he paid $500 a day for police protection. The Crime Commission uncovered a payment of $5,000 to politicians to fix a reckless homicide-driving case. In Gary, in 1961, it was discovered that 77,000 traffic tickets were issued—22,000 were handled and cleared, no one knows what happened to the other 55,000.

The question remains: Will the awakening, the surge of anger, the demand for reform, continue? Do the people of Lake County really want an end to fixes, graft, kickbacks, corruption, gambling and prostitution?

Apathetic citizens have become aroused before. They have even thrown the rascals out of office. But new rascals came in.

"When you vote in Lake County," one disgusted high school civics teacher said, "it's like playing craps with the dice loaded against you."

A few years ago, if you wanted anything in Lake County you had to see "the triumvirate," sometimes called "the Holy Trinity"—Mayor Chacharis of Gary, Sheriff Mandich of Lake County and Mayor Walter Jeorse of East Chicago. Ever since Chacharis and Mandich came under federal indictments, no one knows where to go or who to see.

Today there is no "Mr. Big" in Lake County. Politicians are in disrepute. Home-grown merchants and industrialists are dwarfed by the big national corporations. Big money banks with the Gary National, run by Bob and Bill Gasser. But the bank with the political connections is The First National of East Chicago, dominated by influential, aging Colonel Walter J. Riley (once the powerhouse of Lake County) and run by his nephew William J. Riley. The Rileys also control Union National of Indiana Harbor.

Labor leaders exercise power in their own communities. Orval Kincaid (Gary) and Lester Thornton (East Chicago) of the Steelworkers, for example, make their positions felt locally, but take orders from Joe Germano, District Director of the Steelworkers in Chicago. Others, like Harold Hagberg of the International Brotherhood of Electrical Workers and Michael Sawochka of the Teamsters have no great community interests, but must be reckoned with.

H. B. Snyder, publisher of the *Gary Post-Tribune* and James DeLaurier, publisher of the *Hammond Times,* produce good, interesting, metropolitan papers. Both are Republican, but give Democrats a fair shake. Both raise hell when they catch a Democrat off base. Snyder and DeLaurier are civic-minded and influential. They sometimes lead the county but seldom run it.

Mostly by default, and partly in self-defense, the real job of running Lake County has fallen to the imported managers of the big plants—Inland Steel, U.S. Steel, Standard Oil, Sinclair Oil, Youngstown Steel and Cities Service. Between industry and the political structure, there is a closer tie than the do-gooders like to admit. Sometimes it even benefits the people when, for example, Inland Steel and East Chicago teamed up to put over Jeorse Park.

At the Statehouse in Indianapolis, a Lake County politician confided to a newspaperman: "Lake County isn't as bad as you guys paint it. But when I'm gone, I don't miss it."

three

INDIANAPOLIS

Indiana continues to dominate Indianapolis.
—IRVIN S. COBB

INDIANAPOLIS (population 491,360) is most famous for the 500 Mile Speedway, which is outside the town, and for politics, which is all over town.

It is a city of beautiful parks, lovely homes, stately churches, fine schools, good hospitals and crooked politics.

Publisher Eugene C. Pulliam's down-with-everything *Indianapolis Star* bulldozes the town and makes the *Chicago Tribune* seem New Dealish by comparison.

People who visit Indianapolis go away singing the praises of the picturesque Monument Circle in the middle of town and swearing at the city's peculiar resistance to change.

Back in the 1920's, white-sheeted Kluxers marched down Meridian Street, operated the schools and dispensed "justice" in the courts. Today the city continues to attract every last-ditch reactionary and screwball in the country.

The black-supremacy Muslims are here where the white-supremacy Ku Klux Klan once ruled. Few in number, the Muslims hold meetings in Negro homes and stores along garish, neon-lighted Indiana Ave., once the black belt of Indianapolis, which starts with a pawn shop (Sack's) and ends with a hospital (General). About the Muslims, Richard Caine of the police department's Internal Security Division, says, "They don't want to integrate. They want to exterminate."

Ex-candy manufacturer Robert Welch, who called former President Dwight D. Eisenhower a card-carrying Communist, organized the fanatic, far-out John Birch Society December 9, 1958 in the living room of Mrs. Marguerite Dice's home at 3650 Washington Boulevard.

Who controls the city?

For a time the *Indianapolis News* called the shots. The *News* was owned by then-Vice President Charles Warren Fairbanks. The arrangement was so secret that when Mayor Charles Bookwalter tried to raise money among his Columbia Club pals to fight the *News,* Fairbanks himself contributed fifty dollars.

In the old days, they say, banker-industrialist-politician Will Hays' whisper "was damn near law." In the 1930's, Paul V. McNutt, Bo Elder, Frank McHale and Pleas Greenlee gave Indiana a preview of the New Deal before FDR gave it to the nation. They were undisputed rulers in the capital city.

Big cities have their own built-in power structures. In Indianapolis, you can dismiss the minority groups (Negroes, Jews, Catholics, foreign born) as either too timid, too few or too conformist. The labor unions are tirelessly ineffective in politics, although they have a growing impact on the economy, are effective in raising wages and are remarkably responsible.

Strongman politicians, from time to time, ran the show, behind the scenes and in front—Republicans like George (Cap) Coffin and H. Dale Brown and Democrats like Tom Taggart, Sr. But few politicians ever have had as much influence and power as William Henry Book.

Bill Book runs Indianapolis. He is the power.

Politicians, college presidents, businessmen, civic leaders and editors make pilgrimages to his office to be blessed, en-

Monument Circle in the heart of Indianapolis.

Former Senator William E. Jenner on an elephant during a Republican election rally in Danville, Indiana.

Victor Peterson
Indianapolis Time

Former Senator William E. Jenner (R. Indiana).

Ray Bright, *Indianapolis Times*

dorsed, anointed and indoctrinated with his hold-the-line philosophy. He is positively negative. "Do we really need it now" could well be his motto.

Bill Book has his finger in every slice of community pie —zoning laws, the City Hall budget, hospitals, sports, building laws, taxes, pensions for police, textbooks in schools and property assessments. He has even told the city what time to set its clocks by.

Bill Book is the doer, the prime mover (and roadblock). His title is executive vice-president of the Indianapolis Chamber of Commerce. Department-store owners, industrialists and merchants pay their dues, attend the meetings and listen respectfully when he talks. Book works for them, but you'd never know it. He furnishes the leadership, and some of it is excellent and in the best interests of the community.

William Henry Book was born sixty-two years ago in Virginia, reared in Columbus, Indiana and educated for the ministry at Franklin College in Indiana. He is smallish, soft-spoken and unimposing. In the 1920's he was a reporter on the *Indianapolis News* and worked himself up to assistant city editor. For nine months he was business administrator of Indianapolis Public Schools. In 1926 he joined the Chamber of Commerce as director of government research. What happened since is the history of modern-day Indianapolis.

The bottom dropped out in the 1930's. Jobs were scarce. Hoosiers were hungry and cold with the rest of the nation. Banks closed. A new administration in Washington suddenly took upon itself unprecedented powers, social responsibilities and duties and remade our way of living.

The most bitter, hysterical Roosevelt-hater would not dare suggest removing the economic and social safeguards. Except Bill Book.

He has made a career of fighting Washington and what he calls "government handouts," "socialistic schemes," "federal aid," and "centralization of power." (Some conservatives are genuinely upset by Book's rabid opposition to centralization of power in Washington and his enthusiastic support of it in Indianapolis in the form of metropolitan government.)

How did Book get his power? His protégé and heir apparent, Carl Dortch, describes Book as "a tireless worker, shrewd and with a tremendous capacity for organization." It is no secret, too, that Book ingratiated himself with monied men of power and prestige—respected civic leaders like Arthur Baxter of Universal Lock, Charles Lynn of the world-renowned Eli Lilly drug firm and Guy Wainwright of Diamond Chain.

In Dortch, Bill Book has one of the nation's outstanding authorities on municipal government, a brilliant and knowledgeable researcher who enjoys the respect and trust of politicians, businessmen, editors, civic leaders and school officials. "If Carl Dortch says it, it must be," is a typical comment.

Bill Book has been with the Chamber* ever since he joined, with the exception of two years, 1933 and 1934, when Governor Paul McNutt appointed him state relief director at the height of the Depression. Book's job, in his own words, was to "hand out money to the unemployed." The program was called the Federal Emergency Relief Administration and later became the Civil Works Administration and developed into the Works Progress Administration (WPA). Soup kitchens fed the famished. The desperate and jobless were given work—make-work and part-time work. The Naval Armory on White River and the huge auditorium at Indiana University, which are both still in use today, were built with WPA funds and laborers.

But Bill Book was troubled, he says, by giving away money for nothing. He recalls: "I began to see that Harry Hopkins was trying to change the economy from the free-enterprise system to a socialist system."

---

* At the end of 1963, Book retired as executive vice-president, but will remain with the Chamber of Commerce as a consultant.

Book says he attended a regional directors' meeting in the Muehlebach Hotel in Kansas City where Hopkins said, "This is the revolution. . . ."

"I didn't like it and got out the first chance I got," Bill Book recalls. He hasn't been a card-carrying Democrat since.

WHAT MAKES Indianapolis hick and tick? What makes it a wonderful place to live?

J. Clifton Hirschman owns the largest mattress company in the state, worked in the Republican precincts and ran for public office, served as an officer in the navy and has been active in school reorganization. He is a proud Hoosier whose grandfather came to Indianapolis before the Civil War to get away from Prussian militarism. Hirschman likes Indianapolis, he says, because "the people are conservative, hardworking, patriotic. Their word is as good as a signed statement."

Carl Dortch of the Chamber of Commerce says, "We may not do the most dramatic things in the world, but we like to talk about what we do." Richard Martin, press secretary to Governor Matthew Welsh, has lived in nine states, including New York and California. He is a liberal, an outspoken critic of the "conspiracy of conservatism" in Indiana. "I want to live here for the rest of my life," Martin says. "In Los Angeles you feel as if you are in transit. Here you have a sense of permanence."

Indianapolis is the largest city in Indiana and the state capital. The only larger state capitals are Boston, Massachusetts, Denver, Colorado, and Atlanta, Georgia. Unlike Boston, and any other metropolitan city, Indianapolis doesn't dominate the state or even part of it. It is an overgrown country town, with the advantages of small-town living and big-town industry.

Into it poured not the strangers from exotic lands, but Hoosiers, who moved from farms to hamlets, to towns to the city; or Southerners who migrated from North Carolina,

Virginia, Kentucky and Tennessee. They all came from the wide-open rural spaces, where you keep your distance, where things are always the same, where you don't meet many strangers.

Native Hoosiers, especially from the rural areas, were proud, Protestant and patriotic. They regarded later immigrants from the old country, especially Catholics, as "cheap help" and dangerous rivals for jobs, which they were. Most of the new immigrants were unskilled, unschooled and unemployed, which didn't help their popularity. Employers advertised: "No Irish need apply."

It mattered not that a generation earlier, in frontier Indiana, the brawling Irishers were welcome. They did jobs few Hoosiers or Yankees would do, cutting through swamps and forests, in heat and cold.

JOHN L. McNELIS's father worked in a meat-packing plant. His mother was a maid. It was a golden opportunity for the McNelis family living in the midst of other newcomers—the Irish, the Jews, the Negroes, the Kentuckians. Mom and Pop McNelis came from County Donegal in Ireland, where the potato crop rotted in the ground during a cold, wet and sunless summer.

At St. John's grade school and Cathedral High School, at Xavier College in Cincinnati and the Indiana University Law School in Indianapolis (the old Benjamin Harrison Law School), young McNelis was regarded as a mediocre student, a brash, cocky kid, "but with a heart."

As a young attorney interested in politics, McNelis worked diligently in the precincts, passed out half-pints during election campaigns, took voters to the polls, did what he was told, kept his mouth shut and came to the attention of Billy Clauer, downtown Democratic boss.

Clauer took a liking to McNelis and rewarded him. He promoted him to chairman of the predominantly Negro

Seventh Ward and persuaded Governor Clifford M. Townsend to appoint him judge of the Municipal Court.

If Judge McNelis didn't throw the book at gamblers, drunks, bootleggers and whores, especially from the black belt, you could blame his soft Irish heart—or politics. His reticence to toss anyone in the clink favorably impressed Democratic leaders, who felt here was a man of compassion ideally suited for advancement to Criminal Court. He was nominated without opposition.

In the fall of 1942, at a political rally at 11th and Missouri, under a huge tent near Simpson Methodist Church in the heart of the Negro district, between 700 and 800 colored people turned out to hear the candidates. McNelis remembers that it was cold because there was a lot of beer left over.

A Negro preacher named Reverend Christian wanted to impress the audience with the particular qualifications of McNelis. He began the introduction: "The next speaker is a man that you all love . . . a man that you all know . . . a man who has done freed more niggers than Abraham Lincoln."

IF YOU can stand the heat in the summer, the cold in the winter and the quick temperature changes in between, Indianapolis is where the living is easy. No oceans, lakes, mountains or cities surround Indianapolis to strangle it. It has plenty of room to grow in every direction. If you want to sail, fish, hunt, hike or play golf and tennis you can do it inside the city limits, or get there in minutes.

The city is lousy with civic-improvement associations. A standing joke is that when you see two people talking in the street they are in the midst of electing a president and vice-president of an uplift or down-with society.

There is a monumental civic pride and a fresh, zestful roll-up-our-sleeves-and-get-this-job-done spirit. Cleveland, Ohio, John Gunther once wrote, was where "every rich burgher, returning home at night, is supposed to catechize himself with a dutiful question: 'Have I cooperated well today.' " This was the tradition of Indianapolis when rich and civic-minded citizens like Eli Lilly, J. K. Lilly and J. I. Holcomb ruled the roost. Today their plant managers and the energetic, capable Johnny-Come-Latelys, like Charlie Saville of Sears, Roebuck Co. have organized and channeled the community's men and money into useful projects and programs.

The city brags, and it should. Rotarians and Lions and Kiwanians and Jaycees and Junior Leaguers knock themselves out, almost full time, on civic projects from Americanism to zoo building. Indianapolis has a delightful habit of going over the top on United Fund and other drives. The city took great pride in raising $12 million to build Community Hospital and huge wings on four other local hospitals without tax funds and without a cent of federal aid, which is almost unheard of in these days. The money came from donations, payroll deductions, contributions, endowments, gifts and (like a Salvation Army lassie) shaking a tambourine in public.

The magnificent 500 Festival has become nearly a month-long civic binge tied to the 500 Mile Race in May. It was nurtured and reared through the combined labor pains of such diverse people as former Mayor Alex Clark, promotion man Howdy Wilcox of the *Star* and *News,* Sam Freeman of Strauss' men's store and Mrs. Frank McKinney, elegant wife of banker and former Democratic National Chairman Frank McKinney.

The festival now features a $50,000 golf tournament, movie and television stars, heavyweight boxing matches, colorful two-hour parades, a circus on Monument Circle, cocktail parties, hillbilly dancing in the streets and a fancy-dress coronation ball.

"The tail is beginning to wag the dog," says sports editor Dick Mittman of the *Times.* He fears the race, which is the biggest single sports attraction in the world, is being over-shadowed by the glamour and by the other exciting events.

EUGENE COLLINS PULLIAM is a super patriot. He is forever trying to save America by lashing out against liberals, welfare-staters, do-gooders, Walter Reuther, socialized medicine and one-worlders. He thinks John F. Kennedy has been influenced by left-wing pressure groups and never should have been elected President.

What Pulliam thinks is important. Proud, powerful, profane, Pulliam's prejudices pour out of the printing presses of six newspapers in four cities of Indiana. (He owns and operates the *Star* and *News* in Indianapolis, the *Star* and *Press* in Muncie, the *Sun Commercial* in Vincennes and the *Herald-Press* of Huntington.)

The son of the Reverend Irvin Brown Pulliam, a Methodist home missionary, Pulliam was born May 3, 1889 in Ulysses, Kansas (population 3,157). He attended DePauw University at Greencastle, Indiana, worked on the school paper and became one of the founders of Sigma Delta Chi, national journalism society.

Pulliam was a police reporter on the *Kansas City Star* and later published small papers in Kansas, Florida, Oklahoma, and Indiana. As much a promoter and wheeler-dealer in finance, Pulliam later became a director of the New York Central Railroad. Pulliam's newspapering may be criticized, but there is no question that he has a successful formula.

"When people pick up the paper," Pulliam once told one of his editors, "I want them to say, 'What is that sonuva-bitch saying now?' or 'Look, what a great guy he is.' "

Pulliam's "save America" mission has put him in the company of such conservatives as Burton K. Wheeler, former Democratic Senator from Montana, Dan Smoot, the Texas pamphleteer, Clarence E. Manion, former dean of the law school at the University of Notre Dame, retired brigadier general Bonner Fellers, Hamilton Fish, former Republican Congressman from New York, and John T. Flynn, the New York writer. With them, Pulliam was a member of the "For America movement," whose announced primary purpose was to combat "super internationalists."

Some of the programs advocated by the For America movement were (1) withdraw from the United Nations unless the Communist nations are expelled, (2) limit federal taxes and abolish the withholding tax and (3) end the draft and rely on air supremacy as a war deterrent.

At about the time Pulliam was on the national policy committee of the For America movement, the Indianapolis chapter of B'nai B'rith, a Jewish fraternal and civic organization, named him the "man-of-the-year" for his many civic deeds. Alfred Berman, an Indianapolis lawyer, convinced the B'nai B'rith committee of Pulliam's civic virtues.

While he was compiling the long list of meritorious accomplishments Pulliam's papers supported, the B'nai B'rith's own Anti-Defamation League was putting out its own national report on the For America movement. It was contained in the book *Cross Currents,* written by Arnold Foster and Benjamin Epstein.

Here is what it said, in part, about Pulliam's For America group: "For America seems to be a refurbished and rededicated ghost of the America First Committee which led the pre-war isolationist movement . . . It bears watching."

There were protests in the Jewish community about conferring civic sainthood on Pulliam once the For America record was known. It was also brought up at the time that Pulliam's *Indianapolis Star* had come out against the U.S. Supreme Court's decision on segregation ("We cannot escape the fact that this law was made in the courts and not in the legislatures"). Some Jews painfully reminded others about another Pulliam editorial in the *Star* at the height of the Arab-Israel trouble. ("The natural historical position of the United States should be sympathetic toward Arab nationalism.")

The B'nai B'rith said it was too late to turn back, and Pulliam did get the award. The controversy over this award still persists within the Indianapolis Jewish community.

Pulliam's two Indianapolis papers are currently directed by his son Eugene S. Pulliam. Young Pulliam is respected in the community and in the newspaper profession and is much more moderate politically than his father. However, his father imported two articulate and extremely conservative writers to handle the editorial pages. Jameson Campaigne, author of *American Might and Soviet Myth*, edits the *Star* and M. Santon Evans edits the *News*.

(A guest at the Evans' wedding in Indianapolis in 1962 was former general Edwin A. Walker, who resigned his army commission after being officially admonished by the Kennedy Administration for trying to influence troops under his command toward right-wing politicians. Evans, then twenty-eight, crusaded for Walker when the ex-general said he was being muzzled by the Pentagon. But Evans' editorial page was conspicuously silent when Walker rallied segregationists at the University of Mississippi in an effort to halt the admittance of a twenty-nine-year-old Negro veteran of the Air Force, James H. Meredith.)

Pulliam's financial success hasn't been duplicated in politics. He has cherished the post of Republican National Committeeman for Indiana, but it has eluded him. Politicians say privately that he nursed an ambition to be an ambassador or a U.S. Senator. In one of the hottest political scraps on record, Pulliam tried his best to stop the appointment of Cale J. Holder as a federal judge. Holder today sits serenely on the United States bench in Indianapolis.

There is an evangelical fervor about Pulliam's newspaper crusades. He carries the torch for God and country (and states' rights) and calls down damnation upon all those who knowingly or unknowingly do the devil's work, which could be anyone who doesn't happen to agree with him at the time.

At times, Pulliam has been so carried away by his crusades he has ordered the *Star* not to print the names of the
"enemy." The enemies at times were Congressman Andrew
Jacobs, Sr., Congressional candidate John Carvey and Governor Henry F. Schricker, all Democrats. (In time, the ban on
the "enemy" is usually lifted. In the case of Schricker, there
was a *rapprochement* when Pulliam discovered that Schricker
was conservative to the core.)

In 1958, when Governor Harold Handley, an arch conservative, ran for the United States Senate against "the boy
Mayor" of Evansville, Democrat Vance Hartke, Pulliam went
to work with his customary zeal for a political fight. Like
many Indiana Democrats, Hartke was on the conservative
side himself, and later became a protégé of Vice President
Lyndon Johnson. To Pulliam, Hartke was the enemy, the
front man for Walter Reuther. Pulliam set out to beat him.

On the eve of the election, the late Lester M. Hunt, a
former press agent for the Teamsters Union, wrote stories in
the *Star* attempting to link Hartke to Reuther.

"I have never met Reuther," Hartke protested. "I have
never spoken or written to him, and he would not know
me if we passed on the street."

On October 31, 1958, Pulliam's *Star* carried an eight-
column banner across the bottom of the front page. It said:

DON'T VOTE INDIANA OVER TO THE LABOR BOSSES

The next day, November 1, the *Star* carried a front-page
story by Hunt with the headline:

REUTHER TO GET UNIONS IF DEMOS WIN: HANDLEY

Underneath was an eight-column banner:

DON'T LET REUTHER TAKE INDIANA
VOTE TUESDAY

On November 2, the *Star* front page carried some glee-ful news for the Republicans under the headlines:

GOP TO KEEP 8 DISTRICTS

Handley Win
Expected on
Congress Tide

At the bottom was another of Pulliam's personal polit-ical messages:

STOP REUTHER 'POWER GRAB'   VOTE TUESDAY

The propaganda barrage did not even lift the day before the election or the day of the election, a time when even the most partisan publisher tries to calm down and maintain at least some pose of neutrality or fair play. Not Pulliam.

On November 3, there was another eight-column ban-ner:

WARD OFF REUTHER CONTROL—BE SURE TO VOTE TUESDAY

Election Day, November 4, the headline stretched eight columns across the front page again:

SAVE INDIANA FROM REUTHER CONTROL VOTE TODAY

In the end the *Star,* Pulliam and Handley lost. Hartke won. You might even say Reuther won.

Whether he wins or loses, Pulliam frequently goes into battle with headlines and temper flying. "You Can't Buy The White House," an unsigned and unlabeled editorial on the front page, was Pulliam's journalistic contribution to the 1960 Presidential race between John F. Kennedy and Richard Nixon.

The August 14, 1960 editorial mentioned that the Ken-

nedy millions came "mostly from whiskey," that Kennedy
was nominated by Catholics, that he was under complete
obligation to left-wing pressure groups and the darling of the
Americans for Democratic Action (ADA).

Why won't Jack Kennedy be frank enough to admit
publicly that it was his Catholic friends who gave him the
nomination? The five big states were for Kennedy. Mayor
Wagner, who led New York's delegation, is a Catholic. Governor Lawrence of Pennsylvania, who turned Pennsylvania
over to Kennedy, is a Catholic. Governor Mike DiSalle of
Ohio, who gave the entire Ohio delegation to Kennedy, is a
Catholic. Mayor Daley of Chicago, who controlled the Illinois delegation, is a Catholic. Governor Pat Brown of California, another Kennedy state is a Catholic. The delegations
from these five states, led by Catholics, put over Kennedy's
nomination.

Pulliam's power lies in the relentless, scorching heat of
his newspapers. Few protest. The politicians are too timid
and the people are too cowed. Also, Pulliam is a rough, tough,
tenacious gut fighter. Right or wrong, he has the courage of
his convictions. He is an impressive sight in his crew-cut
when he cusses, damns, threatens and screams. He can be on
the warpath one moment and a gracious and thoughtful host
the next.

Former Congressman Charles Brownson, Indianapolis
Republican, used to say, "I never quarrel with a man who
buys ink by the barrel."

ON THE near northwest side of Indianapolis, in the shadow
of Indiana University's new Medical Center buildings, lives
a family of fifteen Negroes in a four-room shack that has no
running water. The twelve children and three adults (two
pregnant) use an outdoor toilet, get water from an outside
pump (except when it freezes) and boil all their food on a
potbellied stove.

In suburbia, there is one community of forty Negro homes ranging in price from $17,000 to $45,000. They are modern ranch-style homes, either brick or stone.

More typically, the Negro at home in Indianapolis lives in a five-room house with central heating and modern plumbing, a house built over thirty years ago on a small lot. The total value would be about $8,000 on today's market.

Considered by tradition and culture the most Southern of the Northern states, Indiana is no haven for Negroes. Schools were desegregated in 1949 but there is lingering resentment and tension. In Indianapolis, much of this persists despite historic advances in education and income among Negroes. Friction stems largely from (1) the disproportionate amount of crime committed by Negroes, (2) the ineffective leadership among Negroes, (3) the lack of understanding of complicated and sensitive Negro problems by white civic leaders and (4) the bigotry by white and black.

A few Negroes have crashed the white barriers of success. Robert Lee Brokenburr, son of a slave, is a State Senator. Former President Dwight D. Eisenhower once called on him to serve under Henry Cabot Lodge, Jr. as alternate delegate to the United Nations, which he did with dignity and distinction. Gracious and genteel, Brokenburr is a lawyer and a businessman. He has an immense capacity for patience.

This is exactly the one quality which does not endear him to many other Indianapolis Negroes. They respect him, as do most whites. But they are weary and becoming impatient, they say, waiting for equal job opportunities and a chance to live in decent homes.

Ted Knap, one of the nation's best investigative reporters, and now with Scripps-Howard newspapers in Washington, did an exhaustive study of the Negro in Indianapolis. He found, among other things:

Negroes have made significant, but slow gains since 1950. In public schools, the Negro pupil is good or bad depending chiefly on the economic and social stability of his family—

the same as the white pupil and in the same degree. Many Negroes have broken the color line in jobs that have traditionally been denied to them. (For example, the first Negro went on the State Police force in 1963, and half or more of skilled and semiskilled workers are Negroes at Fort Harrison's Army Finance Center, sometimes called the "Payroll Pentagon.")

There are, in Indianapolis, a few pleasant integrated neighborhoods, but most Negroes voluntarily congregate in ghettoes. (Indianapolis' more affluent Jews have the same tendency. On the outskirts of rich, gentile, suburban Meridian Hills, Jews have grouped themselves in expensive ranch-style homes, an area known as "the golden ghetto.")

The housing color line sometimes makes it difficult for a Negro family to get a decent apartment. In integrated neighborhoods, most white neighbors are polite to their Negro neighbors, some are friendly, but few are socially close to them.

Discrimination (and lack of an adequate education) keeps Negroes from enjoying full and equal job opportunities. "Just how much," Ted Knap wrote, "is a matter of opinion, depending on whether you are colored and impatient, or white and unaffected."

The first Negro in Indianapolis was Epriam Ensaw, brought there in 1820 by Dr. Samuel G. Mitchell. The second was a woman, Chaney Lively, who kept house for Alexander Ralston, the surveyor credited with laying out Indianapolis. The third, in 1821, was David Mallory, the city's first barber. In 1827, Indianapolis had fifty-eight Negroes. Today, nearly one in five residents of Indianapolis is a Negro.

THE STORY of Frank E. McKinney is the success story of Indianapolis. In the impoverished South Side neighborhood where he was born, mothers don't want their sons to grow up

to be President, they want them to be "like Frank Mc-
Kinney." McKinney made the fairy-tale rags-to-riches climb,
from grinding poverty to affluence and influence.

He made good in his hometown in ring-a-ding-ding
cash-register style. He was called "Midas McKinney," because everything he touched turned to gold. What he touched,
pushing his way out of a ramshackle house at 29 LeGrande
Avenue in an immigrant neighborhood to a $250,000 estate
in the country, were banks, business, baseball and bipartisan
politics.

McKinney once owned (with Bing Crosby and others)
the Pittsburgh Pirates. Former President Harry Truman
handpicked him to be National Chairman of the Democratic
Party. He is chairman of the board of the American Fletcher
National Bank and Trust Company and has been active in
assorted other enterprises, such as a director of the New York
Central Railroad, the Alleghany Corporation and the Indiana Bell Telephone Company, where his wife Margaret once
worked.

McKinney looks like a banker. He wears conservative
blue serge and dark pin-striped suits, a bland smile and a
ruddy complexion that accents his jet-black hair. He is a
medium-sized, stocky and vigorous man who gives the impression of being a little younger and a good deal larger than
he really is.

But in the center of town, on Monument Circle, he built
a monument to himself—a modern twelve-story, glass and
aluminum and stainless-steel edifice housing the respected,
pioneer American Fletcher National Bank, which he took
over in 1960 by merger. The building significantly carries
the name of the tiny bank in which he maneuvered himself
to the top, Fidelity.

In his ornate, carpeted office overlooking the Circle, or
at a cocktail party, McKinney has a habit of taking you by
the arm and whispering intimately and confidentially in your

ear some trivia as if you were the most important person in the world. It is flattering and good for the ego, especially if someone is watching.

For all his associations with political figures, such as Truman, Vice President Lyndon Johnson and Averell Harriman, McKinney does not have a hard, fast or highly developed political philosophy. He has been described as a conservative who doesn't want to turn back the clock. As Democratic National Chairman, his principal contributions were as a good organizer, a great money-raiser and a splendid smoother-overer.

If "The Chief"—as McKinney still calls Truman—wanted him to push for socialized medicine, or compulsory unions or building a bridge across the Mississippi River lengthwise, McKinney would not stop and debate the merits of the issues. He'd get to work. In 1956, at the Democratic National Convention in Chicago, McKinney directed Harriman's unsuccessful campaign for the presidential nomination only because "The Chief" had given the word.

There are some people who say McKinney runs the town. This is not so. It is a fact, though, that when businessmen and civic leaders want to get some project off the ground they enlist the support of McKinney.

A story currently in fashion in Chamber of Commerce circles is that McKinney, not always considered an angel by big business, wants to settle down, do something for his hometown and reap the respect of an elder statesman. It is known that he wants to bring to Indianapolis big-league baseball and a new hotel. He also wants to change the skyline and build fancy apartment houses downtown so people will move back from the suburbs. For his efforts, the *Indianapolis Times* named him in 1960 "Man of the Year."

Francis Edward McKinney was born June 16, 1904 to Roscoe and Anna McKinney. His first pair of pants were cut down from a pair of frayed fireman's trousers—worn by his father, who years later was to become chief of the Indianapolis Fire Department. Asked about his early life, McKinney replied, "I used to dream I was going to be president of the biggest bank in town."

He had to quit high school in his second year to earn a living. Even when he became president of the small Fidelity Trust Company, other bankers snubbed the brash young man from the wrong side of the tracks. They ridiculed his efforts to bank by using political connections. McKinney didn't wear the old school tie. He was an outsider.

McKinney made his own breaks. When the fabulous Texas wheeler-dealer Clint Murchison bought control of the Indianapolis Water Company, he sent a front man to run it, Tom Moses, a personable young lawyer with plenty of savvy. McKinney became a pal of Moses. In time he asked one little favor, an introduction to Murchison. Apparently McKinney and Murchison understood each other. When Murchison and his sons won control of the Alleghany Corporation, McKinney was named chairman of the Executive Committee.

McKinney started his career as a runner in People's State Bank and later became a teller. Once when he complained bitterly about his lack of a college education, his friend Frank McHale replied, "Why, if you had one, you'd probably still be a teller at People's State Bank."

McKinney says it was the luckiest moment of his life when one of his bank customers, Mrs. Ellen Bush, introduced him to her son Owen J. (Donnie) Bush, a major-league baseball player. Mrs. Bush wanted McKinney to manage her son's money before it evaporated.

McKinney was a good manager. He hit it off with Donnie Bush and saved the baseball player a lot of money. Bush repaid McKinney by introducing him to Billy Clauer in March of 1933. Clauer, serving as Marion County Treasurer, was tired of the job and asked McKinney to run for the political office.

Even as McKinney was elected Treasurer of Marion County in 1934 (taking office on January 1, 1936), the Depression began to lift. Suddenly the Treasurer's office became the most lucrative in the State of Indiana by virtue of its fee system.

By law, the Treasurer was permitted to retain 6 percent of all delinquent taxes collected. For the first time in years, people paid. Overnight the office became good for $35,000 to $40,000 a year.

The Midas touch stayed with McKinney. When he heard that a large block of Fidelity Trust Company stock was for sale for $100,000, he went to a friend in the banking business and signed a note for $100,000 payable in four years. In January 1935, McKinney became president and holder of controlling interest in Fidelity, smallest bank in Indianapolis.

Governor Paul McNutt sponsored a law in the Legislature to reduce the fees in the Marion County Treasurer's office from 6 to 3 percent. It passed, but not before McKinney had his bank stock free and clear.

Once, when McKinney teamed up with Frank McHale, they made headlines across the country. McKinney and McHale joined with a New York promoter, Frank Cohen, to form Empire Tractor Company, which sold tractors for export. In a fast deal with the Argentine government, McHale and his associates cleared a profit of $68,000 for every $1,000 they had invested.

Liquor and politics have always been mixed into a powerful cocktail in Indiana. McKinney's political connections did not hurt him when he owned stock in National Distillers, a wholesale liquor company. He divested himself of interest in the firm when he climbed into the national political spotlight. But he has a knack for getting his friends jobs with the state Alcoholic Beverage Commission, which regulates the liquor and beer industry in Indiana.

McKinney frequently says he no longer wants anything to do with politics, had shunned it all his life and deep in his heart disliked it. He claims it is forced on him.

McKinney's story is that since that fateful day he walked

into Billy Clauer's living room he hasn't been able to extricate himself from the web of politics. This is true to a degree. McKinney feels he has outgrown precinct politics and doesn't want to get mixed up with the mud-slinging, but his friends keep coming back to him for help. McKinney says he becomes involved against his wishes because he feels he cannot turn his back on the people and party responsible for him enjoying the good life.

He helps Democratic friends, but has been known to help Republican friends, too. In 1951 he privately supported Republican Alex Clark for Mayor against Democrat Phillip Bayt, and Clark won. Clark's younger brother James later married McKinney's daughter Claire in a wedding that had, for Indianapolis, significance in social, political and financial circles.

There are people who say it was his banking and business acumen that made McKinney, not politics.

Near Mansfield, Ohio there is a beautiful farm called "Malabar." It was owned by the late author Louis Bromfield. He was proud of it and used to boast that it was strictly a farmer's farm with nary a book on it. But his farm neighbors put it another way: "Louis doesn't keep any books on the farm. But the books keep Louis on the farm."

McKinney tells intimates he'd like to skip politics and concentrate only on banking, but in 1962 he was delighted to serve as chairman of President John F. Kennedy's committee to rewrite the nation's banking laws.

McKinney may not like playing politics at the bank. But politics keeps him in the big league of banking.

Charles Boswell, Phillip L. Bayt and Robert A. O'Neal have been advertised as the good government, clean-as-a-whistle public officials, untouched by human politicians. They played together as youngsters on Ketcham Street on the west side of Indianapolis, in what was once a nice working-man's neighborhood called Haughville. In 1960, when the

Democrats had captured the major public offices, Boswell was mayor, Bayt was prosecutor and O'Neal was sheriff.

Years ago, most of the men in Haughville, including Boswell, Bayt and O'Neal, used to work at one of two plants in the area, Link-Belt Dodge or National Malleable and Steel Castings. O'Neal remembers Ketcham Street as "a Saturday night shopping town."

"We went with our parents and had to stand around while they visited in front of the stores," he recalls. "It was a nice little community, a healthy area of working-class people, not poor or rich. I guess you'd put them between poor and middle class. Any kid in Haughville learned to take care of himself. There were a lot of good, solid, churchgoing families but it was a rough-and-tumble crowd, too."

Republicans as well as Democrats regard Bayt, Boswell and O'Neal as honest. In a city where mayors, prosecutors and sheriffs have shown a willingness to take favors, gifts, money—or, as one gambler put it, "even a red-hot stove"— no one suspects that Boswell, Bayt or O'Neal would take a nickel.

Before the Ketcham Street kids came to power, gambling was wide open, prostitution flourished and the numbers racket and baseball lotteries were big. For many years, under the Democrats and the Republicans, a bookie joint operated by the late Ralph (Hot Horse) Hitch went untouched across the street from the police station, half a block from the sheriff's office and jail and an easy stone's throw from the prosecutor's office.

Hitch was a colorful, 350-pound blimp of a former deputy sheriff, politician, gambler, ex-football star at Butler University and onetime newspaperman whose taste in periodicals ranged from the *New Yorker* magazine to the *Daily Racing Form*. Hitch's gambling establishment also was a bail-bonding company and a meeting place for cops, politicians, newspapermen, whores and touts. A newspaperman once asked him, "How's business?"

Hitch replied, "Business is so bad I had to lay off two cops."

As they came to power, Bayt, Boswell and O'Neal cleaned up the wide-open rackets. What remained were some play-for-pay girls working out of private homes and hotels, gamblers running floating crap games in hotels and motels and bookie joints and lotteries operating on the sly. Racketeers were afraid to run in the county. O'Neal had the reputation of being the cleanest, best and toughest sheriff in Marion County history.

In recent years, as Boswell and Bayt tried to pass City Hall back and forth between them as their personal preserve, they have become recognized more and more for what they are—astute political bosses who know how to crack the whip and give out jobs where it will help the political cause the most. O'Neal has since broken politically with the other two because, he says, they want to keep all the choice jobs for themselves.

Bayt is a lawyer. He flunked the bar exam three times before he passed it "on oral examination." He served, for a year, as a Secret Service agent and handled a variety of New Deal jobs and then went into politics full blast as the protégé of the colorful Al Feeney. Bayt served as deputy sheriff under Sheriff Feeney and as City Controller under Mayor Feeney. Later, he was elected Mayor and Prosecutor on his own.

Boswell was a social worker and earned a reputation as a fine chief probation officer of the Juvenile Court. He became the protégé of Bayt, served as City Controller under Mayor Bayt and later was elected Mayor on his own. He has had two major political disappointments. While he was Mayor he tried to win the Democratic nomination once for Lieutenant Governor and once for U.S. Senator. He lost both times.

O'Neal, whose father was Chief of Detectives in Indianapolis, started out as a career state police trooper, rising to Superintendent of the force. Governor George N. Craig, a

Republican, tried to demote O'Neal and put in a political crony and Legion pal. O'Neal quit and ran for sheriff, which he won against a Republican landslide.

The Ketcham Street Kids are not what you'd call New Frontier Democrats. Bayt once said after a meeting of the Sigma Delta Chi journalism society that his thinking on foreign affairs was similar to the philosophy of former Senator William E. Jenner, the conservative Republican. Boswell takes his philosophy straight from the editorial pages of Eugene Pulliam's right-wing *Indianapolis Star*. At the Columbia Club, a well-known conservative once said he was for Boswell for Senator because Boswell is "far to the right of Barry Goldwater." Down through the years, Boswell, Bayt and O'Neal have turned themselves inside out to "get along" with Pulliam. Alone of all Democrats in Indianapolis, these three got the best notices in the *Star*. They got their pictures in the paper and often.

"Boswell, Bayt and O'Neal all carried the *Star* when they were boys," is a saying in Indianapolis. "And the *Star* has been carrying them ever since."

But the old gang is broken up. O'Neal gave up politics in disgust to become a U.S. Marshal, sponsored by U.S. Senator Vance Hartke. Boswell gave up politics in futility to become Postmaster, sponsored by Senator Hartke. Bayt alone is left in the political arena and has ambitions to become Mayor again.

The Ketcham Street Kids have something else in common, a compulsion to let the Chamber of Commerce help them run things.

When he was elected sheriff, O'Neal appointed John Burkhart, then president of the Chamber of Commerce and conservative finance-committee member of the County Republican Party, as the head of the Sheriff's Advisory Commission.

Not Boswell, not Bayt, nor any other Democrat (or Republican) Mayor in modern times has had the temerity to run City Hall without the constant help, guidance and advice of the Chamber of Commerce. Except one! Mayor Al Feeney told Bill Book and Carl Dortch of the Chamber of Commerce that they were cordially uninvited.

The day Feeney died in office, on November 12, 1950, his protégé, the incoming Mayor Phil Bayt telephoned Dortch of the Chamber of Commerce. "Come on over tomorrow and help me out," Bayt said.

IN INDIANAPOLIS, you climb the stairway to social success, if you climb at all, on the lively arts. There is a competitive cultural compulsion in the city, as if the citizens are trying to prove to the world (and themselves) that they don't live by basketball alone.

Needlessly, it seems, Indianapolis is suffering from a cultural mass inferiority complex. Yet the very provincial pride that infects Hoosiers is the motivating force behind the surprisingly strong cultural activity in town. It is smart to support culture. It's where the socially ambitious young man and young woman can meet the town's elite. Working for the symphony or the art museum may get your name in the society columns. While it isn't a guaranteed social equalizer, it helps.

Few towns of comparable size can boast the number or variety or quality in the arts: Maestro Izler Solomon's work with the highly rated Indianapolis Symphony; Wilbur Peat's direction of the John Herron Museum of Art (which featured in March 1963 the "El Greco to Goya" art exhibit, the biggest and best gathering of classic Spanish work in America); the country's oldest community theatrical organization in continuous operation, the Civic Theater; in winter the professional theater season at the Murat and at Intro, and in summer the wonderful Starlight musicals at Butler University's vast Theatron and the Avondale Playhouse; the multitude of public and private art galleries all over the city; the fresh, enthusiastic amateur theater groups; the jazz musicians and the classical music groups, including the semiprofessional Philharmonic Orchestra.

Coming up next for Indianapolis when the new Clowes Memorial Hall for the Performing Arts is in full swing on the Butler University campus will be a Civic Opera Association and a Civic Ballet Association.

With all this activity going on, there doesn't seem to be a cultural lag. "Sure there is provincialism here," says Henry Butler, music and drama critic for the *Indianapolis Times* and a concert pianist in his own right. "But it is overrated." Butler is the town's leading cultural critic and conscience. He says, "Provincialism is a neurosis here not substantiated by facts."

THERE ARE some politicians who argue that General Dwight D. Eisenhower had an easier time establishing a beachhead on Normandy than he did in Indiana politics.

In 1952, Indiana was the heart of Taftland. Senator Robert A. Taft of Ohio was stronger in the Hoosier state than he was in his own. Indiana Republicans vowed to do or die for him. Blasé politicians, who would deal and double-deal at the drop of a half-pint, talked of Fighting Bob Taft with reverence.

Eisenhower may have been a war hero and a great public figure to millions of Americans, but the Republican pros in Indiana disliked and distrusted him. They considered him, at best, an interloper and an amateur in politics and, at worst, a front man for internationalists and Wall Street bankers.

Eisenhower never did win over the officers and men of the Grand Old Party in Indiana. But he did secure a beachhead in Indianapolis. The man whose generalship turned the tide was H. (for Herman) Dale Brown, the Napoleon of Marion County Republican politics.

Brown used rank-and-file Republicans in the precincts

and wards as shock troops. But he routed the Old-Guard Taft forces (and later the Adlai Stevenson Democrats) with fresh, bright and eager volunteers who had never before participated in politics.

The volunteers were housewives, professional men, businessmen, high school pupils and college students. They didn't know a poll book from a party hack. Brown organized them in a block-by-block crusade for "morality." The amateur volunteers amazed the pros with their zest, enthusiasm and almost uncontrolled and unprofessional capacity for hatred of the enemy, whomever it happened to be.

It was Dale Brown's shining hour in politics. He has been undisputed boss of the Republican Party in Indianapolis ever since.

As leader, Brown has had more than a voice behind the scenes in the issuance of liquor permits for taverns and package stores, for granting zoning variances in restricted areas, for key appointments at City Hall, the courthouse and statehouse, for plush contracts on highway jobs and on political jobs wherever Republicans hold office.

Brown says that most times when he used his influence in liquor cases or on zoning variances it was "to protect the neighborhood." He adds, "One of the reasons I've been successful in politics is because I've had the community at heart."

He is one of the last of the big city bosses around. Smallish, smooth, still in his fifties, and with a taste for fashionable suits, Brown is a cross between an old-fashioned precinct politician and a modern, intellectual political leader versed in philosophy and issues.

When the State of Indiana held a public hearing to determine if the transit company was discriminating, Brown went and testified that Negroes weren't getting their fair share of jobs. When the nonpartisan League of Women Voters needed money to put out a special election newspaper, Brown forked over the dough. When newspapermen needed straight, inside political dope, Brown talked confidentially and truthfully. Most political bosses know how to get along with the do-badders. Dale Brown knows how to get along with the do-gooders.

He is a politician's politician. He works at it day and night and prepares his precincts thoroughly. When a Republican official goes down in disgrace, as happens from time to time, Dale Brown doesn't go down with him. He has an uncanny ability to leap off the back of a floundering public official and onto a new public hero. He was being counted out when he jumped on the Eisenhower bandwagon.

Back in 1956, Brown was bitterly opposed to Senator Homer Capehart. He posed for a newspaper picture with a sign saying: "Send Homer Capehart Back to Washington, INDIANA," which happens to be the Senator's hometown. In 1962, Brown helped plan, organize and execute Capehart's unsuccessful campaign for re-election. Dale Brown's forces carried Marion County for Capehart, and Brown was rewarded in 1963 with being named Republican State Chairman.

Unlike so many political bosses who throw their weight against the public, Dale Brown is a great respecter of and believer in public opinion. He tries to find out which way the public is going and then tries to get out in front. If he sometimes talks one way and acts another, he justifies it on the ground that you can lead the public best if you "let 'em think you're with 'em all the way."

As a longtime political leader, Brown serves at the pleasure of the rank-and-file workers in the precincts. It is not so well-known that he also serves at the pleasure of the "angels" of the party—the men who provide (or collect) the funds for the political machine.

The three principal angels of the Republican Party in Indianapolis are John Burkhart, former president of the Indianapolis Chamber of Commerce, attorney Kurt Pantzer and Silas Reagan, a retired businessman.

Brown tries to minimize the behind-the-scenes role played by the Republican "angels." The truth is that all three have a big voice in the affairs of the party. For example, they had one falling out with a Republican candidate for Mayor, William Sharp, because he would not, in advance of the election, promise to let them pick his top administration officials.

They offered to compromise if he would promise to give them "veto power" over City Hall officials. Sharp refused.

"And where do you think you'll get the money for your campaign?" he was asked.

"I'll raise it myself," he replied.

All of a sudden, Dale Brown and the party lost interest in Bill Sharp. He didn't just lose the election. One Republican official said, "He fought his way to obscurity."

four

THE GAME OF POLITICS

Yes, the old state, as the days have come and gone, has struck a right good average. It has perhaps had no towering mountain peaks, but it has surely furnished as many first-grade second-class men in every department of life as any state in the Union.

—THOMAS R. MARSHALL

NOT ALL the good guys are Republicans. Not all the bad guys are Democrats. And vice versa.

Once you grasp this and stop viewing things through partisan eyes (or with philosophic feelings), it is easier to understand Indiana politics, which is a game played by tough professionals.

There are five basic characteristics which are peculiar to the political game in Indiana. Exceptions are rare (and should be savored). If you want to know the score, you should remember:

1. You cannot escape from politics in Indiana. "You teach your kids how to read outa primers," a politician once told John Bartlow Martin. "In Indiana we begin 'em on a poll book." It is said that the first words of every child born in Indiana are these: "I am not a candidate for office, but if

nominated and elected, I promise to serve to the very best of my ability."

2. Democrats are almost as conservative as right-wing Republicans. A genuine, flaming liberal is about as common as a skyscraper in Kirklin, Shelbyville or Noblesville. If there is an ideological split, it is not between the liberals and the conservatives, but between the patriots and the superpatriots.

3. Hoosiers play politics for their own whimsical amusement, personal prestige, profit and promotion. It is often said that an Indiana politician stands on principle, but only if it doesn't stand in his way of making a buck. It is no secret that every Indiana politician carries in his poll book his timetable to the White House.

4. Farmers dominate the Indiana cities in as unjust, undemocratic and absurd a manner as anywhere in the United States. Indiana cities cannot even make the laws to regulate themselves. Hoosier mayors must go, hat in hand, to the lopsided legislature, controlled by unsympathetic rural politicians, to get back even a portion of the money the cities pour into the state treasury. No Indiana city has any influence beyond its borders, as Chicago overshadows Illinois, or as New York City influences parts of New York, New Jersey and Connecticut, or as Detroit dominates Michigan. "The yokels hang on because old apportionments give them unfair advantages," H. L. Mencken wrote in 1928. Today the real struggle in the State Legislature is as much between the cities and rural areas as it is between the Democrats and Republicans.

5. There is widespread and cynical disregard of good government and the welfare of the people. Politicians who make (and administer) the laws Hoosiers live by cater to the powerful, selfish, special-interest groups. "We have the best legislature money can buy," is a kidding-on-the-square comment heard in the corridors of the Statehouse. Another is: "An honest politician is one who pays income tax on the money he gets for selling his vote." The late A. Brown

(Doc) Ransdall, wise and knowledgeable Indiana correspondent for the *Louisville Courier-Journal,* used to say, "Indiana is ripe for reformers, but no reformers are in sight."

Now let us look at what these five important contributions to the political scene have done for (or to) Indiana. Some of these revelations will shock outsiders, but not Hoosiers. Not only is the politics-as-usual climate accepted in Indiana, but Hoosiers have a pride in the customs, traditions, and heritage of political peccadilloes. They even have a certain grudging admiration for opponents who play the game well.

THE GROCER gets relief business if he kicks back to the township trustee. If he shortchanges the family on welfare, as happens, it is to pay off the trustee.

In the 1930's, the dashing, flashing, white-haired Governor Paul V. McNutt allowed "deserving Democrats" (Frank McHale, Billy Clauer, Tom Taggart, R. Earl Peters, Bill Black, Bill Kunkel and others) to collect a percentage on every case of beer "imported" into the state. McHale himself wrote the law, which gave McNutt's pals a monopoly on the beer business in Indiana. Under Governor Ralph Gates, as World War II ended, Democrats were ousted and Republicans wound up with all the big beer wholesale businesses. Governor Henry F. Schricker came along and forced every Republican beer wholesaler to take a Democrat partner in what were accurately labeled "shotgun marriages."

Some of the biggest law firms in the state have partners on both sides of the political fence so they can do business with Democrats and Republicans. Policemen go up and down the ladder, depending on their friends in City Hall. Politicians write utility laws with built-in rate increases for water, gas, electric and transit companies. There's political fixing, favoritism and just plain meddling in schools, mental health, organized labor, business, civic affairs, street paving,

road building and getting elected president of the Broad
Ripple High School PTA.

Selfish interests hire powerful lobbyists to influence the
State Legislature, a shadowy no-man's land where every pressure group is represented and the public is not. Out of it
come mechanic's lien laws, which force innocent home-own-
ers to pay twice for repairs. Hoosier workers are caught in
the web of too-easy credit (and fantastically high and hidden
interest rates) because loan sharks and political sharks infest
the Statehouse corridors.

Once there was a nationally advertised bourbon whiskey
with strange political connections. If you displayed it on the
counter of your tavern or package liquor store, you could
have crap games, take bets on horse races and have lottery
jars openly on the table without interference from the police.

Governor George N. Craig handpicked as the state's
mental-health commissioner a woman who had limited experience, if any, in a state mental hospital, Dr. Margaret
Morgan. A gay, bronzed skiing enthusiast, she was called (by
enemies) "the society psychiatrist" and (by friends) "the Joan
of Arc of Psychiatry." Dr. Morgan's family owned the Morgan
Packing Company and was a powerhouse in Indiana politics.
Her brother Jack was a Republican district chairman and
member of the GOP State Committee, ruling body of the
party.

The storm warnings went up early in Dr. Morgan's
reign. Hospital administrators quit. Politicians ran the wards.
At the Muscatatuck School for Retarded Children in North
Vernon, the superintendent Alfred Sasser was forced to resign. He made the mistake of trying to run the institution,
which displeased Marvin Thompson, the business administrator. Thompson was the son-in-law of the Republican County
Chairman Fred Matthews, who also happened to be the judge
of the Jennings Circuit Court. (Having a political boss for
judge doesn't faze Hoosiers.)

Sasser was accused of poor management. One of the hospital workers was charged and indicted on a morals count (later dropped). Much of the political shenanigans in mental hospitals was cleaned up in succeeding administrations of governors Harold Handley and Matthew Welsh.

Yet, in 1962, when Muscatatuck hired a retired police chief as security officer, Governor Welsh's executive secretary Jack New and other Democrats set up a howl. The new security chief, it seems, was a Republican.

Indiana politics is on a year-round basis whether or not it is an election year. For example, the Democrats and Republicans always maintain big headquarters staffs—clerks, secretaries and press agents. Where does the money come from?

When the Democrats are in the Statehouse, all employees are expected to "voluntarily contribute" 2 percent of their wages to the party. Those who decline to volunteer are usually no longer needed. Republicans who screamed in anguish when the Democratic war chest bulged knew a good thing then they saw it, and adopted their own version. Republican workers generally are asked to contribute one week's salary each year to the GOP. Now city halls and courthouses all over Indiana have their own fund-raising gimmicks. You can safely say that nearly every person who works in a political office in Indiana is obliged to contribute part of his salary, no matter how small, to his boss's campaign or to the party headquarters. Richard Martin, press spokesman for Governor Welsh, defends the practice. It is, he says, "cheaper than an employment agency fee."

Of course, the prime requisite for filling a job in Indiana is not what you know, but who you know, and in what political party. The first of the great political Statehouse machines was created under Governor McNutt. His pals fired every Republican in the Statehouse and replaced them with Democrats.

In the State Highway Department, a pretty Republican secretary remained on the job. Pleas Greenlee, McNutt's patronage secretary, was furious.

"We can't fire her," said Frank McHale, "she's sleeping with one of the Statehouse reporters."

"Hell," roared Greenlee, "get him a Democrat secretary to sleep with."

Years later, McHale went before Governor Handley's Alcoholic Beverage Commission to try to prevent a national distiller from coming into the state to make an Indiana-bonded bourbon. Noble Ellis, a gentle, understanding farmer from Orleans, perhaps the most honorable man ever to sit as chairman of the liquor commission, started to explain what the law was by reading the book.

"Don't tell me, Sonny," snapped McHale, "I wrote the law."

You cannot get a tavern license unless you play ball with the downtown politicians. Insurance agents with the right connections get the city, county and state insurance plums. Construction firms have at least one prominent Democrat and one well-known Republican to play both sides of the street. You get your automobile license plates and driver's license from a ward chairman or a precinct committeeman, who divvy the profit with the state. The respected Indiana State Police is untouched by merit system or civil service. It is bipartisan. (Politicians who wrote the law insisted that half the troopers be Republicans and half Democrats.)

"POLITICS is the most unfair of callings," Stewart Alsop wrote. "In no other vocation do professionalism and experience count for so little."

The exception, of course, is Indiana.

Alsop rightly pointed out that twice in the last twenty-five years the Republican Party has turned down the professional and offered its greatest prize to a rank amateur. This just doesn't happen in Indiana. The amateur doesn't beat the Hoosier pro.

When Wendell Willkie won the Republican presidential nomination in 1940, and Dwight D. Eisenhower in 1952, they were both amateurs. They were also bright, shining new faces on the political horizon, easier to sell, the party leaders said, than the same tired old politicians. More than anything else, the Eastern political leaders in particular liked the new, exciting brand of Republicanism they were preaching. It would help get votes in the big cities.

One GOP strategist said, "What the party needs above all else is a winner."

In Indiana the old pros said, "What kind of victory is it when you desert the ship . . . when you abandon Republican principles? Why win?"

Willkie and Eisenhower, the amateurs, the interlopers, the modern Republicans, were disliked, if not actually detested, by Hoosier conservatives of the Grand Old Party.

The situation hasn't changed. Twenty years after Willkie threw out his hands and proclaimed this "One World," his son Phillip, burning with ambition and egotism and brilliant in a helter-skelter way, threw himself on the mercy of the Indiana old guard. Phillip begged for support from the Taft-Jenner wing of the party. "What can I do, what can I say, how can I ever get you guys to back me?" young Willkie pleaded.

"Repudiate One World," shot back Lisle Wallace, then Republican chairman of the Sixth District.

Young Willkie did not repudiate One World. He also did not get the nomination for Governor, Lieutenant Governor or Secretary of State, all offices he wanted and made a stab for. At the Republican National Convention in Chicago, he made a spectacle of himself by running himself for Vice President. The Indiana GOP reluctantly gave him the nomination for Superintendent of Public Instruction and he campaigned on a conservative platform of "no nonsense frills" in education. He got the political thrashing of his life. Thousands of Indiana teachers marched en masse to the polls in protest, at the skillful direction of teacher-lobbyist Robert

Wyatt. Willkie ran far behind the GOP ticket and was one
of only two Republicans defeated. The other was Crawford
Parker, who lost the Governorship to Democrat Matthew E.
Welsh.

IN 1952 on a hot July day in Chicago, the Stockyards Amphitheater aisles were jammed with weary, sweaty delegates,
milling and pushing. They sang and stomped, whistled and
cheered and tooted noisemakers.

The Grand Old Party had once again turned its back on
"Mr. Republican"—Senator Robert A. Taft—and given its
most coveted honor to a man who had never before voted,
General Dwight D. Eisenhower.

"Lincoln was assassinated again—this time by Republicans," said Lisle Wallace, a down-the-line Taft man. "It was
a fight between the millionaires and the billionaires," commented reporter Dan Kidney, "and the billionaires won."
Taft said it was a victory for Wall Street. George Diener and
H. Dale Brown, the original Eisenhower men in Indiana,
called it "the beginning of a moral crusade," a defeat for
reactionaries and a victory for the middle of the road. It
was a triumph, said then-Senator William E. Jenner "for
One-Worlders, internationalists and big spenders." Melo-
dious-voiced, Bible-quoting Senator Everett M. Dirksen had
pointed an accusing finger at Governor Thomas E. Dewey of
New York and bitterly warned, "We followed you before,
and you took us down the road to defeat." Editor Walter
Leckrone of the *Indianapolis Times* said the liberals had re-
captured the Republican Party.

The Indiana delegation had gone to Chicago with thirty
votes for Taft and two for Eisenhower. The Ike delegates
were the late Big Bill Hutcheson of the Carpenters Union
and publisher Eugene Pulliam, who was more conservative
than Taft but felt the only hope the Republican Party had
of winning was by nominating Eisenhower. Arthur Summer-

field of Michigan approached the Hoosiers: "Ike needs Indiana to put him over." Furious and red-faced, Pulliam
turned to Cale J. Holder, chairman of the delegation, and
said, "We only lack nineteen votes for Ike. You've got a
chance to be a hero." Holder replied, "Hell no."

Finally, Harold E. Stassen's Minnesota delegation
abruptly changed its mind and threw all twenty-eight of its
votes to Ike. It was all over.

One by one, the Taft states jumped on the Ike bandwagon. "Mis-tah Chairman," shouted the man into the mike
over the din. "Wisconsin wishes to change its vote. Wisconsin
now wants to cast all of its votes for the next President of the
United States, Dwight D. Eisenhower." More cheers.

Up at the Blackstone Hotel, in a suite of rooms occupied
by the Ike campaign headquarters, a group of Hoosier girls—
volunteer clerks and secretaries recruited in the Eisenhower
crusade—were clustered around a television set, sobbing their
eyes out. I never could find out whether it was a mass trau-
matic experience because Indiana did not endorse Ike, or
because they were proud the Hoosier delegation had the
courage to stand fast.

On the convention floor there was bedlam. Taftman
Clark Springer, former State Chairman, slugged United Press
photographer Stanley Tetrick. Delegations marched riotously
and joyously behind Ike placards and state standards. But
not Indiana. The Hoosiers went down fighting at the barri-
cades for Taft.

There took place on the convention floor an episode
that revealed the intense dedication of the Hoosiers for Taft.

Joey Goldstein's loyalty to the Grand Old Party and the
Taftmen who ran it knew no bounds of propriety. He did
political odd jobs. But the oddest of all was when he sym-
bolically placed the Indiana standard between two rows of
chairs and deliberately broke it in half. Taft may have lost,
but the Hoosiers took satisfaction in the knowledge that the
Indiana standard was not paraded in the Eisenhower victory
demonstration.

Note: Only three other Taft states besides Indiana refused to jump on the Ike bandwagon: Ohio, Illinois and Utah.

IN 1962, Charles Boswell was the Democratic Mayor of Indianapolis, biggest city in the state, when he decided to run for United States Senator. At the time, I wrote: "Boswell is campaigning on a platform designed to win the vote of Barry Goldwater."

Boswell was a nice guy, a good golfer, financially on the square, a social-worker-turned-politician. But nothing in his background indicated that he would embrace, as he did, the slogans, philosophy and catch-words of the Chamber of Commerce and publisher Eugene Pulliam. Boswell was aghast (and against) such Democratic programs as federal aid for slum clearance and flood control. He had a field day slugging Indiana AFL-CIO president Dallas Sells ("he's trying to remake the Democratic Party in the image of Walter Reuther"), the Democratic candidate for Congress Andrew Jacobs, Jr. ("immature, unfit for federal office, selfish, spoiled brat") and his own Governor Matthew E. Welsh ("he has the backbone of a fishing worm"). The Republicans never had a better hatchet man.

You could say that Boswell, while tearing the Democrats to pieces, showed remarkable restraint in not saying an unkind word about Republican Congressman Donald Bruce, onetime employee of publisher Pulliam (as radio news commentator). In his freshman year, Bruce prided himself on voting no in Congress to such an extent that he earned the sobriquet, "The Abominable No Man."

Perhaps Boswell visualized a conservative triumph—Senator Boswell, Democrat, and Congressman Bruce, Republican? How do you go about attacking a man who is on record for practically everything you want to espouse?

Boswell's extreme conservatism and name-calling finally got him in trouble with the Democrats. He was defeated for

the Democratic Senate nomination by thirty-four-year-old
Birch Bayh, Jr. of Terre Haute, who ran as a Kennedy
Democrat.

Boswell is not alone among Democrats as a conservative.
Senator Vance Hartke was influenced by Vice President
Lyndon Johnson, a stranger on the New Frontier. The political Bobbsey Twins, Frank McHale and Frank McKinney, who
ran the Democratic Party in Indiana for nearly twenty years,
are big-business oriented. Former Governor Henry F.
Schricker, by comparison, makes Senator Harry Byrd of Virginia seem like the last of the big spenders. About the only
Democrat with a statewide reputation who approaches being
a liberal is Governor Welsh, and he is a lawyer with a banking and business background.

Try as they might, though, the Democrats just cannot
be more conservative than the Republicans, especially in an
election.

Republican Homer Capehart did not run against Democrat Birch Bayh for Senator in 1962. Republican William
Jenner did not run against Democrat Henry Schricker for
Senator in 1952. Republicans rarely run against their opponents. They run against Harry Truman, Walter Reuther,
socialism, the United Nations, the "Democrat War Party,"
the "unconstitutional income tax," the international conspiracy of communism and Democratic "softness on Reds,"
all of which, the theme goes, will getcha if you don't watch
out.

When Governor Harold Handley ran for Senator in the
middle of his term, his campaign bogged down in the cities,
where he was blamed for increasing taxes and for allowing
the right-to-work bill to become law. Panicky Republicans
held a supposedly secret strategy meeting in a huge room of
the Severin Hotel in downtown Indianapolis. Closed doors
notwithstanding, reporters outside could clearly hear the
fiery burn-your-bridges-behind-you advice of Senator Jenner.
He blurted out,

Forget the God-damned cities. Draw a circle around every single one and don't set foot in them. Forget 'em. Concentrate on the farms and the towns. If we can't win in Indiana, we can't win anywhere. We've got the most conservative press and the most conservative people in America, from Lake Michigan to the Ohio River. Pour it on. Call the Democrats dupes, dopes, pinks and finks.

Democrats say they like to hear Jenner rave, particularly when he gives the world twenty-four hours to get out.

Handley lost. In addition to higher taxes and the right-to-work law, many Hoosiers became disenchanted with Handley because he was running for another office in the middle of his term as Governor.

WORD portraits of men in politics are difficult, not so much because politicians try to be all things to all men, but because what a politician says or does means one thing to one man and something else to another. It is not possible to be entirely fair (or just) about living politicians. Everyone enjoys some political prejudice—the truck driver, the professor and the writer.

Here are some of the men who have shaped Indiana politics in the last twenty years—the old pros and the new breed —and my impressions of them. All have a passion for politics. All are colorful and interesting.

LIKEABLE Ralph Gates can't say no. His friends josh that if he were a girl, he'd always be pregnant. The small town lawyer and banker was elected Governor in 1944. One Republican grudgingly paid him the supreme political compliment: "Ralph Gates knows how to tell the truth . . . and maneuver out of it." He is a politician's politician, perhaps the ablest in all Indiana. Gates says he is successful in it be-

cause it is his avocation and not vocation, meaning he doesn't
need the money.

Robert Bloem, city editor of the *Indianapolis Times,*
and onetime press agent for the Democratic Party in Indiana,
was a political reporter when Republican Gates left the
Governor's office. Bloem wrote: ". . . He will leave the in-
delible mark of a colorful and progressive administration."

Gates rescued mental hospitals from near collapse, reorganized the public-health program, started a statewide avi-
ation program, expanded the state-park system, made
advances in flood control and created the Department of Commerce and Public Relations. The list is long, but in spots
Gates' record has been controversial and the going rough.

Apparently one of the reasons it was rough is that Gates
couldn't stay out of a fight. "If someone petitioned the State
Highway Department for a traffic light, Gates would get involved," one of his own department heads said.

The chunky Gates, who always seemed to be peering
down the lower part of his glasses to see, was born February
24, 1893 at Columbia City, the rural seat of Whitley County
in northeast Indiana, where he still lives. In 1963, at the age
of seventy, he worked from 9 A.M. to 7 P.M. in his law office.

There is a difference. Years ago, for amusement, he used
to come to Indianapolis to spend long, nocturnal sessions
with fellow Republican politicians in smoke-filled rooms. Today he is growing flowers in his spare time. Beautiful flower-
beds surround his new home on Crooked Lake, eight miles
from his law office. The house is shaded by a small grove of
big sycamore trees. On a hill at the rear are pine trees, en-
hanced by wild flowers and dogwood and redwood.

Life would be complete for Gates if his son Robert followed in his footsteps to the Governor's Mansion. Like his
father, Robert joined the Navy in wartime, became state
commander of the American Legion and Republican Chairman of the Fourth District.

Ralph Gates has been described as "downright jolly,

handsome in a rough, unadorned way, all plain, intelligent
Hoosier, a friendly, sympathetic man to whom anybody could
take his troubles." He is probably the most underrated Governor, lobbyist, lawyer and politician Indiana ever had. He is
country smart.

In 1953, the railroads were taking a licking in the State
Legislature, even though a former railroad lawyer, George N.
Craig, was Governor. The rush call was put out for "the best
friend the railroads ever had in Indiana"—Ralph Gates.

Here is how I reported it at the time for the *Indianapolis Times* of February 7, 1953:

> Former Governor Ralph Gates was getting full credit
> today for engineering the railroads' first big victory in the
> State Legislature.
>
> Lawmakers and lobbyists alike credited the former Re-
> publican Governor with putting the brakes on the "full
> crew" railroad law which requires a second brakeman on
> long trains.
>
> Whether he did or not—and he claims he was not the
> conductor—the fact remains the House yesterday passed the
> railroad-sponsored bill, 52–45, while he was very much in
> evidence.
>
> The same measure failed to pass the day before by only
> five votes.
>
> Gates is an attorney for the Pennsylvania Railroad. He
> told the *Times* he was in the Statehouse "only to do some
> legal work for clients."
>
> He was seen at various times conferring with legislators.
> So packed was the chamber with lobbyists—union and rail-
> road—that when the controversial bill came up for a final
> vote, Speaker of the House James D. Allen ordered the doors
> closed and the floor cleared of spectators.
>
> State Representative Phillip Willkie, Rushville Repub-
> lican (and son of Wendell Willkie), said he had been ap-
> proached by lobbyists on both sides. He admitted former
> Governor Gates had given him "the railroad side of the case."
>
> Willkie was one of five Republican lawmakers who voted

in favor of unions Thursday and switched in favor of the railroads the next day. Others were: Walter Barbour, Indianapolis; Edwin Brubeck, Indianapolis; Maurice Chase, Bedford; and Herbert Copeland, Hanover. (Two GOP lawmakers switched from railroads to unions and four Republicans who did not vote the first day cast their votes for the railroads the second time.)

Through the years, politicians in Indiana have picked up a stratagem from Gates' vast political repertoire: "If there's something good to be done and it'll improve your record and stature and you can do it, do it. If you can't do it, appoint a committee and then take credit for doing it."

BULLETIN
LA PAZ, BOLIVIA, NOV. 11 (UPI)—STREET FIGHTING BROKE OUT HERE TODAY AS A FULL-SCALE REVOLUTION BY THE FASCIST FALANGE PARTY THREATENED TO OVERTHROW THE GOVERNMENT.

The words gushed out of the printer in the United Press office on the second floor of the *Indianapolis Times*. It was hardly front-page news in 1953 in provincial Indiana, except for one thing. Senator Homer E. Capehart was in Bolivia on a State Department-sponsored fact-finding and good-will tour. The *Times* tried all day to locate Capehart by long-distance telephone. Either they were having a prolonged siesta down there, or the lines were cut or he was lost. United Press had, all of a sudden, stopped sending news about the revolt. Early the next day we placed a call to the United States Embassy in Santiago, Chile, next stop on Capehart's itinerary. Our luck was good, he was there.

"Are you all right?" I inquired breathlessly.

"Yep, yep, yep," said Senator Capehart.

"Did you see the revolution?"

"We heard shooting. We saw people running around with guns. In the middle of everything we were trapped for thirty minutes in an elevator. I had to climb out through the top with a ladder."

"Were you frightened?"

"What? What? I can't hear you."

I shouted. "Were you frightened?"

"No. I have had enough experience in Indiana politics," Capehart said, "so that I know how to start a revolution, fight a revolution and end a revolution."

Capehart looks like an overstuffed farmer in Sunday-go-to-meeting clothes and talks like one: "I just got back from sloppin' the hogs." He is a farmer, likes to climb on the plow or run the wheat binder or stack wheat at harvest time. There's nothing he can't do on the farm. But a country bumpkin he is not.

Chomping on a perpetual cigar, Capehart is a warm, friendly, impatient man who wants to do everything right now. In 1941, before he was a Senator, a reporter described him as Indiana's "super supersalesman, America's jukebox king and the original Gladhand Charlie."

Born in Algiers, Indiana, Capehart got his formal education at Washington (Indiana) high school. When World War I broke out, he was just a big farmer boy working on what is called the Graham Farm in Daviess County. The height of his ambition was to own a big farm like that. To-day, across the road, he has the farm, only bigger (2,000 acres).

After the war, Capehart temporarily abandoned farming and took to selling. He worked for several corporations selling milking machines, then tractors, then threshing machines and popcorn machines. Later he picked up a patent for a device that shifted phonograph records. Thus started Capehart Corporation, which wound up in receivership after several years during an expansion program in the midst of the Depression.

Homer didn't stay out in the cold long. He sold himself to the Rudolph Wurlitzer Company as vice-president and proceeded to put that company on the map with jukeboxes and musical-instrument sales to schoolchildren. In 1940, Capehart started his own Packard Manufacturing Corporation for musical devices.

He located his company in Indianapolis in typical Capehart style. He blew in one day as if he were going to a fire, shouted for lists of available factory sites, and for a real-estate man to show him around. Ten minutes later he was on his way, and within an hour he had signed a lease.

The sad plight of the Republicans in 1938 gave Capehart a chance to demonstrate to Republicans his gift of salesmanship and showmanship. On the banks of the Wabash, with Franklin D. Roosevelt's New Deal in full bloom, Capehart decided to stage the now-famous Republican Cornfield Conference. On August 27, 1938, from his farm, Capehart announced he was "sick and tired of the New Deal and intended doing something about it." He fed nearly 20,000 Republicans baked clams and chicken under forty striped tents. Federal Judge John S. Hastings said it was "the greatest political rally ever staged in the United States since the great Whig rally on the battlefield of Tippecanoe in May 1840." The mass meeting, widely heralded as a grass-roots conference, wowed the Grand Old Party, revived it and established Capehart as a Republican on the way up.

In 1940 he directed arrangements for the official notification at Elwood, Indiana of Wendell Willkie, Republican nominee for President. In 1941 he headed the British War Relief and organized and directed a huge Indianapolis rally opening the U.S.O. drive. In 1942 he was elected Republican chairman of the Seventh District. In 1943 he was Indiana chairman of Navy Day. And in 1944 he was nominated and elected to the United States Senate.

For eighteen years, Capehart was indestructible in politics. He started out by defeating the champion Democratic vote-getter Henry F. Schricker. Then he polished off Assistant United States Attorney General Alex Campbell in 1950 and six years later he defeated former Secretary of Agriculture Claude Wickard. In 1962, however, he was upset by Senator Birch Bayh, Jr. by 10,000 votes.

Capehart's influence in Washington was greater than many of his own Indiana political associates realized. He was a member of the Senate Committees on Banking and Currency, Foreign Relations, Government Operations and also served on the Joint Committees on Defense Production and Aeronautical and Space Sciences. Capehart got those choice assignments because of his own interests and because of the seniority system, which rules Congress. (When he was defeated, Capehart was the third-ranking Republican in the Senate and fourteenth-ranking in either party.)

The portrait of Homer Capehart as a bumptious conservative, an unreconstructed reactionary trying to drag the world, screaming, back into the 18th century, may have been true once. It hasn't been true since General Eisenhower captured the White House and routed the Republican Old Guard. Capehart's reputation for being an old-fashioned Midwest isolationist is revived every six years when he runs for reelection. This is simply because Capehart himself resurrects his old conservative speeches and lets fly before appreciative Indiana Republican audiences.

But read Dan Kidney's dispatch in the *Indianapolis Times* of March 29, 1953:

Washington, March 29—"Senator Capehart is doing a splendid job. He has taken a lot of criticism from members of his party. But I'm convinced he's putting his country above past considerations."

This praise for Senator Capehart was broadcast over a national network by Senator Paul H. Douglas (D., Illinois), noted economist and long a leading Senate liberal. He was talking about Capehart's fight for standby war emergency economic controls as Chairman of the Senate Banking and Currency Committee . . .

Long labeled as a business spokesman, Capehart now

finds some of the more extreme spokesmen for certain business groups calling him "socialist."

"Maybe I'll be tried before some future McCarthy Committee," he laughed. "It sure is easy to be a liberal in this
Congress."

The very next month, April, Capehart broke with Indiana Republican Congressman Charles Halleck. Capehart
joined Senator Robert A. Taft of Ohio in pushing for a
federal appropriation for public housing. (Halleck said he
never had felt that public housing should be considered part
of Republican Party policy.)

Capehart made his views public:

> I am for private enterprise as everyone knows. But un-
> less you have some public housing you will never get slum
> clearance. The two go together, and one is useless without
> the other. There are some things that private business can-
> not do, and this is one of them. For private business must
> operate at a profit if the concern is to function. There is no
> profit in slum clearance. That makes public housing neces-
> sary.

This is not to say that Capehart is a flaming liberal, a
Hubert Humphrey in conservative clothes. There was a time
when Capehart was a full-fledged member of that hardy band
of stand-patters, the Senate's last-ditch, hold-the-line boys—
Jenner, Welker, McCarthy, Malone. (Oregon's liberal, sharp-
tongued Senator Wayne Morse once called Capehart "a
rancid tub of ignorance.")

"In eighteen years in the Senate you sometimes change
your views," is how Capehart explains his flexibility. "I'm
not the smartest man in the world. Sometimes I change my
opinion. Sometimes I'm wrong."

What hurts Capehart most of all is that the do-or-die

Taft and Jenner Republicans in Indiana don't love him. Perhaps they could forgive a deviation in philosophy here and there. But in Indiana, where political realists say, "If yer not fer me, yer agin me," Capehart has committed heresy. He liked Ike in 1956. And if this was not bad enough, he was suspected of secretly liking Nelson Rockefeller in 1962.

What I remember best about Capehart is the 1950 election campaign, riding along the country roads of Indiana in the back seat with Ben Cole of the *Indianapolis Star.* Capehart was saying, "Of course, it's possible for me to be President. Why not? How do you think they're picked? It's whatever the big boys on Wall Street say."

VANCE HARTKE was born May 31, 1919 in the small mining town of Stendal, Indiana, where his father was a teacher, a local political leader and postmaster.

In the book Hartke co-authored with John Redding, *Inside the New Frontier,* Hartke says that when he was a pupil of his sister Ruth, he wrote a theme on what he was going to be when he grew up. He said he would be Governor of Indiana—or Senator. And, the book happily reports, Senator he was, within thirty years. Modesty, perhaps, keeps Hartke from revealing at this time what his ultimate schoolboy ambition was.

Robert Flynn, political writer for the *Evansville Press,* did a great deal of research on Hartke. He says that Hartke indeed had political aspirations, but that he actually confided to schoolmates he was going to be President. This is not so much a correction as it is notice to Jack Kennedy, Bobby Kennedy, Teddy Kennedy and any other Democrat who has his eyes on the White House in 1964, or 1968, or 1972 or 1976. (In 1976, Hartke will only be fifty-seven.)

What Makes Sammy Run? was the story of a boy who parlayed a burning ambition with ingenious tricks to get to

the top in Hollywood. Hartke could be the Sammy of Democratic politics. He's consistently on the run.

At thirty-six he was elected "the boy mayor" of Evansville. Two years later he was elected U.S. Senator, the first
Democrat elected to represent Indiana in twenty years. As a
freshman Senator, thanks to ingratiating himself with Vice
President Lyndon Johnson, Hartke got two choice Senate
Committee assignments, Commerce and Finance, and later
became chairman of the Democratic Senatorial Campaign
Committee, something that has never before happened to a
brand-new Senator.

Hartke lives, breathes, sleeps and eats politics. His wife
Martha has as much driving ambition as Hartke and works
as hard to put him across.

People still remember the furious campaign Hartke put
on for Mayor. On Halloween night 1955, some youngsters
came "trick or treating" to the door of Mrs. Jack Breskow.
After the candy was dispensed, one youngster pushed his mask
off his face and shouted, "Thank you. And don't forget to
vote for my daddy, Vance Hartke."

Behind the happy-go-lucky, young-man-in-a-hurry Hartke
image there is as calculating a politician as Indiana has ever
produced.

In 1962, for example, Senator Hartke came up with a
something-for-everyone plan. It would rid Indianapolis
Democrats of their own Mayor, Charles Boswell, who was
knocking the party and dragging his feet on the eve of the
election. It would bring harmony to Marion County Democrats. It would help Governor Matthew Welsh elect the
Democratic lawmakers from Marion County he needed to
support his program in the State Legislature. It would give
Prosecutor Phillip Bayt a running start for Mayor in 1963.
And, to the surprise of no one, it would help Hartke win the
loyalty of the Marion County Democratic organization if he
needs it to fight Governor Welsh for the Senate nomination
in 1964.

Hartke then unveiled what is probably the most brazen and cynical political plot ever attempted in Indiana:

Charles Boswell would resign as Mayor to become Postmaster.

Albert Losche would resign temporarily as City Controller.

Phillip Bayt would resign as Prosecutor to become City Controller and then automatically succeed Boswell as Mayor.

Losche would be rehired as City Controller.

Judson Haggerty, Democratic candidate for Prosecutor, would be named Prosecutor, replacing Bayt and giving Haggerty on-the-job training.

Boswell also would resign as County Chairman to be replaced by a harmony political boss.

As fantastic as it sounds, this game of musical chairs with high public office was almost successful. The deal collapsed when Bayt threw in the towel after realizing it was causing a bad taste in the mouths of the public. The *Indianapolis Times* let its readers vote on the issue, with a front-page coupon: "Do you want Boswell for Mayor or Postmaster? Why?" There were no prizes offered. More than 3,000 replies poured in, including telegrams and special-delivery letters. There was almost unanimous condemnation of the deal. People who wanted Boswell to remain as Mayor said he had an obligation to stay in City Hall. People who wanted him to be Postmaster said they wanted to get rid of him as Mayor. (Only one part of the deal went through: Boswell resigned to become Postmaster. He was succeeded by City Controller Losche, seventy.)

At grade school, high school and at Evansville College, Hartke was a top-ranking student. He was president of the student body in college and captain of the basketball team. World War II interrupted Hartke's study of law at Indiana University. He served both in the Coast Guard and Navy and came back to Bloomington to get his law degree.

In Evansville he practiced law, became a deputy prosecutor and was named Democratic chairman of Vanderburgh County, which he used as a springboard to Mayor.

Like most river towns, Evansville was noted for its gambling dives and brothels. Hartke cleaned them up, tried with some success to end traffic-ticket fixing, built swimming pools and filled in chuckholes. He was, at the same time, a good Mayor and a tough political boss who dispensed jobs only through his political machine and on a basis of "what can you do for me?"

Hartke's around-the-clock campaign for Senator was notable in that he did not line up with any single faction and no faction was for him at the start. His friends organized each county. He criss-crossed the state from sunup to sundown. In his book, Hartke tells how he campaigned and served as Mayor at the same time:

> . . . (Hartke) purchased a recording machine and took his work with him as he drove, dictating as he went. Many a stenographer in Evansville in City Hall got to know Hartke's voice without seeing his face. . . . Hartke made as many as eight speeches a day. . . . He was up by eight, ready for the road by nine. He was never in bed before two and more generally three or four in the morning. . . . Many times Mrs. Hartke would substitute for her husband if he was late or detained. Everyone carried something that had on it a huge heart with a key through it—Hart-ke. The Hartke family of five children (now seven) made all the church suppers, picnics, fish fries and barbecues with their parents.

Hartke claims to be an insider on the New Frontier. It would be more accurate to label him a cowhand on the Lyndon Johnson political ranch. What surprises and dismays many Indiana Democrats is that Hartke will kiss and make up with his worst enemy even if it means hurting a friend.

Hartke is personable, an indefatigable campaigner, burning with ambition, a splendid organizer and a ruthless political operator. In his book, he says, "You only learn to take a punch in the nose by being hit on the nose."

There's a line forming in Indiana anxious to teach him how.

CHARLES ABRAHAM HALLECK'S driving ambition, plain for all to see in the Rensselaer High School yearbook, has so far eluded him.

> *Charlie Halleck, our editor in chief*
> *One in whom we have much belief,*
> *Has hopes and ambitions today*
> *Of becoming President of the U.S.A.*

Instead he has become one of the roughest, most highly skilled in-fighters in Washington, D.C. As Republican boss in Congress, Halleck has given his party its most effective legislative leadership since the regime of Illinois' tough, pink-bearded "Uncle Joe" Cannon as Speaker (1903–1911).

Halleck has exerted more influence on national legislation than any Democrat or Republican from Indiana. With Democratic Congressman Howard W. Smith of Virginia, Halleck has formed a coalition of Republicans and Southern Democrats which, at times, is the party in power in Congress. As a reward for his efforts, President Eisenhower wrote Halleck: "You are a political genius."

Yet for all his great strengths and abilities (he is a gut fighter, cold and calculating and a ruthless party disciplinarian), Halleck is not admired (or appreciated) by party leaders back home in Indiana.

Hoosiers who issue right-wing credentials by-pass Halleck every time, despite his conservative record. He was an isolationist before World War II, fought against selective service, strongly opposed New Deal–Fair Deal programs, and plunked hard for a balanced budget and against waste and extravagance.

What makes down-the-line conservative Republicans distrust Halleck are his connections with Eastern Republicans. Indiana, even more than Ohio, is the heart of Taftland, and three times, at least, Halleck crossed Taft.

In 1940, Halleck nominated Wendell Willkie, onetime registered Democrat, campus liberal at Indiana University and Wall Street lawyer. (Halleck's reward was basking in the national limelight after an exciting speech, but back home he was hurt politically and within a year broke with Willkie, who wanted aid for Britain.)

In 1948, Halleck adroitly swung the Indiana delegation to Governor Thomas E. Dewey of New York on a promise he would be Dewey's running mate. (Dewey reneged on the deal, fearful that Halleck's conservatism would hurt the ticket.)

In 1952, Halleck was denied a seat at the nominating convention because the Taft forces, tightly gripped by Indiana State Chairman Cale J. Holder and Senator William E. Jenner, felt he would be working (and voting) for Eisenhower on the convention floor, even though he wore in his lapel what has been described as the world's smallest Taft pin. (Halleck went to Chicago anyhow, removed his tiny Taft pin, and worked effectively behind the scenes for Ike.)

It may be that Halleck reached his political peak when Eisenhower was in the White House. On January 2, 1959, after twenty-four years of working toward it, Halleck assumed the top spot among House Republicans, shoving aside Congressman Joe Martin in the process. Halleck's political performance for Ike was brilliant, even when he personally disagreed with the bills. ("I don't like it," Halleck once told Eisenhower about a particularly onerous bill, "but if you say so, Mr. President, I'm with you.") Robert C. Albright reported in the *Washington Post:* "Halleck is Ike's good right arm on Capitol Hill."

When Ike and Mamie departed from the White House, the Halleck image suffered in competition with President

Kennedy, the Kennedy Cabinet and the Kennedy family. With Illinois' velvet-voiced Senator Everett M. Dirksen, Halleck gave the Republican view on a TV press conference labeled the "Ev and Charlie Show." This caused an undercurrent of dissatisfaction with the Halleck performance within the House. Some of it came from younger GOP members who regarded Halleck, at sixty-two, as "old-fogyish" and "too negative." Some of it was instigated by vengeful Taft followers and friends of the deposed Joe Martin.

In 1962, two days after Eisenhower made a personal pilgrimage to Halleck's hometown of Rensselaer to publicly praise "Charlie, my Boy," the Americans for Conservative Action in Indiana dumped the dean of the Hoosier Congressional delegation from its endorsement.

Don A. Tabbert, a protégé of Bill Jenner, former U.S. District Attorney and president of the Indiana chapter of Americans for Conservative Action, pledged $2,800 toward the election of eight Indiana congressional candidates, all Republicans, including five incumbents. Congressmen endorsed were E. Ross Adair of Fort Wayne, Donald Bruce of Indianapolis, Ralph Harvey of New Castle, Richard Roudebush of Noblesville and Earl Wilson of Bedford. (One Republican Congressman was missing from the list besides Halleck: the able, conscientious William E. Bray of Martinsville.)

The Indiana chapter of the Americans for Conservative Action is not alone in dismissing Halleck from the ranks of the "true blue" conservatives. When *Time* magazine presented a favorable profile of Halleck, the *Fort Wayne News-Sentinel* ripped the conservative buttons off Halleck's political tunic. It called Halleck an ultraliberal who with Willkie and Tom Dewey had let "all manner of internationalists, liberals and ultraliberals and worse" into the Republican Party.

The *Time* magazine article, in fact, tells some interesting things about Halleck. How he "led a pleasantly Tarkingtonian life, hunting coons and skunks in the nearby Kankakee marsh, mowing neighbors' lawns for spending money, playing halfback on the high school football team." And how he has come to insert a "Lincoln" in his father's name (Abraham Halleck) because, as a brother explains, it "sounds good to say that in Lincoln Day speeches."

Halleck's boyhood town is Rensselaer (population 5,500), a rigidly Republican farming village in the northwest part of the state that inspired the song "Back Home Again in Indiana."

At Indiana University, Halleck met his future wife Blanche White, was graduated Phi Beta Kappa and was student-union president in his senior year. Even before he finished Indiana University's law school, Halleck ran for prosecutor of Jasper and Newton counties in 1924. He won and has never lost an election since. In 1934, when the New Deal was at its zenith, Halleck was the only Republican elected to Congress from the state. On the day he first walked into the chamber of the United States House of Representatives, the GOP side of the aisle rose, cheering.

In his twenty-eight years in Congress, Halleck has not been rigidly predictable. Ultraconservative Republicans are often made nervous by his flexibility. Modern Republicans are dismayed, they say, because Halleck makes a contemporary Republican sound prehistoric. Democrats like to dig up his old speeches and play them back to him. In good-natured fashion, Halleck tries to put everyone at ease: "There comes a time when a man must put his party ahead of his principles."

FRANK McHALE looks like a political boss should look. He's rough, tough, gruff, smooth-pated and flabby-jowled. For twenty years he had as much power in Indiana as Boss Hague in New Jersey, Pendergast in Kansas City and Kelly in Chicago.

Frank McHale was Paul McNutt's Jim Farley. He helped put McNutt into the Governor's Mansion but, try as he might, he was unable to make him President, as Farley did for Franklin D. Roosevelt.

The 1930's were troubled times when McNutt rode into the political arena, seemingly a Messiah. McNutt pushed through the State Legislature a series of social reforms for the health and welfare of the people. He rewrote the banking laws and reorganized and centralized state government. He awarded jobs to desperate Democrats. Before Roosevelt gave the New Deal to the nation, McNutt gave it to Indiana. The state was cheered and galvanized by McNutt's show of force.

If in the process, McNutt crushed all opposition and shoved through the Legislature laws to further his own ambitions and to create a monopoly in the beer business for his pals it was hardly noticed at the time.

McHale did a good deal of McNutt's skull work and between them they developed a political machine which the late Raymond Clapper said that "for sheer efficiency would have put Boss Kettering of General Motors to shame."

Today McHale justifies the liquor laws he wrote in the McNutt days by saying (1) it kept the bootleggers out of the business in Indiana, (2) it did away with the roadhouse speakeasy (all taverns must be inside a city), (3) it eliminated brewery control over taverns and (4) it kept some "deserving Democrats" from starving, including Clarence Jackson, father of the gross-income-tax law in Indiana, later president of the Indiana State Chamber of Commerce and now chairman of the board of American United Life Insurance Company.

Perhaps McHale's most remarkable contribution to Indiana politics was as the brains behind the "Two Percent Club" law. Under it the Democrats would charge every jobholder 2 percent of his earnings for the privilege of working for the state. The money was supposed to go into the Democratic kitty, to help with election expenses. Governor McNutt justified the law on the theory that everyone knew it took money to run a political campaign and that you had to get your money either from the utilities or special-interest groups—or from your own workers. Although the "Two Percent Club" became a campaign issue in 1935, 1936 and 1938, with the Republicans screaming bloody murder, it is now generally accepted by both parties as "the best way" to raise campaign funds.

FDR was suspicious of McNutt and his growing Indiana political machine. He felt that McNutt posed a constant threat to him. McHale says that Roosevelt flashed the word to eliminate McNutt from politics. Forty-four agents of the Treasury Department's Fraud Division were sent into Indiana, headed by the great investigator John L. Sullivan, who had nailed Al Capone and destroyed the Pendergast machine in Kansas City. For eight months, the T-Men investigated McHale and other top McNutt Democrats, but they found nothing.

McHale is a stout but nimble lawyer. His political and legal careers were brilliantly successful, and it would be hard to say exactly how much one helped the other. So formidable has the McHale name become that the great majority of his biggest clients are wealthy Republicans.

It is easy, almost too easy, to stereotype lawyer-banker-politician-businessman McHale as a political boss solely interested in big fees and profits. He is chairman of the board of his hometown bank, the Logansport National. He was a stockholder, director and counsel for the Empire Ordnance Corporation, one of the most criticized and investigated munitions companies of World War II. In 1941, Missouri's Senator Harry Truman denounced Empire's efforts to buy political influence in Washington as "anything but ethical." McHale today says the guns Empire supplied enabled British tanks to blast General Rommel's Afrika Corps out of the desert. (McHale has a picture of the tanks on his desk in the Chamber of Commerce building in Indianapolis.)

There is not one McHale, there are many: McHale the politician, the gambler at Churchill Downs, the stand-up fighter (in a courtroom, a political brawl or a business deal), the champion of the underdog, the sentimental son of Irish immigrant parents.

Even Indiana politics can't entirely explain the phenomenon of McHale. Five years after World War I (he was stationed at Kelly Field in the Air Corps), McHale came back home to Logansport to practice law. He had helped the veterans of Cass County organize an American Legion post, but he had no intention of going into politics. (Later, he became state commander of the Legion.)

The Saturday before Labor Day 1924, McHale was standing in front of the Ragan & Fansler Pool Room. Off in the distance he heard a band and saw a parade of white-sheeted Kluxers marching down the street. McHale was furious. Everyone in the parade was wearing a white hood and robe except the band, whose members were dressed resplendently in their American Legion uniforms.

As the parade passed down the streets, bystanders were ordered to remove their hats and throw money into the huge flag they were carrying. McHale not only refused to throw money, he wouldn't doff his hat. The parade stopped in front of McHale. Again he was ordered to remove his hat.

Now McHale was a strapping 230-pounder, a former football player at the University of Michigan, but he was all alone. He stepped into the street and challenged anyone to knock his hat off. There were no takers.

The next issue of the town's Klan paper said McHale had a gun in each hand when he issued his "cowardly challenge." McHale says it was this incident which got him interested in politics. "I went out to beat every sonufabitch connected with the Klan," he says.

Politicians, clergymen and reporters have just about given up trying to figure him out. When Sister Lydia, the administrator of Saint Vincent's Hospital in Indianapolis, ordered five doctors removed from the staff for performing unnecessary surgery, McHale, a Catholic, sued the Archdiocese for one dollar. One of the doctors was a poker-playing pal of his and McHale felt the hospital was discriminating against a non-Catholic. (McHale dismissed the suit when the administrator subsequently was transferred to another hospital.) Years later, when the Archdiocese was denied permission to build a school and Catholic Church inside Meridian Hills, a wealthy suburb on the outskirts of Indianapolis, McHale took the case without a fee. He won it in grand style and was honored by the Pope as a Knight of Saint Gregory.

McHale has long been associated in business and politics with Frank McKinney. It was McHale who persuaded President Truman to pick McKinney as National Chairman of the Democratic Party. Both McHale and McKinney handled bankruptcies handed out in the Federal Court of Judge William E. Steckler, who was sponsored politically by McHale. (One of the biggest involved Tom Taggart's mammoth French Lick Springs Hotel now owned by the Sheraton chain. McKinney's old Fidelity Trust Company was named trustee and McHale served as attorney.)

McHale says there are a lot of people who think that "politics is a license to steal." He himself was criticized for representing clients before government agencies while an influential and powerful member of the Democratic National Committee. "I am strictly within my legal rights," he said at the time.

McHale will be remembered in Indiana for having made a technical science out of politics. He took no chances. As McNutt's chief legislative assistant, McHale had a dossier on every legislator, Democrat or Republican. He always wanted to move sure-footed with every politician, know his strengths and his weaknesses. He wanted to be familiar with everything he'd ever said or done. McHale told me, "We knew how much each legislator had in the bank, whether he played with girls. Did he drink? Whether he was married and who were his best friends. We knew if his business was going good or bad and how much he owed."

This screening system helped McHale become one of the most influential men in the Midwest when he was Democratic National Committeeman for Indiana, long after McNutt left the state to become Commissioner of the Philippines.

Unlike Pendergast, Kelly and Hague, McHale did not need a political machine to stay in power. He relied instead on the powerful friends he cultivated and handpicked to high public office. The political misfortunes which beset the Democrats in Indiana helped McHale. So long as the party was winning the White House with FDR while Indiana Democrats were losing, National Committeeman McHale was the chief dispenser of federal jobs in the state. Without having to consult with temperamental Governors, Senators or Congressmen, McHale named postmasters, federal judges, federal district attorneys and put other Hoosiers on federal payrolls, commissions, bureaus and departments.

McHale persuaded McNutt to let Clifford Townsend follow him into the Governor's Mansion. When Earl Crawford had been designated by the Democratic organization as Lieutenant Governor, organized labor objected and McHale removed Crawford's name and wrote in Henry F. Schricker. McHale sponsored William E. Steckler, Luther Swygert and Nathan Swain to the federal bench and Michael Fansler and Paul Jasper to the Indiana Supreme Court. Four federal district attorneys—Matthew Welsh, Marshall Hanley, Gilbert Haney and Alex Campbell—were boosted by McHale. In addition, McHale had secured for Wayne Coy first the WPA regional directorship and later the chairmanship of the Federal Communications Commission. Meredith Nicholson was named minister to Uruguay and John W. Kern, Jr. went on the United States Tax Court, thanks to McHale's influence.

"I checked every damn one of them," McHale says. "I

knew every man's background. I checked it myself. I never had a man go sour. I turned down some of my best personal friends. You couldn't trust 'em."

SAMUEL LUBELL, the door-to-door pollster, came back from South Bend, Indiana with startling information.

"Homer Capehart is in trouble on Medicare," Lubell declared in the city room of the *Indianapolis Times*. Lubell is a highly regarded political forecaster. But he had been in Indiana only three days. Seasoned Indiana politicians and veteran reporters could not, or would not, believe that after eighteen years the undefeated champion of Indiana politics would be upset. Every other poll in the state suggested a Capehart landslide in 1962.

"People in Indiana want Medicare," Lubell persisted. "Not just old people, but their sons and daughters who have to pay their expensive medical bills."

Only one thing kept Lubell from predicting right then and there, three months before the election, that Capehart would lose. On Lubell's sensitive popularity meter, the needle did not register plus or minus at the mention of the name of the Democratic challenger Birch Bayh (pronounced "by").

If Lubell had stayed in Indiana, his needle would have jumped all over the place at the mere mention of the thirty-four-year-old Terre Haute lawyer-farmer. In two months the Democrats had everyone in the state singing about Birch Bayh. In Muncie, Mary Lou Conrad, wife of Bayh's campaign manager, wrote a jingle that made popular overnight Bayh's unusual Welsh-derived name. Sung to the tune of Lucille Ball's "Hey, Look Me Over" (from the Broadway musical *Wildcat*), it went like this:

Hey, look him over; he's my kind of guy
His first name is Birch; his last name is Bayh!

Candidate for Senator of our Hoosier State,
For Indiana he will do more than anyone has done before.

So, hey, look him over; he's your kind of guy,
Send him to Washington; on Bayh you can rely.
In November remember him at the polls,
His name you can't pass by, Indiana's own Birch Bayh.

For the first time since Governor Paul McNutt, the Democrats poured out the campaign funds for radio and TV time. The catchy song was played daily on virtually every radio and TV station in the state. In the final days of the campaign the song really got a workout. You couldn't watch two television programs in a row without hearing the song. Kids were singing it. While they did the housework, women hummed it and kept time with a dustcloth. Men whistled it going to work.

Once, at the Columbia Club, citadel of the Republican Party in Indiana, the orchestra struck up "Hey, Look Me Over." H. Dale Brown, county and state Republican chairman, became so irritated he ordered the Broadway melody banned forever in the club.

When the votes were counted, Bayh won by slightly more than 10,000. It was the biggest upset of the 1962 election.

Bayh's an old hand at belting big boys out of the ring —he was light-heavyweight boxing champ at Purdue. He's also an old hand at coming up a winner. At seventeen he was the champion tomato-grower of Indiana's 4-H clubs. At twenty-two he was president of his senior class at Purdue. At twenty-six he was elected to the Indiana State Legislature. And by the time he was thirty-one he was Speaker of the Indiana House of Representatives.

Only once can Bayh's friends recall a failure to win. That was in a national oratorical contest sponsored by the Farm Bureau. Bayh finished second to a beautiful girl from Oklahoma and, since he couldn't outtalk her, he married her.

Marvella Bayh, Indiana's answer to Jackie Kennedy, is honey-haired, hazel-eyed and slender, with the scrubbed smartness of a Junior Leaguer modeling at tea. She made few speeches, but appeared everywhere with her husband and did extremely effective work.

Bayh was at a disadvantage on the serious side of the campaign. Capehart, a member of the Senate Foreign Relations Committee, had access to private reports. He loudly demanded that the United States invade or blockade Cuba. Bayh ridiculed the idea while his supporters snidely asked if Homer planned to lead the first charge. Bayh backers worked up a slogan: "Vote for Capehart and get a free ride to Cuba."

Then President Kennedy pulled the rug out from under Bayh. He announced what Capehart had been seeking—a naval blockade. That seemed to cinch things for the veteran Republican. The President himself—whom Bayh had been strongly supporting—was joining his opponent. It looked so good, in fact, Capehart slowed down.

Bayh didn't. Caught with his defenses down, Bayh rewrote his Cuba speeches. He said the President's action was based on "facts, not emotion" and charged that Capehart's demand still was irresponsible, as of the time it was made. Bayh kept punching away, right up until the polls closed. His margin of victory averaged two votes per precinct.

Going to Washington was nothing new for Bayh. He lived there most of his first fifteen years. His father, an ex-basketball coach, was an army colonel. (Bayh, Sr. is still in Washington as physical-education director of District of Columbia Schools.)

At fifteen, young Bayh went back to Indiana to live on his grandparents' farm near Terre Haute. After growing his champion tomato patch (and winning a $200 prize), he enrolled at Purdue, but then enlisted in the army.

Learning he was going overseas, he bought four dollars worth of garden seeds. In the town of Hoefgen, Germany he organized ninety German youngsters into an American-style 4-H group, taught them how to grow vegetables and flowers and turned Hoefgen into one of postwar Germany's best-fed towns.

Once back home he finished at Purdue's Agricultural School, went to the State Legislature, studied law and got his law degree from Indiana University in 1960.

As young as he is, Bayh started a precedent in Indiana politics. After he was elected he toured the state and made personal appearances at factory gates and luncheon clubs, trying to thank the voters for sending him to Washington.

GEORGE NORTH CRAIG, who was born August 6, 1903 in Brazil, Indiana, had the rare ability to strut while eating. He was the first World War II veteran to become national commander of the American Legion. A ruggedly handsome lawyer, and with considerable ability and a powerful personality, Craig seemed destined for great things in Republican politics and on the national scene. His election as Governor in 1952 was no surprise, since Eisenhower was at the head of the ticket. Craig's nomination, however, was a surprise. It was expertly directed and executed by Republicans opposed to the Jenner-Taft machine and by some of Craig's Legion buddies.

Four Taft men were running against Craig for Governor: Leland Smith of Logansport, John Van Nuys of Rensselaer, Sam Harrell of Indianapolis and W. O. Hughes of Fort Wayne. Taft forces controlled the state convention but declined to make a choice between their four men. Craig, who was secretly for Dwight D. Eisenhower, publicly said nothing. He won when the Taft candidates could not agree among themselves as to which ones should drop out and which one should stay in and fight Craig.

Craig's regime as Governor ended, for a while at least, his furious ambition for high national office. He appointed first-rate men to second-rate jobs and second-class men to first-class jobs. He had monumental battles with the State Legislature, and his own Republican lawmakers refused to approve his sweeping program to centralize state government, à la McNutt.

When Craig was absent from his office, which was often, lobbyist and public-relations counselor Doc Sherwood used it to make and receive telephone calls (the better to impress clients). Once, at a Press Club affair, veteran newsman Jep Cadou, Sr. publicly asked Craig, "If something should happen to Sherwood, would you become Governor?"

Eventually little Doc Sherwood went to State Prison in connection with a highway scandal and two of Craig's state officials went with him—Highway Chairman Virgil (Red) Smith and Administrative Assistant Bill Sayer, sometimes called the "Assistant Governor." Craig never was implicated in the scandal. But from it he learned an old Indiana political lesson: "It's not your enemies you have to worry about, it's your friends."

Craig has a future in Washington, D.C., where he is practicing law and still has many friends.

HAROLD HANDLEY, born November 27, 1909, was one of the few Governors Indiana produced in modern times who was not a lawyer. He is a good-natured, down-to-earth, friendly fellow who is well-liked. A Republican, he sounds more conservative than Barry Goldwater and Marie Antoinette put together and, in my opinion, it's an act.

Handley wants to belong to The Establishment, which to him would be the industrialists and big businessmen. Before, during and after his term as Governor (from 1957 to 1961), Handley kept up a running attack on the federal government. Some of his criticisms:

> The federal government is the biggest threat to America's eminently successful free-enterprise system.

The Portland Mills Bridge in Parke County.

The Indiana World War Memorial in Indianapolis.

. . . In Indiana we have consistently opposed federal grants for our schools because we want to perpetuate absolute home rule in education.

We have spurned federal grants for library service because there are few communities in Indiana—urban or rural —which are not within short driving distance of fine public libraries. All the federal dollars in the world cannot force a person to read.

The tax dollar of a city council or a state legislature operates openly for all to see. Not so with the carefully hidden dollar of federal bureaucracy, intertwined with federal aid.

Handley was the political protégé of Bill Jenner, who was his friend at Indiana University. The Jenner forces put Handley over for Lieutenant Governor in 1952 and for Governor in 1956. In 1958, Handley ran for U.S. Senator at the urging of Jenner—and lost. (Two things hurt him. He was called "High Tax Harold" because he had raised taxes and he was running for Senator in the middle of his term for Governor.)

Handley's state administration was between mediocre and fair, which is good for Indiana. His greatest political asset was his charming wife Barbara.

The real Handley, to me, was the one I saw instinctively and affectionately hug a Negro child in his office. Organized labor rose up against another Handley, the conservative politician who allowed the right-to-work bill to become law without his signature.

Labor leaders thought Handley double-crossed them on the right-to-work law. Jenner thought Handley was "too soft." Handley ruled, I once wrote, with "hasty indecision."

MATTHEW E. WELSH, who was born September 15, 1912, got into politics (he told five inquisitive cadets from Culver

Military Academy) to "advertise the availability of a struggling young lawyer."

In a dignified, soft-spoken way, he is perhaps Indiana's most articulate Governor. A Democrat, he has friends and relatives in both parties. His sister Margaret married Alex Clark, former Republican Mayor of Indianapolis.

Welsh is a small-town lawyer (Vincennes) grounded in business and banking and seasoned politically in the State Legislature. He has been called ultraliberal. He isn't, except perhaps by comparison with the radical right wing. When the General Assembly appropriated more money than the state could expect to take in, Welsh warned it would bankrupt Indiana. When it came to pass, Welsh drastically cut back spending, withheld millions the Legislature had allocated for construction and ordered a 5-percent across-the-board reduction in personnel.

Welsh enjoys the support of schoolteachers, the college communities, organized labor, minority groups (whose causes he champions), as well as many conservative Democrats, including banker Frank McKinney and lawyer Frank McHale.

The Governor has surrounded himself with some bright, able, young men, notably press spokesman Richard Martin and executive secretary Jack New. His political advisers are in the Indiana tradition—ruthless, professional and tough, including attorney John Hurt and "assistant governor" Clinton Green. Welsh has the charm, poise, intelligence and political machine to climb to national prominence. He has one drawback—an ambition deficiency.

IN HIS detailed and exciting study *Indiana: An Interpretation,* John Bartlow Martin observed:

> Now, a healthy body politic can stand a lot of corruption. But not an endless amount. Healthy Indiana was in 1900. But look what she had to sustain for forty years:

breeders of hate and intolerance, capitalists and bankers who thwarted industrial growth, wealth that resisted change and wanted nothing for the community but lower taxes, unions that resisted change and wanted nothing but shorter hours and more money and more dues, politicians who wanted nothing but a treasury to plunder and an office.

Are times changing?

On April 16, 1962, Governor Welsh sent sixty of his top state officials back to school to learn more about government management. They heard a lecture from Lynton K. Caldwell, director of Indiana University's Institute of Training for Public Service. His message "The Statehouse needs more management and less politics. We're coming to the time when it won't do Democrats or Republicans any good to appoint a bunch of political lunkheads."

He said more problems are being taken to the federal government to solve, because state governments are slow to respond or are deaf to them.

In all Indiana, only one man in public office made a crusade to give cities and towns fair representation in the State Legislature so that metropolitan areas would have an equal voice with rural areas. His name was State Senator Nelson Grills of Indianapolis, a lawyer, former law professor at Indiana University and wartime commander of a navy blimp shot down over the Atlantic.

Year after year, Indiana state lawmakers violated the Indiana State Constitution by not fairly balancing the Legislature. Grills protested. He begged, fought, cajoled and threatened. He dramatized the issue. He made Hoosiers in cities understand, once and for all, that they did not have a fair voice in the Legislature, that restrictive and punitive laws were being made for them by farmers with no interest in city problems.

Grills did not even get a chance to run for reelection. He was defeated by his own Democratic Party in the primary.

One Democratic faction headed by State Revenue Commissioner James Courtney pushed Jack Bradshaw, a bright young attorney in Frank McHale's law office. The City Hall-Courthouse Democratic machine, headed at the time by Mayor Boswell and Prosecutor Bayt, found Grills distasteful. Neither Boswell nor Bayt could dictate to Grills, who was an independent thinker. As a result, the Boswell-Bayt faction also supported Bradshaw. Only the independents were for Grills. Unfortunately, in a primary election, the machine vote more than offsets the independent people vote.

The Democrats, the self-styled champions of equal and just reapportionment, defeated the only leading advocate of it.

five

ON THE CAMPUS

*We have grown some ivy, but we have not yet
taken on moss.*

—GEORGE ADE

TERRY BRENNAN may have been Knute Rockne's
ghost when I wrote the following poem in the Notre Dame
press box late in September 1954 for the *Indianapolis Times*.
It was his first game as head coach and the Fighting Irish had
shut out a formidable University of Texas team, 21 to 0.

> *Remember the Rock of Notre Dame?*
> *He started the Irish on the road to fame*
> * Four horsemen rode and Gipper ran*
> *   To gridiron glory for the man.*
> *Elmer Layden and Frank Leahy*
> *Each built his own dynasty*
> * Plunge and pass, around the end*
> *   And Lujack there to defend.*
> *Is this the end of the mighty clan?*
> *Is young Brennan the right man?*
> * Out of the South, the Texans came*
> *   And lost to Brennan's Notre Dame.*

Harken all ye men of green . . .
This is what my eyes have seen:
An Irish team that will not bow
Rockne's ghost is coaching now.

Brennan was a Notre Dame law school graduate, bright,
articulate, a gentleman with a pleasing personality and a
gifted football player. But a Rockne he was not. In five years
Brennan's teams won 32 games and lost 18. In his last three
years, Brennan lost more games than Rockne did in a lifetime of coaching—15 defeats against 15 victories. From 1918
to 1931, Rockne coached Notre Dame to a record of 105 tri-
umphs, 5 ties and only 12 losses.

(To me, this proved not only that my poem was wrong,
but that writing history on deadline is dangerous.)

When Brennan was hired to coach the Irish, he was
scarcely older than some of the players. To think Notre
Dame would entrust its football fortunes to a twenty-six-year-
old was hailed as fresh evidence that the best-known Catholic
university in the United States was de-emphasizing football.
(When Frank Hering went to Notre Dame to coach football
in the fall of 1896, he "had a hard time working up enough
enthusiasm to get a squad on the field," according to Arthur
J. Hope's history of the university.)

When Brennan was fired, just before Christmas 1958,
it was widely interpreted (even in Catholic circles) as an
indication that Notre Dame was more interested in football
victories than in academic achievement. The *Indiana Catholic,* now the *Criterion,* official newspaper of the Indianapolis
Archdiocese, edited by the Reverend Father Raymond T.
Bosler, blamed it on pressure from the alumni. The paper
said: ". . . the priests and laymen at Notre Dame who were
trying, successfully, we believe, to remake the public image
of Notre Dame from football factory to first-class university
have really suffered a setback."

Many observers close to the university, however, doubt

whether it listens to the alumni. In Cleveland, one old grad complained, "We have as much voice in the affairs of Notre Dame as the alumni of Sing Sing."

Colliding head-on with the win-every-Saturday alumni is the Reverend Father Theodore Martin Hesburgh, president of the University of Notre Dame. *Look* magazine said Father Hesburgh "is a man who runs far ahead of his interference. Sometimes he would be better off wearing a football helmet instead of his priestly black biretta."

Football made Notre Dame. But under Father Hesburgh it isn't bigger than Notre Dame. It is no secret, though, that his cry for academic excellence is not fully appreciated by many who were attracted to the campus by the Knute Rockne legend. After losing a football game in 1961, some Notre Dame students ridiculed Father Hesburgh's high scholastic standards in a protest march carrying aloft placards saying: "Down With Excellence." The undergraduate *Scholastic* magazine complained editorially that the emphasis on academic excellence "leaves the student reeling."

This suits Father Hesburgh. He is more concerned about how history will judge Notre Dame than the value this year's sophomore puts on a winning team. Stung by criticism from top Catholic educators, Notre Dame has risen above an undistinguished academic record and is now reaching for the influence and renown of the Ivy League universities.

Father Hesburgh's predecessor the Reverend Father John J. Cavanaugh may have lit the fuse that sent Notre Dame into academic orbit. "Where are the Catholic Salks, Oppenheimers, Einsteins?" he asked. He was not alone. Jesuit theologian Gustav Weigel of Maryland's Woodstock College said, "The general Catholic community in America does not know what scholarship is."

Under Father Hesburgh, Notre Dame has embarked on a $66-million program of excellence, which includes new buildings, libraries, more books, an increased endowment and a bigger operating budget to attract top faculty members.·

Father Hesburgh has tossed out some vocational courses, toughened the admission standards, held down undergraduate enrollment and let the graduate school enrollment grow.

Much as he dislikes the fund-raising part of the presidency, Father Hesburgh's eyes light up when he describes the new $8-million library or the new radiation laboratory or the Committee on International Relations.

"Of course we will give him what he asks for," one alumnus said, "but I do wish he'd spend a little of that money for a couple of tackles."

What isn't understood, even by Catholic educators, is that Father Hesburgh, although uncompromisingly committed to academic excellence, is shooting for Notre Dame to be more than a Catholic Harvard, or a Catholic Yale. He wants Notre Dame to do more than education and research. He has added a new dimension to higher education: dedicated service to the vexing and complex problems of mankind.

Father Hesburgh told the 1962 graduates of the Massachusetts Institute of Technology,

> I am not interested in better dog food when people are hungry. I have seen people dying on the streets of Calcutta; I have seen hungry refugee children on the sampans and in the shacks of Hong Kong; I have seen unnecessary disease in Uganda, in Pakistan, in Brazil and Chile. I have sensed the hopelessness of many of the 900 million illiterates of the world. Against this background, I am slightly nauseated when I see science and technology dedicated to trivial purposes like better deodorants and better detergents, better cosmetics and more aesthetic telephones, better garden sprinklers and better remote control of wrestling and horse operas on television.

To lead the way, Father Hesburgh throws himself into public service. In 1961, as a member of the United States Civil Rights Commission, he wrote a notable attack on police brutality against Negroes. *The New York Times*, hailing it as a "declaration of conscience with significance for every American," said: "Father Hesburgh has pointed a glowing road toward human betterment and decency."

He is the Vatican's personal representative to the International Atomic Energy Agency in Vienna and is considered an effective negotiator. He votes on where $40 million in grants should go for medical and welfare projects as a member of the Rockefeller Foundation. He helps award federal research projects as a member of the National Science Board. He has visited almost every country in Africa, Asia, Europe and South America. If, when he comes back to the campus, he is impatient with mediocrity and stiffarms the football zealot, it is because his sense of values recoils at fun and games as a total way of life.

It so happens that Father Hesburgh understands the contribution football and Knute Rockne have made to Notre Dame. Until Rockne teamed up with Gus Dorais and passed Army silly, 35 to 13, in 1913, tiny Notre Dame was virtually unknown. Father Hesburgh understands, too, that it was football that unlocked the sources of money that now help pay for Notre Dame's increasing academic quality.

Unlike some Catholics, Father Hesburgh doesn't fear that a relentless monotony of Notre Dame football victories would lead to resentment from non-Catholics and an increase in bigotry. He believes good athletes and good students are compatible. After all, the gravel-voiced, smash-nosed Rockne was a brilliant chemistry student who was graduated *magna cum laude* in 1915. Father Hesburgh would not, however, sacrifice a jot of excellence in academics for the best quarterback in the United States. If he had the choice between developing an undefeated, national football championship team or a Nobel Prize scholar, football would come second.

Some intellectuals insist that religious dogma is incompatible with the scientific spirit of skeptical, free inquiry in a great university. Father Hesburgh says, "We must cherish both values. . . . There is no conflict between science and theology except where there is bad science or bad theology."

James E. Murphy, director of public information at Notre Dame, tells something of the impact of Father Hesburgh on the campus:

> I have heard him say on more than one occasion, 'Never settle for second best.' And this is an across-the-board conviction with him. He means our scientists should never settle for second best in their research; our students should not settle for second best in picking a wife; the University should not settle for less than the best it can obtain in the way of students or faculty members. This notion of excellence pervades his whole thinking. He has raised everyone's sights at Notre Dame, except maybe the football team's.

The Roman Catholic spiritual tradition is well nourished at Notre Dame, but it does not smother non-Catholic students or faculty. Rabbi Albert Plotkin not only is a graduate of Notre Dame, but he heads the University's fund-raising drive in Phoenix, Arizona. Harvey Foster, a Methodist, is a 1939 graduate of the law school and formerly was special agent in charge of the New York FBI office. John Scott, former mayor of South Bend and now publisher of the *Lafayette Journal and Courier,* is a 32d-degree Mason who was graduated from Notre Dame. All are enthusiastic Notre Dame boosters and are impressed, they say, with the democratic atmosphere in academics and religion.

Almost all of the 5,500 undergraduates are Catholic. Of the 487 full-time faculty members, there are several Jews and more Protestants than priests or lay brothers.

If the future Notre Dame graduate comes out less concerned about Saturday's football score and more concerned about his fellow man, Father Hesburgh will have produced, finally, the significant man.

WHEN he took over Indiana University in 1937, Herman B Wells weighed 228 pounds and was considered a lightweight. When he retired twenty-five years later, he weighed 280 and was considered on many U.S. campuses the heavyweight champ of college presidents.

He put Indiana University on the world map. In record numbers he gave provincial Hoosiers culture with their book learning.

In the summer of 1962 he voluntarily retired and was succeeded by Elvis J. Stahr, jr., forty-six, Kentucky-born lawyer, Rhodes scholar, educator and onetime Secretary of the Army. (Wells and Stahr have one thing in common: an idiosyncrasy in spelling their names. Wells uses the middle initial B with no period after it. Stahr uses "junior" after his name with a small "j.")

It was Wells, son of two schoolteachers in Jamestown, Indiana, who was responsible for the way Indiana University developed from an unranked Middle Western state school to one of the leading institutions of higher learning in the U.S. You can separate the roly-poly Wells from Indiana as easily as you can separate Einstein from the theory of relativity.

The wife of an IU professor once explained her status: "A faculty wife is a person married to a faculty."

It has been said that bachelor Wells is married to Indiana University. A grateful school honored Wells on his retirement with a title it never before used: "Chancellor." He now heads the Indiana University Foundation, which finances research and handles private gifts.

The immense 1800-acre Bloomington campus in the rolling, wooded hills of scenic southern Indiana is the home of the university, now as when founded in 1820, one year after Thomas Jefferson established the University of Virginia.

IU started with ten students and one professor. When Dr. Wells became the eleventh president, the university had less than 5,000 students. Wells shattered the calm of campus life. He alarmed hidebound Hoosiers with his penchant for dressing up in a coonskin coat and roaring around town in a bright blue touring car with the top down.

Today there are 25,000 students on campus and at extension centers in cities around the state. Still fun-loving, Wells manages to confine his exuberance to fine food, world travel and buying antiques.

At a campus reception for the cast of South Pacific, Wells and actress Janet Blair kissed and an alert photographer for the *Daily Student* recorded the smooch. Wells protested that Miss Blair was bringing greetings from an old friend. Miss Blair, however, was ecstatic.

"Undoubtedly, Dr. Wells has a tremendous advantage as Dr. Kinsey is on the faculty," she said. "How else could a man look like Santa Claus and kiss like Cary Grant? Wow!"

Eleven colleges, schools and major divisions make up the university, one of the most beautiful in the country.

Dr. Wells is the first to admit that brick and mortar—no matter how pretty or how well decorated—do not make a great university. He has been described as a politician. School administrators say he was a gifted administrator. Some called him a diplomat. He had been a teacher and dean of the business school. His enemies (and he has some) said he was an operator. His avocation is banking.

The truth is that Wells is a politician, diplomat, administrator, banker, scholar and operator, and what cements all of these qualities into a unique university president is a genuine fondness for people.

He proved to be a master at charming cash out of economy-minded farmers and rustics in the State Legislature, and he used it to buy academic quality. No football coach recruited a quarterback with the finesse and persistence of Wells looking for a Nobel Prize winner.

Up surged the English department, the music, medical and law schools. The faculty blossomed with top scholars: heart surgeon Harris B. Shumacker, Jr., Nobel Prize-winning geneticist Hermann J. Muller and the late biologist-turned-sexologist Alfred C. Kinsey.

The academic strength of IU is in its distinguished and internationally ranked professors, the expansion of the curriculum, the increase in research activities and the development of extracurricular activities. Before he left IU, Wells had started an honors program to attract outstanding students.

Because Dr. Wells had been considered political-minded and sensitive to public opinion, some faculty members at one time questioned whether in a crisis he'd sacrifice intellectual integrity, the backbone of higher education. The answer came for skeptics at the height of the controversy over the late Dr. Kinsey, whose much-publicized and unprecedented book reports on the sexual behavior of men and women created a nationwide controversy. Parents threatened to take their youngsters home from Bloomington. The clamor to oust Dr. Kinsey reached the halls of the State Legislature. At the height of the storm, on August 21, 1953, Dr. Wells calmly issued a statement:

> . . . the human race has been able to make progress because individuals have been free to investigate all aspects of life . . . only through scientific knowledge can we find the cures for the emotional and social maladies in our society. I have large faith in the values of knowledge, little faith in ignorance.

The whole state revolves around Indiana University, which is the way Wells planned it. Unions hold training programs on the campus. Businesses send executives there for trade seminars. Newspaper editors from all over the state come to Bloomington once a year for a journalism institute. Teachers, policemen and politicians have career programs there.

It has been called the intellectual and cultural garden spot in Hoosierland. Its School of Music includes on the faculty thirteen members with a Metropolitan Opera Company background, including conductors and singers. The ivy-covered limestone buildings, blasted out of nearby rock quarries, house some of the finest rare books in the world, a big-league auditorium, a high-ranking language center and medical, law, dentistry and business schools rich in respect.

After scrutinizing sixty campuses, Princeton's former president Harold W. Dodds glumly reported in his book *The Academic President—Educator or Caretaker?* that college presidents often spend only 10 to 20 percent of their time on educational matters. Snarled in business management, public relations and fund-raising, said Dodds, they should be devoting half of their time to real academic leadership.

A newspaperman once called Dr. Wells "a correspondence-school president" because, the reporter felt, the IU president was directing the affairs of the school by mail, usually from abroad.

Three Presidents of the United States have called on Wells to serve the nation: Franklin D. Roosevelt, Harry S Truman and Dwight D. Eisenhower. In 1943, Secretary of State Cordell Hull named Wells special economic adviser for liberated areas and to membership of the United Nations Relief and Rehabilitation Conference. He has been an alternate delegate to the United Nations and once was called on to oversee elections in occupied Greece. Wells was cultural adviser to General Lucius Clay in Germany in 1947, and at the United Nations charter meeting at San Francisco in 1945 he was chairman of the American Council on Education.

The globetrotting educator has visited Greece, Germany, Russia, Pakistan, Scotland, Turkey, Finland, France and Thailand, to name a few. "Herman Wells not only has spread the fame of Indiana University to all parts of the world," one associate said, "but he has brought the rest of the world a little closer to Indiana."

Perhaps the most important aspect of his travels is that Dr. Wells made the university cognizant of its international responsibilities. Thousands of foreign students come to the Bloomington campus, where they are welcomed with open arms. In Pakistan, Wells set up an Indiana University extension center.

When he was on campus, Wells made time for the students. Through the years he listened to student problems in his famous Tuesday afternoon conferences. That afternoon, Wells set aside for students without appointments. He listened to problems from sex to finances, and never with an eye on the clock. He saved many a youngster from dropping out.

Ernie Pyle, the late and great war correspondent, was a student at Indiana University. He once wrote: "Students bring their troubles to Hermie, their love affairs, their financial troubles, the little jams they're in."

A firm believer in the fraternity and sorority system (he was once president of IU's Sigma Nu chapter), Wells likes to drop in unannounced at Chapter houses and dorms.

Indiana University has a strong extracurricular-activities program, which includes the usual hoopla of queen contests, bicycle races (the Little 500), proms, sports and parties. Dr. Wells was particularly upset when one member of the faculty wrote an article in a national magazine exposing hi-jinks on the campus. He believes in student participation in more than scholastic affairs.

He said, for example, our most cherished memories are of the college years—the exciting period of life which marks the end of adolescence and the beginning of adulthood. He encourages students to enjoy many university experiences: debating, drama, rah-rah, dates and football games as well as trying to grow intellectually.

Before he turned his office over to Stahr, Wells kept an original newspaper cartoon by George Lichty in his office. It depicts a college president and a professor in conference.

"You're jumping to conclusions in asking for a raise, Professor," the college president says. "No sooner do we lose a few football games and you get the idea we're going to over-emphasize education."

MEN OF science are not noted as romantic types, but Frederick Lawson Hovde may achieve notoriety for carrying on a flagrant love affair with Purdue University. How else could you explain why he turned down a chance to become president of his alma mater, the University of Minnesota?

The temptation, he admits, was real. In facilities and full-time students, Minnesota is almost as large as Indiana and Purdue combined. It was on the athletic fields, in the classrooms and on the campus of Minnesota in the late 1930's that Fred Hovde bloomed into adulthood.

In sticking with Purdue, educators say Dr. Hovde made a "mature decision," like a man fondly remembering a childhood sweetheart, but not letting puppy love interfere with the real thing.

In the heart of the cornfields of Indiana, Purdue has become the largest technical school in America—and possibly the world. Each year it turns out more engineers than all of the top-ranked technical institutions of the U.S., including the Massachusetts Institute of Technology, Georgia Tech and the University of California. Each Purdue graduate has a choice of four or five jobs from which to pick, even in lean times.

"Purdue is not a factory which takes high school graduates as raw material and processes them into scientists, engineers, farmers, businessmen or teachers," Dr. Hovde once said. "The best we can do is provide an environment in which the student may learn."

Immediately after the Civil War and through World War II, Purdue played an important state and national role in the continuing industrial revolution under the leadership of such presidents as Richard Owen, Abraham C. Shortridge, Emerson White, James Henry Smart, Winthrope E. Stone and Edward C. Elliott.

In 1945, at age thirty-seven, Dr. Hovde came to the west Lafayette campus of Purdue University on the banks of the Wabash River as its seventh president. It was then, as now, a coeducational university supported by state and federal funds to teach mechanics, home economics, science education and agriculture. It has been called a "cow college," or a "high-grade vocational school."

Dr. Hovde had been head of the United States rocket development in World War II. Today, in what has been described as the infancy of the scientific revolution, Dr. Hovde orbited Purdue into the big leagues of technology. The result has been tremendous, with remarkable contributions from Purdue to the state of Indiana, the nation and the world.

From his campus window in the stately Executive Building, Dr. Hovde can look out at the famous Purdue Mall leading to the main gate. The wide boulevard, dotted with oak trees, is lined on both sides with classrooms and laboratories housed in red brick and red-tile roofs trimmed in the gleaming white of Indiana limestone. It is a glorious sight, especially in winter with snow on the ground. Under this peaceful campus scene is a bustling activity and building to keep pace with the explosion of knowledge.

Dr. Hovde is unafraid of bigness. There are disciples of small colleges who look on universities of the Big Ten as educational factories. Dr. Hovde says:

> Diversity is a good thing in colleges. Our country is safe so long as we have it. Colleges have different functions. I want all kinds, big and small, private and public.
>
> There is no man, no government, I would trust to dictate what kind of education we should have. As soon as one man or one group controls it within his own educational limitations, it automatically is subverted for some other purpose.
>
> The fear of largeness doesn't bother me. Students who are lost in a big school will be lost in the world, which is pretty big, too. Personally, I favor big schools. They offer wider opportunities, have more research facilities, more student organizations and many activities from stamp collecting to space pioneering.

Purdue has its own planes and airport (first college in America to own one) where students fly and study aeronautical engineering; a missile lab where students study rockets and jet propulsion under Dr. M. J. Zucrow, an internationally known authority; a fabulous coed recreation gym, where students are encouraged to swim indoors or outdoors, ice skate, practice crew, shoot rifles or pistols, play volleyball, basketball, table tennis, softball, tennis, horseshoes, squash, archery, badminton or even the old Italian game *bocci*. There are even seven boys for every girl (if you consider dating as recreation).

Purdue has fine libraries, research labs by the hundreds, exotic greenhouses where students study banana and pineapple plants, modern classrooms and perhaps the nation's finest marching band for a university without a school of music.

Purdue owes its life to the Morrill Act signed by President Lincoln July 2, 1862. By this law, the federal government offered to turn over public lands to any state which would use the proceeds to establish and maintain a college to teach agriculture, mechanics and train military leaders (ROTC). Dr. Hovde has hailed it as "the greatest act passed by any parliament of man."

Prior to the Civil War, college was limited to the study of religion, medicine, law, military science—the regular professions. Usually, only sons and daughters of the select attended. State universities opened opportunities to the sons and daughters of the working classes. And the federal land-grant colleges made a fine science of agriculture and mechanics—researching new ways to grow food where none grew before and developing new techniques in travel and automation.

Educators say an outstanding university must have more than fine buildings and a scenic campus and extensive research facilities and a high-caliber faculty. It must also have, they say, bright students, which traditionally have been identified with the private liberal arts colleges. Seventy percent of Purdue's students usually are in the top third of their high school classes, 26 percent in their second third and only 4 percent in the lower third.

"I have no quarrel with Columbia or Harvard or Yale," Dr. Hovde says. "If you pick the best students, they'll turn out to be the best."

The classic fight in education today is between liberal arts and vocational training, with some schools turning to five-year courses in an effort to equip students with professional skills and a broad background in philosophy, history and religion to help them put everything in perspective. Dr. Hovde's position is that education is a lifelong process and that Purdue must of necessity concentrate on the fundamentals of technology while the student is in class.

One of the flyingest college presidents in the U.S., Dr. Hovde may be either in Washington for a top-level meeting with defense officials, in Indianapolis for a civic meeting, in Detroit with industrialists, in his office, on campus visiting classrooms or watching a football or basketball practice. ("I'm just like any downtown quarterback," he says, "only more so.")

His extracurricular duties include: director of General Electric Company, member of the Ford Scholarship Board, trustee for the Advancement of Teaching, member of the Defense Science Board and member of the Fundamental Education Board. How does the university operate with such a busy president? Dr. Hovde delegates authority. He says he's proud of the competence of the Purdue staff.

Fred Hovde and his wife live in the university president's house in Lafayette, off the campus. They have three children. At Minnesota, Hovde was halfback and signal-caller on the team with the great Bronko Nagurski. In addition he was a Rhodes scholar and was hailed as "the Yank at Oxford" when he won his Oxford Blue playing rugby against traditional rival Cambridge. Today Hovde plays golf in the high

70's. His enthusiasm for athletics, science, scholarship and engineering make him the symbol of the ideal Purdue man.

Dr. Hovde is a strong advocate of the Reserve Officer's Training Program, which is why Purdue has exceptional air force, army and navy ROTC units. "So long as the world is divided, all men have an obligation to defend the nation," he says. Besides, he feels military discipline is wonderful supplemental training.

Few educators or outsiders know the battles Dr. Hovde has waged for academic freedom. When the chemistry lab was dedicated some years ago, some influential and powerful members of the American Legion at the Indianapolis headquarters objected to the main speaker, Professor Linus Pauling of California Tech. Pauling was suspected of left-wing social and political views. Five times Dr. Hovde went to Indianapolis at the request of the Legionnaires. Each time he refused to remove Dr. Pauling from the program. As a compromise, the Legionnaires asked Dr. Hovde to consult with them with respect to all future speakers invited to the campus. Dr. Hovde said he did not intend to abdicate his job as president of Purdue to any group.

Hovde has also been criticized, from time to time, for permitting Purdue's Great Issues course, a program that sometimes brings radicals of the right and left to the campus for discussions with juniors and seniors.

Dr. Hovde told one critic, a newspaper publisher, "The purpose of the course is essentially to present the ideas behind the great issues which divide men everywhere so that our students, when they leave the university, have more than emotional acquaintance with the great intellectual issues faced by men not only here, but in all nations."

Purdue has made important advances in jet propulsion and rockets. It has sent more graduates into the U.S. space program than any other institution in the U.S. It has created a huge airborne television program for Midwestern schools, which already is making enormous changes in educational patterns. Work already completed has related remote control to nuclear reactors and military systems. The university is pioneering in space, electrical engineering, breeding and highway research.

What about the future? H. L. Solberg, associate dean of engineering, reports, "Hovde revised our curriculum to provide graduates with an education that will permit them to cope with the problems they will be facing in the next ten to twenty-five years in an area in which technology is expanding with explosive violence."

If Hovde sounds like a man with a mission, it is because he is dedicated to the proposition that technology can, if properly used, bring to the world full bellies, comfort, work, pleasure and perhaps peace. He once told Purdue graduates, "In this world of complexity and organizations, and baffling problems such as race relations and world tensions, every new generation of young people will need to be better educated and better trained. In a nutshell—the preservation of our society requires more and more competence."

INDIANA has its own "Little Ivy League." DePauw University at Greencastle and Wabash College at Crawfordsville are the prestige, private liberal arts schools in the state. Traditional rivals, both are nonsectarian and rank academically with some of the finest small liberal arts colleges in the U.S., including Williams, Amherst, Haverford, Oberlin and Carlton.

THE METHODIST EPISCOPAL CHURCH founded De-Pauw in 1837 as Indiana Ashbury University. It has an attractive campus, fine faculty, bright students, conservative leadership and a knack for providing the leaders of Indiana's business and professional community. In 1963, it acquired a new president, Dr. William E. Kerstetter, who succeeded the late Dr. Russell Humbert. In the DePauw tradition, Dr. Ker-

stetter is a Methodist minister with a strong educational background. (He had been president of Simpson College of Iowa.)

Although it has no journalism school or department,
DePauw has strong ties to the news media. On its campus
the Sigma Delta Chi journalism fraternity (now society) was
founded. There are enough DePauw alumni clustered at the
Wall Street Journal to hold a good-sized reunion. (Among
the DePauw graduates there are Bernard Kilgore, president
of the *Wall Street Journal* and Buren H. McCormack, vice-
president and editorial director of the paper.)

DePauw is coeducational, with over 2,000 undergraduates. The university seems to exercise more control over its
students than most colleges, private or public.

Educators have their own way of evaluating a college.
Youngsters look at it through different eyes. Here's a random,
yet typical comment about DePauw in 1963 by a coed, Miss
Susan Fortune of Indianapolis: "I like the atmosphere. I like
to walk to class and smile and say 'Hi' to everyone."

Among DePauw's noted alumni: U.S. Supreme Court
Justice Willis Van Devanter, Senator Albert J. Beveridge and
historian Charles A. Beard.

THE PRESBYTERIANS, who dominated higher education
in early Indiana, founded Wabash in 1832 at Crawfordsville.
Today it is a private, liberal arts college dependent upon
neither church nor state.

In an era of bigness, Wabash is small—654 undergraduates. In an era of coeducation, it is for men only. In an era of
decreasing personal contact, it is a community of scholars
who are preparing not so much for earning a living as for
living a life.

Wabash has high-spirited, well-motivated students, an
exceptional faculty, enlightened administrative leadership
and a stimulating climate for learning on a lovely forty-acre
campus.

Apart from the scholars and professors on campus, it is important to know what the students themselves think of Wabash. William Lowery, class of '63, from Munster, Indiana, put it this way: "There's a strong intellectual tradition on the campus."

Among Wabash's famous sons are former Governor James T. Goodrich, former Vice President Thomas Marshall and General Lew Wallace, who wrote *Ben Hur*.

JERROLD K. FOOTLICK of the *Indianapolis Times* won the national education writers top award at Atlantic City in 1963 for "broad, crusading coverage." A recognized authority on colleges and public schools in Indiana, Footlick rated as the state's superior small, liberal arts schools: Wabash, DePauw, Earlham, Hanover, Butler, Franklin, Manchester, Marian and Indiana Central.

Footlick regards Rose Polytechnic Institute as an outstanding engineering school. The two state-owned teachers colleges came in for a special evaluation from Footlick. He said about Indiana State College (Terre Haute) and Ball State Teachers College (Muncie), "Both still are primarily teacher colleges, and pretty good at that job. Both are working to improve liberal arts. Significantly, Indiana State got the word 'teacher' taken out of its name two years ago."

BUTLER UNIVERSITY of Indianapolis is growing into one of the fine, private universities in the Midwest as it toughens its admission standards, raises faculty sights and encourages the performing arts on its campus under Alexander Jones, a scholar and authority on Mark Twain. In 1963, Dr. Jones succeeded Dr. M. O. Ross, who retired. Butler was founded in 1855 as Northwestern Christian University by the Disciples of Christ in Irvington. It is nationally known for its coach, Tony Hinkle, who builds character and wins basketball games, too. (In his forty-second year at Butler, Hinkle has turned out more successful high school basketball coaches in Indiana than any other mentor.)

Earlham College at Richmond is Quaker-operated, with a highly respected educator, Dr. Landrum R. Bolling, an ex-newspaperman and former foreign-service officer, as president. It is a coeducational, liberal arts college.

Franklin College at Franklin was founded in 1837 under the name Indiana Baptist Manual Labor Institute. It is now considered one of the best bargains for a good liberal arts education under the flexible, yet generally conservative leadership of Dr. Harold Richardson.

Hanover College at Hanover is a Presbyterian-related, coeducational liberal arts school. It is bolder than most. Hanover has embarked on an experimental program, cutting the number of courses in half. Students get strong, concentrated doses of liberal arts and have few electives.

Manchester College at North Manchester received world attention as the school where Andrew Cordier taught. Cordier was an effective administrator at the United Nations, and is now dean of Columbia's School of International Affairs. Manchester is respected as a liberal arts school.

Marian College at Indianapolis is a Catholic School only twenty-six years old. It has been coeducational (boys added) since 1954. Constantly improving, it is willing to try new things, including public-service political forums, far-out drama and jazz concerts.

Indiana Central at Indianapolis has developed a strong liberal arts program under the no-nonsense administration of Dr. I. Lynd Esch. Strongly Brethren Church-oriented, Indiana Central is growing and improving.

TRI-STATE COLLEGE at Angola is an engineering and commerce school. It has the support of such organizations as Timken Bearing Co., Freuhauf Trailer, General Motors,

Northern Indiana Public Service and the Indiana Motor Truck Association. This school features concentrated doses of practical courses on the four-quarter system. There are few, if any, extracurricular activities. Serious-minded students, anxious to start working, finish the normal four-year course in thirty-six months, going full time with no break for summer vacation. James Nicholas, a trustee from Indianapolis, describes Tri-State as "the realistic approach" to education, with many students studying for specific jobs, such as aircraft engineer, draftsman or motor-transport management. The school is growing (nearly 2,000 students) and improving, with twenty-one nations represented in 1963. Other Tri-State trustees include Fred Zollner of Zollner Piston Co. of Ft. Wayne and J. T. McCormick, prime contractor at Cape Canaveral. There is no liberal arts course at Tri-State.

John Herron Art Institute at Indianapolis awards college degrees for specializing in art. Affiliated with the John Herron Museum of Art, students work under some of the finest artists in the Midwest.

Evansville College at Evansville is an example of a good four-year liberal arts college which serves the community. Students from the entire southwestern Indiana area use its facilities. The school is a great asset to the town.

Two excellent Catholic colleges for girls are St. Mary's College at Notre Dame (South Bend) and St. Mary-of-the-Woods (Terre Haute). St. Meinrad Seminary (St. Meinrad) is a respected Jesuit college that prepares students for the priesthood.

Other progressing four-year colleges in Indiana include Taylor (moved to Ft. Wayne from Upland), Valparaiso University (Valparaiso), St. Joseph's (Rensselaer), Anderson (Anderson), Huntington (Huntington) and Goshen (Goshen).

THERE are a number of superior private secondary schools in Indiana, including Park (for boys) and Tudor Hall (for girls) at Indianapolis, Culver Military Academy (Culver), Howe Military Academy (Howe) and Brebeuf Preparatory School, run by the Jesuits at Indianapolis. All stress academic excellence and a well-rounded program. Culver, however, maintains an outstanding national reputation for developing scholarship and instilling a sense of values in its cadets. In Indiana, private prep schools compete with exceptionally strong public high schools. For example, in the Indianapolis area, North Central, Shortridge, Broad Ripple, Speedway and Southport are the academic equal of many of the better private schools. (In a few isolated areas of the state, however, the schools are almost primitive, where grade and high school pupils go to ancient schoolhouses and are obliged to use outdoor toilet facilities.)

THE QUIET revolution in Indiana educational circles is to establish junior colleges patterned after historic and respected Vincennes University, at Vincennes, Indiana. Robert Wyatt, the influential executive director of the 44,000-member Indiana State Teachers Association, says community colleges are "the only solution" to the coming tidal wave of college-bound high school graduates. Strong opposition to the junior college concept comes from the two big state universities, Indiana and Purdue, which are fighting for all the educational dollars they can get from the State Legislature. (Vincennes University is a state and community supported liberal arts two-year college which also offers courses in business, nursing, engineering, secretarial work, agriculture, and has a strong program of adult education.)

six

HOOSIER SPORTS: AUTO RACING AND BASKETBALL

All gates I've crashed, I'm here to tell
I'll crash St. Pete and then crash hell.

—ONE-EYED CONNELLY (famous gate-
crasher at the Indianapolis Speedway)

Babe Ruth of the New York Yankees, taunted by the Cubs and booed by the fans, strode to the plate in a 1932 World Series game at Chicago's Wrigley Field. With his bat he majestically pointed to the centerfield flagpole 400 feet away, where he promptly belted the ball.

Did the Babe really call his shot? Experts disagree to this day whether this was an audacious act or whether the Bambino was just waving his bat.

There is a similar legend at the Indianapolis Motor Speedway, also the subject of heated controversy. In 1912, second year of the 500 Mile Race, Ralph DePalma was out in front with only 100 miles to go. His nearest competitor, Joe Dawson, was 15 miles behind.

With five laps to go, DePalma's big Mercedes developed mechanical trouble. A connecting rod had broken and it tore a hole in the crankcase. The car spurted oil. DePalma nursed his ailing monster around, but its speed dropped—from 60 to

40 miles an hour. Less than a mile from the finish line, on the northwest turn, DePalma's leaky, wounded Mercedes died.

The car's heart gave out, but not DePalma's. He got out and told his riding mechanic Rupert Jeffkins, an Australian, to start pushing. Together they propelled the car through the turn. Dawson still had three full laps to go.

Here is where the dispute comes. Insiders at the track say DePalma was only pushing his car back to the pits. Al Bloemker, publicity director of the 500 Mile Race, says as much in his book *500 Miles to Go*.

Another version, which I like to believe, is that De-Palma, a magnificent competitor, was trying to push his car across the finish line first. Failing that, he was going for the checkered flag, anyway.

Whatever version you accept, here is what actually happened. A murmur of voices arose as DePalma and Jeffkins pushed the Mercedes down the homestretch. It grew into a cheer. Wild applause shook the stands.

Dawson raced to the finish line ahead of them. But DePalma, a born showman, was undaunted. With a wave of his hand, he acknowledged what was now a tumultuous ovation. He marched the remaining 600 yards to cross the finish line—if not a winner, a legend.

Brave men risk their lives to drive around the two and a half oval track at speeds up to 180 miles an hour on the straightaway. In its first fifty years, twelve winners have subsequently died racing, including the incomparable Bill (Iron Man) Vukovich, who won the race twice and was leading on two other occasions. Mechanical trouble once stopped him from winning less than three laps from the checkered flag and, in another race, death flagged him.

After every accident, cries of protest echo across the country to "stop the carnage," to put an end to the Roman-holiday orgy of thrills, spills and chills. If you spend any time around race drivers you know their philosophy: it can't happen to me. But it does.

Oscar Fraley, sports writer for United Press International, reported the Memorial Day in 1955 when Vukovich was killed. Before the race Iron Man was showing friends a letter from his daughter.

"Put your foot through it," she wrote, "I need a new dress."

Vuky put his foot through it—all the way.

When the race was over, with more than its share of crashes and pileups and the final checkered flag for Vuky, Bob Sweikert maneuvered his car into Victory Lane and looked in astonishment at his sobbing wife.

"You certainly didn't think it could happen to me, did you?" he asked, a broad smile on his face.

It did, on another day, at another track.

Race drivers wouldn't have it otherwise. They know the risks. They gladly take them for gold and glory and for whatever else it is that makes adventurous men want to go higher or faster than someone else.

ANTON (Tony) HULMAN, Jr. owns the Speedway. He is a mild and modest merchant who was born rich in Terre Haute, Indiana on February 11, 1901 and grew up to be a multimillionaire.

His friends joke that he is the only Democrat who ever went broke in the beer business. This isn't exactly true. The beer company, Cook's of Evansville, did go bust. But the Hulman family fortune was intact, protected by a baking powder, Clabber Girl, and numerous other business, financial and real-estate interests. Despite his wealth, Hulman lived in comparative obscurity until age forty-four, when he bought the Indianapolis Motor Speedway. The Speedway cost $750,000, for which Hulman got 433 acres of real estate, a brick and asphalt race track going to weeds, a collection of old grandstands and instant fame.

The shy Hulman has been in the limelight ever since. An estimated 250,000 fans come to the track on race day with picnic baskets, blankets to spread out on, and refreshments. This is the largest crowd to attend a single sports event in the United States. Hulman, who doesn't like to discuss money, won't say exactly how many people come in or how much he makes. But he does plow the profits back into the track—in new stands, new buildings and bigger prizes.

At sixty-two, Hulman stands 5 feet 11 inches and weighs 170 pounds, which is what he weighed when he was an All-American end on the undefeated Yale football team of 1923. In 1948 he was a member of the American team in the International Tuna Cup Match off Nova Scotia. In 1919, Hulman was considered "the best schoolboy pole-vaulter in the U.S."

"I wouldn't say I have a hunger for speed," Hulman says. "But I am fascinated by it, no matter in what kind of sport—boats, automobiles, running."

Hulman is married to the former Mary Fendrich of Evansville, who inherited the La Fendrich cigar fortune. They have a daughter, Mary Antonia, who is married to race driver Elmer George.

The list of business and civic organizations in which Hulman is active is so long that Hulman himself can't remember them off the cuff. One with which he was prominently identified is the Indiana Flood Control and Water Resources Commission. Once mentioned as a candidate for Governor on the Democratic ticket, Hulman joked, "I might run for Governor if I thought it would get me off the flood-control commission."

As a businessman, Hulman at first didn't take at all seriously to the idea of buying the Speedway. But a sentiment which might best be described as "provincial patriotism" colored some of his thinking. And there was the natural lure of Hulman's hobbies.

The Speedway, owned by Captain Eddie Rickenbacker of Eastern Air Lines, had been closed during the four years of World War II. Rickenbacker planned to let it go. The late

Wilbur Shaw, a Speedway champion in three races, heard it was to be cut up for a real-estate development. Shaw thought somebody ought to save it and Indiana's historic 500 Mile Race.

"I guess some of the optimism of Wilbur Shaw rubbed off on me," Hulman says. Hulman & Co. closed the deal in November 1945 and Shaw, a colorful personality in his own right, was installed as president. Hulman stayed in the background.

"Even at that time it was difficult for me to realize so many people over the country were interested in the continuance of the 500 Mile Race," Hulman says. "I couldn't realize there were people so enthused about it as there were."

What makes auto racing so attractive to so many people? Hulman's answer: "Keen competition, rather than speed, makes auto racing the great sport it is."

The circumstance of Shaw's death in a plane crash in 1954 brought Hulman to the center of the stage, where he's been ever since. It is Hulman who, like Shaw before him, heightens the tension before the race by alerting the thirty-three daredevil drivers in their sleek racing machines: "Gentlemen, start your engines."

IN NO sport is the competition rougher or keener. And in no sport will the competitors help each other more.

It is not unusual for one driver to take his closest competitor's car out for a spin to see if he can iron out some of the kinks or suggest ways to get a jot more speed out of it. In 1961, Tony Bettenhausen, a popular driver, was killed test-driving a car for Paul Russo, another leading driver.

The 500 Mile Race is the big league of auto racing. It is possible the close cameraderie and sportsmanship of the drivers and mechanics is a natural result of the nearness of disaster. No one puts sand in his competitor's gas tank.

What about the fans? Do the huge crowds come in record numbers to satisfy some morbid curiosity or in the sadistic spirit of the spectators who watched the gladiators fight lions in the Coliseum in ancient Roman times? There may be a ghoul or two in the crowd of 250,000, and even some who come to boast that "the crash happened right in front of me."

For the most part, though, people come to see the excitement of the race. There is nothing quite like thirty-three race cars roaring into the southwest turn at more than 145 miles an hour to start the race. Or a wheel-to-wheel duel to the finish such as Jim Rathmann and Rodger Ward staged in 1960.

(On the 197th lap, with the lead changing hands at every turn, Ward noticed that continued high speed would end in almost immediate tire failure and probable disaster. Ward, one of the greatest drivers at the track, and the winner in 1959 and 1962, played it safe and coasted. Ward later said, "It's tough to finish second when you know you have a car fast enough to win. But it isn't as bad as going to the hospital instead of collecting $45,000 or more for second place at the Victory Dinner.")

Back in 1955, Bill Vukovich was leading with the same spectacular pace he zoomed around to win the race in 1953 and 1954. Fans in the sun-drenched Tower Terrace and the front grandstand amused themselves by watching Vuky pass the slower cars on the straightaway. They waited for him to come around again. He didn't. Nor was he in the pits for a change of tires or gas.

The yellow flag cautioned drivers to slow down and hold their places in the field. Still no Vuky. After a lengthy interval, the Speedway loudspeaker broadcast a terse bulletin: "There has been a mixup on the backstretch. There is no report yet if anyone is injured."

Reporters stationed around the track at strategic places phoned details into their newspaper offices. Trying to avoid hitting a couple of cars that had collided in front of him,

High school basketball during the state tournament.

The Indiana War Memorial at Indianapolis.

Madge Oberholtzer, Statehouse secretary who was murdered by **D. C. Stephenson,** Ku Klux Klan grand dragon.

D. C. Stephenson, former grand dragon of the Ku Klux Klan in Indiana.

Vuky veered off and vaulted the backstretch rail. He was killed instantly.

Fans in the stands were notified of Vuky's death by newspaper extras that were rushed to the track while the race was still in progress and by transistor radios. Sid Collins, voice of the vast Speedway radio network, first double-checked to make sure Vukovich was dead and that Vuky's wife Esther knew it before he broadcast the news. Then Collins went into a dramatic off-the-cuff eulogy of Vukovich that brought him a tremendous response from Coast-to-Coast.

(Collins, who had been broadcasting the 500 Mile Race for fourteen years, did not see the accident. He saw his first Speedway accident in 1961 when Jack Turner flip-flopped forty feet in the air on the main straightaway. Most of the accidents are on the turns and are phoned in to him by a team of reporters stationed around the track.)

The Vukovich death smothered the Speedway like a blanket of gloom. Some fans left, while others stayed in stunned silence. They hadn't bargained for this.

Whether the track is a laboratory for automotive products and safety engineering is something else. It is true that the rear-view mirror was invented here. Ray Harroun, who was one of the first drivers without a riding mechanic, put it on the car to see who was coming up on him.

Other automotive developments on tires, sparkplugs, brakes, engines, torsion-bar suspension and fuel-injection systems have been made. Whether they would have been made without the 500 is something else again. Medicine might learn some valuable lessons about the impact driving long distances at high speeds has on a driver. (The 500 Mile Race is said to be equivalent to 50,000 miles of pleasure driving, which is why many manufacturers regard it as a superior test for equipment.)

Oddly enough, the man destined to become the Speedway's first 500 Mile winner didn't want any part of the race.

"Too long," said Ray Harroun. "It'll wear out the drivers and the cars. Why that's almost as far as driving from Indianapolis to Washington, D.C." He won the race at an average speed of 74.59 miles per hour. It took him 6 hours and 42 minutes of steady driving to do it. Rodger Ward won the race in 1962 in 3 hours and 33 minutes, at an average speed of 140.29 miles per hour.

Four men have been largely given credit for starting the world's greatest race course at Speedway on February 9, 1909: Carl Fisher, Arthur C. Newby of the National Motor Vehicle Company, Frank H. Wheeler of the Wheeler-Schebler Carburetor Company and James A. Allison, who started the Allison Division of what now belongs to General Motors.

But it was really the inspiration and driving force of Fisher, who had a constant craving for excitement, adventure and grand and gaudy business promotions. He was a born gambler and competitor. He raced in cars against a horse at the Fairgrounds. He piloted bucket-seat race cars around treacherous dirt tracks. He was a member of the American team that went to Europe for the Vanderbilt Cup auto races —and lost.

Fisher started as a youngster in Greensburg, Indiana, racing neighborhood kids on roller skates and ice skates. He gambled his savings on a bike-repair shop and became a professional bike rider.

Two different reasons have been given for Fisher's decision to start the Speedway. One is that on a trip to Greenfield to try out a new car, Fisher was upset because it broke down on the way back, not once but many times. "There ought to be a track to test these cars out before the public gets 'em," Fisher is quoted as saying.

Another version is that Fisher brought the idea home from Europe because it appealed to his competitive nature, his love of racing and his shrewd business sense.

Reporters close to racing say that there is truth to both

stories and that Fisher wanted both a track to (1) test cars and also (2) because he could envision the promotion and profit in a grand sports spectacle.

Fisher's biggest crap-shooting deal was not the Indianapolis Speedway or even when he and his chum Jim Allison borrowed a thousand dollars each to back an inventor, P. C. Avery, on the Prest-O-Lite battery, which gave automobiles headlights. It came later when Fisher put his bankroll on some swampland where a hot sun caressed the seaweed and the Atlantic Ocean crashed over the sand dunes. Fisher developed and promoted it. It is now called Miami Beach.

At Miami Beach, and at the Speedway, Fisher was assisted by one of the best-known press agents in the country, Steve Hannagan, who later went with former Democratic National Chairman James A. Farley to Coca-Cola. Hannagan wrote in 1925 that Fisher "has the agile mind of a press agent."

Will Rogers said of Fisher, "He's the man that took Miami Beach away from the alligators and gave it to the Indianians."

IN INDIANA you can easily spot the old, dilapidated, one-room, red schoolhouse. It is usually attached to a modern basketball gymnasium. Hoosier hysteria, as high school basketball is known in the state, is an obsession with far-flung psychological, social and educational effects.

In tiny towns, where there are less than 100 teen-agers, the communities refuse to consolidate their back-woodsy high school with the adjoining town's high school a few miles away, even though it would mean a better education for their children at less cost. That their sons might be able to use a science lab and their daughters a well-stocked library makes no difference. Hoosiers want school consolidations like Indiana farmers want hoof-and-mouth disease for their livestock.

Why? Because of the chance that their town will, like

David, slay Goliath to win the state basketball championship. In Indiana, basketball is the great equalizer. You do not need a thousand pupils, and thousands of dollars, to start and outfit a team. All you need is a gym, a coach and five boys who know how to throw a round ball through a hoop.

When the high school basketball season gets underway, it isn't just a matter of a few good games, but a maniac preoccupation that seizes the state and grows and grows in some 680 town gyms until the finals in Indianapolis in mid-March.

During the 1961–62 season, according to former commissioner L. V. Phillips of the Indiana High School Athletic Association, total paid attendance at sectional, regional and final games was 1,554,454 persons for a total ticket take of $1,044,850. This, of course, does not include a full-season schedule of nontournament games.

Kurt Freudenthal of United Press International reports that high school basketball gets bigger and bigger, creating new gyms, which cost millions and seat increasing numbers. At least a dozen high schools built gymnasiums for the 1961–62 season, including Anderson, Franklin, Goshen, Silver Creek, Arlington of Indianapolis, Sunman, Warren Central, Clinton Prairie, Eastern of Green County, Brown County, Carroll and North Miami.

Huntingburg, a hotbed of basketball in southern Indiana, can pack its entire town population of 4,146, plus another town, into its new gym, which seats 6,260 comfortably. But it is not alone in this distinction. Carmel, with only 1,442 people in town, has a gym seating 4,500. Clay City has 500 people in town and a 3,000-seat gym. Monon boasts 1,417 townspeople and a gym seating 3,056. Zionsville, which is trying to convert and revert its downtown character into Early American, has a gym seating 3,775 in a town of only 1,824 people. Knox can seat all but fifty-eight people of the town in its gym, which holds 3,400 fans. Brownsburg's gym is modest by comparison. It can seat only 4,027, which means that at some games 451 people in town might not be able to see the team play.

At tournament time, when a team is playing away from home, the town is deserted. Everyone is either at the game or watching it on television. Even the firemen and cops leave. Officials from neighboring towns volunteer for extra-duty to protect the town when a team is playing away from home in the tournament. They expect the same kind of neighborliness when and if their home-town team advances in the tournament.

This fanatical devotion to basketball has been called juvenile, maniacal and worse. But it does have its boosters. Robert S. and Helen Lynd, in their social study of Muncie, took note of the annual fever that grips Hoosiers when "through the sycamores the basketballs are flying." They saw basketball as a form of community boosting, boasting and belonging. There is another way of looking at it: What else is there to do?

"Basketball should be declared a felony," says Asa J. Smith, the Indianapolis lawyer. "The coaches should be dismissed, the players expelled and the principals horse-whipped." He is overstating his position, but he means it. Basketball, to him, is blown all out of proportion to its value.

Eugene Cadou, Sr., dean of political writers in Indiana and father of Jep Cadou, Jr., sports editor of the *Indianapolis Star,* doesn't share his son's enthusiasm for the game. "It's a silly game," he says, "watching a bunch of snot-nosed kids running around in their underwear."

These are minority opinions. Adults are more excitable about basketball than their kids. And adults cause the most trouble, as any harassed principal will tell you when he hasn't enough tickets to go around for the big game.

Charles W. White, who is a free-lance writer and a sort of Hoosier philosopher, points out that basketball can sometimes get in the way of adults, but basketball always comes first. He tells about the wife of a Muncie lawyer who wanted to attend the state tournament at Indianapolis but unfortunately was expecting a baby at the time.

"The doctor told me I could go," she said, "but I mustn't allow myself to get excited. So I sat still and didn't yell at all and everything went fine."

Another family crisis occurred at Anderson during a sectional game leading to the Hoosier finals. A farm family had tickets for the game. One of their sows, however, died (perhaps of excitement, White suggests) the day before the tournament was to start. Worse, she had just given birth to a litter of fine pigs needing attention. The Indiana farm family solved the problem by putting the piglets in a basket and taking them to the tourney, giving them their bottle between halves.

BACK in 1954, Milan was a sleepy little town nestled in Ripley County and not far from the Ohio River. It had a population of 1,150 people (on Saturdays when the farmers came to town to window-shop and buy groceries). The total Milan high school enrollment was 162—with only 75 boys.

In basketball, Milan had its hands full just playing teams like traditional rival Sunman, enrollment 125, give or take a few kids playing hookey.

Out of the 751 teams which started the high school tournament, tiny Milan became, before long, the people's choice. The starting five had to play most of every game because there were only five other boys in school who could dribble the ball, let alone put it through the hoop.

Coach Marvin Wood is now teaching and coaching in big (enrollment 2,793) and beautiful North Central High School, a public school in a fashionable suburb of Indianapolis. At Milan in 1954, Coach Wood couldn't afford to substitute much. He depended mainly on Bobby Plump, Bob Engel, Gene White, Ron Truitt and Ray Craft. These five he drilled and drilled. Occasionally he would use as substitutes Rollin Cutler, Kenny Wendelman, Glenn Butte, Bill Jordan and Roger Schroder.

During the season, Milan lost 2 games and won 28 preparing for the state tournament. One of the losses was to Aurora, considered one of the good teams in the state. Milan dropped the game by 9 points.

When Coach Wood's team played Aurora in the elimination contest of the state tournament, Milan won. There was some slight excitement, a spark of interest around the state. (Milan was not the smallest school in the tournament, Hebron was—with an enrollment of only sixty-five pupils.)

Indiana's high school basketball tournament is played on four successive Saturdays. Milan won the title game of the semifinal tournament the evening of March 14 by upsetting Crispus Attucks, a great Indianapolis Negro high school team. The whole state took notice.

One of the players on the Attucks team was the fabulous "Big O"—Oscar Robertson. Robertson did everything on a basketball court except take tickets. He propelled Attucks to the state championship for the next two years and started a basketball dynasty at the school. He went to the University of Cincinnati, where he was an All-American for three seasons and proclaimed the greatest college performer of all time. Later he went on to star for the Cincinnati Royals professional team.

On this day, however, senior Bobby Plump outscored sophomore Oscar Robertson, 28 to 22.

How did Milan beat Attucks?

Instead of the razzle-dazzle, fast-break, run-and-shoot offense so typical of Indiana basketball, Coach Wood slowed down the pace. He figured his boys were too small and too slow to run with the bigger, sturdier teams. He deliberately used a "cat-and-mouse" system. His boys dribbled and passed to perfection until they had an opening to shoot.

Four teams were left in the final tournament at the Butler fieldhouse the next Saturday night—Terre Haute Gerstmeyer, Elkhart, Muncie Central and Milan. In the afternoon games, Muncie knocked off Elkhart, 59 to 50, and Milan, using the "cat-and-mouse" system again, defeated a tall and talented Terre Haute Gerstmeyer, 60 to 48. That same Saturday night, March 21, Milan was pitted against Muncie Central high school in the state-championship game.

Newspapers in Indianapolis, Fort Wayne, Terre Haute, South Bend, Evansville, Muncie and Lafayette headlined the exploits of "the mighty men of Milan." Radio commentators speculated on the David and Goliath meeting of Milan and Muncie (enrollment 1,662), considered the finest team in the state in many years.

It was some buildup. Milan again was the underdog. But the whole state was pulling for the little guy to knock off the big guy.

John V. Wilson of the *Indianapolis Times* visited Milan before the game. He wrote: "A critical water shortage perils this Ripley County town of 1,150, but it couldn't care less. It is more concerned about its team in the state basketball finals."

Milan was allotted only 900 tickets. It was estimated that 300 Milan townspeople were forced to stay home. The rest went to Indianapolis for the game. Twenty-one of the town's twenty-four firemen went, too.

It was a typical Milan cat-and-mouse game. The Milan team could not match Muncie in size or speed. It played a possession game. The boys dribbled, passed, dribbled, passed and stalled. It was a low-scoring game and, once or twice, Muncie threatened to break the game open with its speed. Milan hung on, played for the openings and shot.

With three seconds left to play the score was tied 30–30. The boys worked the ball to Bobby Plump, their deadliest shot. He drove in and took a one-hand jump shot from fifteen feet out and won the game.

It was a tumultuous evening all over the state. The little guy had beaten the big guy. It warmed the hearts of Hoosiers in hamlets and big cities, on farms and in big industries. At Milan, the 300 stay-at-homes built a huge bonfire. Jimmie Angelopolous, perhaps the outstanding prep school authority in Indiana, wrote in the *Indianapolis Times:* "It was the greatest day in forty-four years of Indiana basketball."

Coach Wood and his team went home to Milan in Cadillacs supplied by Chris Volz, a hometown backer. Some 40,000 Hoosiers lined thousands of cars bumper-to-bumper for at least thirteen miles to welcome home the victors.

Jimmie Angelopolous described the eighty-mile trip home through the villages, towns and hamlets of Indiana:

> A plane circled overhead. In Shelbyville, two little boys, one holding a basketball, waved at the champs. Another kid shooting baskets with a little girl outdoors in Greensburg paused to salute the team.
>
> A fire truck and police escort screamed sirens at Greensburg. Another fire truck waited at 1 P.M. at Batesville. The procession of cars snowballed by the hundreds entering Ripley County. Traffic slowed behind police and fire truck escort. Hundreds of cars lined the road at Penntown, thirteen miles north of Milan. It took thirty-five minutes to creep eight miles from Batesville to Sunman.
>
> Traditional rival Sunman, enrollment 100-plus, was just as proud of its neighbor. It greeted the team with a band reception. Flags lined the street.

To Hoosiers, Milan is Cinderella, Dink Stover at Yale, Frank Merriwell and Tom Swift all rolled into one. It's our fairy tale come true.

seven

HOOSIERISMS

*All living Indianians are active politicians and
frequently the dead ones are, too; they've voted
them in close elections, out there, often.*
—IRVIN S. COBB

PART OF the charm of Indiana must be the names
of the various towns. The sophisticated *New Yorker* magazine laughed in print about some high school visitors from
Bean Blossom. The editors should talk to some of the youngsters from Gnaw Bone, Pumpkin Center, Carp, Zulu, Bobo,
Daisy Hill, Bogle Corner and Lena.

And that's not all. Towns are named after many lands:
Brazil, China, Chile, Cuba, Denmark, Hindustan, Ireland,
Klondyke, Norway, Peru, Scotland, Siberia, even Russia-
ville. Romantic faraway cities have their namesakes in Indiana, too—Athens, Cairo, Paris, Rome, Shanghai and Vienna.

Other Hoosier cities and towns are named Brooklyn,
Denver, Manhattan, Memphis, Miami, Reno and Topeka.
There are even cities named after other states: Nebraska,
Nevada and Vermont.

But the most colorful names offer anything a reasonable
man might ask for: Hope, Harmony, Leisure, Surprise,
Friendship, Economy, Free, Onward, Handy and Fickle—
even Popcorn.

On the Indiana map, you can enter West Point, climb Mount Olympus or scale Pike's Peak, find your Waterloo, bow to Mecca, go to Leavenworth or worship Buddha.

ARTURO GODOY, a clownish character, had forced Joe Louis to go 15 rounds to win a decision. Mickey Rooney found love and tears in the "Andy Hardy" films. In her squeaky voice, Wee Bonnie Baker repopularized "Oh, Johnny, Oh." You could buy a Chevy coupe for $660. John Steinbeck's sad book about the Okies (*The Grapes of Wrath*) was made into the most-talked-about movie of the year.

It was the spring of 1940. One of the violent topics of conversations in offices and barbershops was whether FDR would break with tradition and go for a third term and whether the Republicans would nominate Senator Robert A. Taft of Ohio, who seemed to be the favorite or the young racket-busting attorney from New York Tom Dewey. There was little talk, if any, of Wendell Willkie, head of Commonwealth and Southern, a large utility. He was an unknown.

Willkie's whole career was intimately associated with the interests of big business. In an effort to disassociate himself from the big business and vested utility-interest labels, he decided to campaign for the White House from his hometown of Elwood, Indiana. Opponents cynically called him "the barefoot boy from Wall Street."

The galleries at the Republican national convention in Philadelphia were packed with supporters who chanted "We want Willkie." Delegates were startled to receive telegrams from friends at home pleading with them to vote for Willkie. The delegates were swayed by the seemingly spontaneous demonstrations which were skillfully rigged behind the scenes. They bought Willkie. The amateur Willkie had blitzed the convention.

The old party pros were not sold, least of all James Eli Watson, who had represented Indiana in the United States Senate from the high-tariff days of William McKinley to

Franklin D. Roosevelt's New Deal. Watson was titular head of the GOP in Indiana. Sunny Jim wanted nothing to do with Willkie, whom he regarded as an upstart who didn't go through the political chairs and wouldn't know a precinct from a poll book.

Willkie, a warm, big, bearlike person, saw Senator Watson walking out of the Columbia Club on Monument Circle. He ran after him in the street.

"Why won't you be for me, Jim?" he asked. "After all, if I were a prostitute you'd let me pray in your church."

"I wouldn't mind you coming to my church if you were a whore," Sunny Jim snapped. "But damned if I'd want you leading the choir the first week."

YOU MIGHT have read or heard about the Claypool Hotel of Indianapolis. This is where one impatient and fastidious gent, Victor Lively, tired of waiting for a girl, Dorothy Poore, to come across with a little loving. He killed her and stuffed the body in a dresser drawer. The unsolved WAC murder took place there, too.

Down the years, the Claypool Hotel has been known affectionately as "the Cesspool." But it was also where Abraham Lincoln stopped to make a speech enroute to the White House. Then the Claypool was known as the Bates House and its guests were more sedate.

It was, and is, the home-away-from-home for Hoosier politicians. In Indiana the legend persists that an honest transaction is a bundle of unmarked bills in a black satchel thrown over the transom of a room in the Claypool.

FORMER Vice President Alben Barkley frequently told this story about himself. But it actually happened to Senator James Watson. In 1938, Watson attempted a political comeback.

In the preconvention maneuvering, Watson was surprised to encounter an old political friend who was supporting his opponent Raymond E. Willis. Amazed, Watson reminded his old friend of past favors: a postmastership for his brother-in-law, a census job for his aunt, an appointment to West Point for his son.

"Yes," the delegate agreed. "But what have you done for me lately?" (Watson lost the nomination.)

WHEN Zoologist Alfred C. Kinsey forsook the birds and bees for men and women, his scientific studies shattered the tranquility of Indiana University's Bloomington campus.

He became the center of a raging controversy. Sermons, editorials and shocked housewives warned that the reports might encourage the sex practices which Kinsey described as widespread.

Imagined or real, the fears were: Would a wife hesitating on the brink of an affair be encouraged to proceed by learning that one-fourth of all married women had sexual relations outside of marriage? Or would a husband, secure in the knowledge that half of all men commit adultery, revel in extramarital romances? Or worse, in a society already preoccupied with sex, would teen-agers accept the Kinsey reports as a new "doing-what-comes-naturally" moral code?

There were endless debates over whether Kinsey was a great scientist or a sensational grandstander and a seducer of American morality. Rose La Rose, the stripteaser, took time from an engagement at the Fox Burlesque in Indianapolis to berate Kinsey as "a literary Peeping Tom." Moralists were outraged and some scientists who questioned Kinsey's reliability were infuriated. One member of Congress sought, without success, to have the Kinsey Report barred from the mail. A few parents wrote the university that they would not feel safe having their children on the same campus with Dr. Kinsey.

Then there were those familiar with the Bloomington campus who suggested that Kinsey, with all his research, could learn more from the students than they could from him. A trustee of the university, C. Walter (Mickey) McCarty, executive editor of the *Indianapolis News,* humorist and an accomplished after-dinner speaker, impishly referred to Indiana University at banquets and luncheons as "Kinsey College."

The colossal publicity that greeted publication of the report on the female species overshadowed in many communities the news of Russia's experiments with the hydrogen bomb. In Europe the story got bigger headlines than the coronation of Queen Elizabeth. *Time* magazine quoted Mrs. Kinsey as saying innocently, "I hardly ever see him at night anymore since he took up sex."

Dr. Kinsey, who died in August of 1956, was a quiet scientist and sociologist who went around the campus wearing an unpressed suit and scuffed loafers. Nothing in his previous academic life had prepared Indiana University for the two bombshells he dropped: *Sexual Behavior in the Human Male* in 1948 at six-fifty a copy and *Sexual Behavior in the Human Female* in 1953 at eight dollars a copy. The high price tags did not keep them off the best-seller lists.

Born in Hoboken, New Jersey, in 1894, Kinsey was the son of a self-made man who had started as a shopboy at Stevens Institute of Technology and later headed its department of mechanical arts. He was a sickly boy. Years later he remembered when his family moved ten miles from smoggy Hoboken to the rolling green hills of South Orange, where he became wildly interested in birds and flowers. At sixteen, he was graduated from South Orange high school with top honors and worked his way through Maine's Bowdoin College, where he majored in biology and sociology. At the Zeta Psi fraternity house, he played the piano with abandon, developing a lasting interest in classical music.

Kinsey moved on to Harvard as a graduate student and

later joined the Indiana University faculty in 1920 as assistant professor of zoology. There he lived the sheltered, almost monotonous life of a normal member of the faculty. He married Clara Bracken McMillen in 1921 when she was a graduate student in chemistry. They had three children. On Sunday nights, Kinsey himself presided over record-player recitals for faculty friends. At school he concentrated on researching the gall wasp and, in the narrow circle of gall-wasp scholars, he became known.

Why did he switch from birds and bees and gall wasps to humans?

E. Ross Bartley, a former newspaperman entrusted with handling the public image of Indiana University in 1962, made the answer an official part of the school's history.

In the 1930's, said Bartley, Kinsey joined eleven other teachers in giving a marriage course.

"Students asked him about sex," Bartley reports. "Kinsey was amazed at how much the students didn't know and how few scientific answers there were. He felt that this was a field neglected by scientists, and so he set out to find some answers. Once he turned his attention to sex behavior, he never went back to the gall wasp."

Kinsey became the George Gallup of sex. With three other trusted associates, they secretly journeyed across the United States for fifteen years. They sought private interviews with men and women in homes, saloons, colleges, club meetings, after meetings of YWCA's, in prisons and in burlesque houses. They took notes in a code which they learned by heart and was never written down, to protect the names of their informants.

On the campus, at the Institute for Sex Research, Kinsey and his associates acquired from the Orient, Africa, Europe, and America perhaps the largest pornographic library in the world. It contains everything from crude stag movies, sado-masochistic literature, erotic pamphlets, filthy pictures, lewd photographs and drawings to material on biology, medicine, psychiatry, religion, art and law. The U.S. Customs once tried without success to stop pornographic and erotic material from being shipped to Bloomington from abroad. Officially, the University says, "The collections of the institute are important not only because they enhance the research of the institute, but also because these materials are being preserved for scholars of the future."

No students or faculty members can peek at the collection for their own amusement, according to Paul H. Gebhard and Wardell B. Pomeroy, who are carrying on Kinsey's work.

The Indiana University alumni magazine predicted "the monumental Kinsey report will undoubtedly contribute to revision of our present moral and legal codes." Looking into the future, the Columbia University Press compiled a list of eminent persons living in March of 1954 who would be remembered 200 years later. On the list were Hemingway for novels, Picasso for painting, Thurber for satire, Stravinsky for music, Einstein for physics (and math), Jung for psychology, Hutchins for education, Toynbee for history and, you guessed it, for sociology with a capital S (for sex), Dr. Alfred Kinsey.

One of the amazing stories concerns the Kinsey Report and politics. In the beginning of the McCarthy era it was revealed that some eighty-odd State Department officials had been fired because of homosexual tendencies. Republicans seized with delight on this issue and, for a time, it almost rivaled the Communist issue. In his book *Nixon and Rockefeller,* Stewart Alsop wrote that one story making the rounds in Washington was that some bright young man in Republican headquarters read the Kinsey Report and alarmed party officials with statistics: there must be several million American homosexuals of voting age. Alsop frankly reported that he personally could not prove the story, but that nevertheless "the homosexual issue was instantly dropped."

WHEN Thomas R. Marshall returned to Indiana after serving two terms as Vice President, he was interviewed by Felix Bruner of the *Indianapolis Times*. Marshall's quote became famous: "What this country needs is a good five-cent cigar."

HERB SHRINER, who has made a career of being a Hoosier, is not even a native of Indiana. He was born in Toledo, Ohio and moved to Indiana, he says, "as soon as I heard about it." Herb tells about his success at WOWO radio in Fort Wayne, Indiana as "Harmonica Herb." "I made quite a name for myself," he reports, "and I left there when I found out what it was."

Shriner likes to reminisce about small-town life in Indiana. "Boy, did we use to have excitement Saturday nights!" he exclaims. "It was nothing for us to go down to watch a few haircuts."

There were others:

"They tried one-way streets, but it didn't work. We only had one street."

"Fellow who runs the Fix-It shop has to sleep there. The lock on the front door is busted."

"Indianapolis is a big city where the meters run faster than the cabs."

While Shriner is most closely identified with Indiana, the state has produced some native sons and daughters who made good as entertainers. Among them are Anne Baxter (Michigan City) of the movies; Richard Bennett (Cass County) of the movies and father of Joan and Constance Bennett; Monte Blue (Indianapolis), pioneer cowboy actor; Joe Cook (Evansville), comedian; Irene Dunne (Madison) of the movies and the United Nations; Jan Garber (Indianapolis), orchestra leader; Phil Harris (Linton), orchestra leader and actor; Carole Lombard (Fort Wayne) of the movies; Marjorie Main

(Acton) of the movies; Noble Sissle (Indianapolis), orchestra leader; Harry Von Zell (Indianapolis), radio announcer and actor; Claude Thornhill (Terre Haute), orchestra leader; Clifton Webb (Indianapolis) of the movies; and the incomparable Red Skelton (Vincennes), one of the great natural comedians of modern times.

If you asked the mothers and fathers of today's collegians who were their favorite entertainers way back when in Indiana, they'd most likely mention Dick Powell, who was born at Mountain View, Arkansas on November 14, 1904. Powell alternated with Louis Lowe as singer and banjo player with the Charlie Davis band at the Ohio Theater, Indiana Roof and the Circle Theater. Dick Powell made a tremendous impact on Hoosiers in the two years he sang all around central Indiana in 1927 and 1928.

HOAGY CARMICHAEL wrote "Stardust" on a sentimental return to his beloved Indiana University campus. At the "Book Nook," the hangout where he spent most of his college days and nights, Hoagy picked out the melody, partly on the piano, partly whistling. In 1929 he went to Hollywood to try to interest Paul Whiteman in "Stardust" and "Old Rockin' Chair." Whiteman, the king of jazz in those days, was unimpressed and turned down Carmichael's songs.

Hoagy wrote many other haunting tunes, among them "Little Old Lady" and "Lazy Bones," but it was "Stardust" which became the great American standard.

(Hoagy's mother Mrs. Howard Carmichael played piano for the same sorority and fraternity dances at Indiana University in 1903 and 1904 for which her son played "hot piano" twenty years later with his own band.)

Other Hoosiers were great music composers. Paul Dresser, who studied for the priesthood in Terre Haute, wrote "On the Banks of The Wabash" and "My Gal Sal." One of the all-time greats, Cole Porter, was born rich in Peru,

Indiana and spent most of his time living in Paris. He wrote "Night and Day," "Begin the Beguine," "You're the Top," "I Get a Kick Out of You," "My Heart Belongs to Daddy," "Wunderbar," "In the Still of the Night," "What Is This Thing Called Love," "Anything Goes," and many others.

Remember the song "Margie"? It was written by J. Russell Robinson of Indianapolis. It was not an Irishman but Thomas Payne Westendorf of Plainfield who wrote "I'll Take You Home Again, Kathleen."

One of the giants of the music industry came from the south side of Indianapolis, wrote some of the best-remembered songs of all time, and is little known. He composed more than 3,000 songs, including "Take Me Out to the Ball Game," "I Want a Girl Just Like the Girl Who Married Dear Old Dad," "Wait Till the Sun Shines Nellie," "Only a Bird in a Gilded Cage" and "I'll Be With You in Appleblossom Time." His professional name was Albert vonTilzer. His real name was Harry Gumbinsky and his father Jacob owned a hair-goods store that specialized in wigs, switches, puffs, rats and fuzzy false bangs—in an era (1884) when "falsies" were curls of real hair. Father, mother (Sarah) and the six Gumbinsky boys—Julius, Louis, William, Albert, Harold and Harry—lived over the store at 193 East Washington Street.

Harry Gumbinsky, probably the most prolific musicman who ever lived, had fun with music, composing such ditties as "I'll Bake a Cake Like Your Mother Used to Make, If You Make the Dough Like Dad," and "I'll Lend You Anything I've Got, Except My Wife, and I'll Make You a Present of Her." But the songs he wrote that captured his own fancy were "In the Evening, by the Moonlight" and "All Alone."

MORE than a year before John Dillinger engineered Indiana's greatest prison break at Michigan City in 1933 and swashbuckled into the nation's newspaper headlines, bank robberies in the Hoosier state already had reached epidemic proportions. Three a day wasn't unusual. There was one red-letter day for newspapermen when nine Indiana banks were stuck up.

The bold robberies of Dillinger held a bizarre fascination for a public disillusioned about the Depression.

This, though, is not a story about the surly Mooresville boy who blazed a trail of crime and terror through the Midwest before he was shot down by FBI agents when "the lady in red" fingered him outside a Chicago theater in 1934. It is about an overworked and underpaid newspaperman who benefited from every Dillinger caper. He worked for the International News Service and scooped his bigger rivals the Associated Press and United Press every day on the bank lootings.

Jack Cejnar, bureau manager for INS in Indianapolis, could hardly keep pace with the larger AP and UP staffs covering the state capital, let alone the rash of bank holdups breaking out all over the state. He had a limited budget for long-distance telephone calls and nothing for paying correspondents. It was in the basement of Mike Hanrahan's saloon, while slopping up news, that Cejnar got a brainstorm. He dashed to the office of Eddie McClain, then state insurance commissioner.

"What companies carry bank-robbery insurance in Indiana?" he inquired.

"That's an easy one," McClain replied. "American Surety carries 98 percent of the business."

Under the insurance policy, the bank was obliged to flash holdup news to the company in Indianapolis even before it called the police. Cejnar made a deal on the spot. For an immediate tip on every bank robbery, Cejnar agreed to give the insurance company a professionally prepared news report of the crime—within fifteen minutes—so insurance investigators could start their own probe before the trail got cold. (In those days a suspicion persisted that many bank holdups were inside jobs and Dillinger was credited with more stick-ups than he ever carried out.)

Day after day, Cejnar scooped his rivals. The AP and UP were baffled to the point where they sent investigators into Indiana from New York to find out what was going on. The timing was so close many suspected Cejnar was in ca-hoots with Dillinger.

As enterprising as Cejnar's system was, State Police Superintendent Al Feeney unwittingly gave him an even bigger advantage. With no police radio as yet available, Feeney set up a system of county blockades whereby the sheriff would block off all the roads after a bank job and commandeer all telephones so he could organize a posse of deputies. Cejnar was always able to get his phone call through before the sheriff shot into action. By the time reporters for AP, UP and newspapers were alerted to what was going on, all the telephone lines were busy.

As the Dillinger era engulfed Indiana and bank rob-beries got more spectacular and gained national dimensions in headlines, the secret technique paid off for Cejnar in big-ger exclusive stories. Cejnar reports budget-conscious INS sent him professional kudos, but kept him pure of com-mercialism. He did not get a raise in pay or a single bonus for his sensational Coast-to-Coast scoops.

AN INTERESTING footnote to the Dillinger story: Cap-tain Matt Leach of the State Police had the responsibility of solving the stickups. Before he could move to one town there was a bank robbery in another town. He was miserable. The public clamored for action. Political heat from the State-house scorched the department.

At the height of the tension, Jack Cejnar of INS picked up a book at a secondhand store in Detroit for ten cents and sent it anonymously to Captain Leach. The title was *How to Be a Detective*. Leach was so outraged that Cejnar was afraid to tell him he was only playing a joke. It didn't help matters when the UP sent all of its newspaper clients across the nation a story speculating that Dillinger had sent the do-it-yourself detective book to Leach.

WESTBROOK PEGLER, the acid columnist and former sports writer, years ago spent considerable time in Indiana. Knute Rockne, coach of Notre Dame, always referred to him as "Eastbrook Heckler."

THE 1920's were no more roaring in Indiana than anywhere else in the dry U.S.A.—and no less.

The most powerful organization in the state was the Indiana Anti-Saloon League. The most powerful man in the state was the superintendent of the Indiana Anti-Saloon League—the Reverend Edward Seitz Shumaker, a Methodist clergyman. He virtually controlled the State Legislature.

In 1917, Reverend Shumaker appealed to the State Legislature to pass a statewide Prohibition bill and it dutifully responded—70 to 28 in the House and 38 to 11 in the Senate. The law went into effect April 2, 1918. Thirty breweries, six distilleries and 6,044 saloons were forced to close.

Harold C. Feightner, old-time Indianapolis newspaperman, shrewd political observer and later spokesman for the beer industry, wrote: "With Hoosier boys falling in France, with the draft coming closer and closer, with meatless days and lightless nights, nobody paid much attention to the social and economic changes that had been wrought."

Again in 1919, Shumaker cracked the ecclesiastical whip and the State Legislature ratified the Eighteenth Amendment to the federal Constitution. Unlike its ally, the Ku Klux Klan, the Anti-Saloon League sought no members—only donors—and it was eminently successful. It was built around and in the evangelical pulpits and styled itself the "church in action."

Feightner tells about the time Eugene Jepson Cadou, Sr., the famous INS correspondent, and the Reverend Shumaker were comparing ailments. The head of the Anti-Saloon League avowed that he had obtained relief from a certain patent medicine. Cadou called at a drugstore and, to his delight, found it contained 20 percent alcohol. The resulting big story hit the front pages everywhere.

THE WRIGHT BONE DRY LAW was passed at the insistence of the Women's Christian Temperance Union (WCTU). It made possession of liquor in an automobile a felony and, in the event of conviction, the judge was prevented from suspending sentence. It was easy to get convictions under this law. The prosecutor got a twenty-five-dollar fee for every liquor conviction. In Lake County the prosecutor made as much as $200,000 a year tax free. The law was repealed in 1933.

The Baker Law of 1908 made it an offense to smoke a cigarette on the street. Still on the books is a law which prohibits a white person and a Negro to marry.

GOVERNOR George N. Craig had bitter foes inside his own Republican Party as well as outside. In an effort to heighten his public image, Craig hired a high-powered press agent from Chicago, Bill O'Connell. This brought Craig favorable attention in the press, more outside the state than inside.

Down in southern Indiana, around the towns of Bedford, Oolitic and Paoli, Republican foes of Craig made their own evaluation. Said Hugh Gray, a back-woodsy rustic with a degree from Indiana University, about the Craig regime, "It's jest like an outhouse. You can whitewash it and plant honeysuckle all around, but it still stinks."

IN SOME Indiana newspaper offices any person automatically becomes a Hoosier if (1) he does something notorious or meritorious and (2) either lives, lived or flew over Indiana in a plane.

By these standards, you cannot quarrel with me if I list three Hoosier Presidents of the United States: Abraham Lincoln of Spencer County (the sixteenth), Benjamin Harrison of Indianapolis (the twenty-third) and William Henry Harrison of Vincennes (the ninth).

Indiana also has had three others nominated for the Presidency: Republican Wendell Willkie of Rushville, Socialist Eugene V. Debs of Terre Haute and Prohibitionist John P. St. John of Franklin County.

Sometimes called the "mother of Vice Presidents," Indiana has given the United States four "Veeps": Republican Schuyler Colfax of South Bend (1869–73), Republican Charles W. Fairbanks of Indianapolis (1905–09), Democrat Thomas A. Hendricks of Shelbyville (1885) and Democrat Thomas R. Marshall of North Manchester (1912–19).

Four others were nominated for Vice President: Democrat William H. English of Indianapolis (1880), Abolitionist and Free Soil Party George W. Julian of Centerville (1852), Democrat John W. Kern of Indianapolis (1908) and Southern Democrat Joseph Lane of Vanderburgh County (1912 and 1916).

KENESAW MOUNTAIN LANDIS, first commissioner of baseball, came from Logansport, Indiana. He was at one time judge of the United States District Court in Chicago.

His brother Frederick Landis was a writer (*Copperhead* and *Lonesome Hill*), a Congressman and the father of the present Indiana Supreme Court Judge Frederick Landis.

Kenesaw asked his brother Fred to visit him in Chicago during the treason trial of Victor Berger, former Mayor of Milwaukee. Fred was impatient with hanging around the courtroom and told his brother so. Kenesaw spit out the tobacco wad in his mouth, turned and said, "It won't take but two hours to give this bastard a fair and impartial trial and send him to the pen."

THE FIRST city anywhere to have all its streets lighted by electricity was Wabash, Indiana, the Rock City. Brush Electric Light Company of Cleveland guaranteed that four of its lights placed atop the courthouse would cast a light for a distance of one mile. The courthouse was high on a hill overlooking the rest of the city. Cost of this pioneer experiment was $1,800 for the installation plus $1.15 extra each night.

On March 1, 1880, 10,000 people came to witness the historic event. An awed correspondent for the *Chicago Tribune* reported: "For a mile around, houses and yards were distinctly visible, while far away the river glowed like a band of molten silver."

OLD-TIMERS SAY the most colorful Hoosier was Lieutenant Governor Harold Van Orman, who owned hotels in Logansport, Evansville, Bloomington, Fort Wayne and Lafayette.

He had a reputation as a Casanova and wound up marrying a circus bareback rider. Van Orman distributed hotel cards which read: "Good rooms, good meals and pies like your mother used to make." On the other side, it said: "Tarts like your father used to make."

PAUL V. McNUTT was considered Indiana's ablest and most qualified Governor. Also, its most brazen political boss.

He ruled with an iron fist. He had been dean of the Indiana University Law School and used the American Legion as a springboard to Democratic political fame.

When McNutt was running for Governor, however, Republican Gaylord Martin hit him with a political speech that got under McNutt's skin. Martin said, "Who is this great American the Democrats are offering, this great lawyer, this great soldier? He is a lawyer who never tried a case and a soldier who never fired a gun." It was true.

COLONEL JOHN JACOB LEHMANOWSKY, who served under Napoleon, and afterward settled in Indiana, died thinking he was responsible for giving Indianians the nickname "Hoosiers." His story was that while embroiled in a dispute with some natives in Kentucky he tried to tell them he was a "hussar." According to the Lehmanowsky family, the Kentuckians then applied the name "Hussar" or "Hoosier" to everybody from Indiana.

James Whitcomb Riley had his own private version. He said,

> These stories commonly told about the origin of the word "Hoosier" are all nonsense. The real origin is found in the pugnacious habits of the early settlers. They were vicious fighters, and not only gouged and scratched, but frequently bit off noses and ears. This was so ordinary an affair that a settler coming into a barroom on a morning after a fight, and seeing an ear on the floor, would merely push it aside with his foot and carelessly ask: "Whose ear?"

Another theory was that the Indiana men who manned the flatboats on the Ohio River were athletic and pugnacious and were accustomed, when on the levees of the Southern cities, to jump up and crack their heels together and shout "Huzza!"

There are other versions and variations. Some say it was a corruption of a French, or a German, or a Spanish, or even an English word. Others say it was derived from the words "Who's Here?" Louis Kossuth, the Hungarian patriot, said he was told on his visit to Indianapolis in 1852 that it came from "hoosa," the Indian name for corn. Another theory traces it back to an Indiana prizefighter named Aaron Short (when he crushed his opponent, the crowd would cry "Hurrah for the Hoosier," meaning the formidable "husher" who could hush all comers). Other theories: the pioneer's wary greeting to newcomers, "Who's yer?" and a canal foreman, Sam Hoosier, who prefered to hire shovelmen from the Indiana side of the Ohio River.

Most of the theories carry two features in common:

1. The word was first applied to a rough, boisterous, uncouth, illiterate class of people and the word implied this character.

2. The word came from the South, or was first applied by Southern people.

It is interesting to note that even today the word has one meaning to natives of Indiana and quite another to outsiders. To people in Indiana, the word "Hoosier" is a gracious, kind and proud word, conjuring someone who has roots and belongs to the forests, trees, rivers and lakes of the state. To outsiders, "Hoosier" is an uncomplimentary word, meaning usually a rustic or peasant or someone who is uncouth and straight out of Tobacco Road.

The man who has perhaps done the most research on how and when Indiana acquired the nickname is Jacob P. Dunn. His conclusion is that the word originated as "hoozer" in the Cumberland dialect of England, from the Anglo-Saxon word "hoo," meaning high or hill. Dunn traces the word to a hill-dweller and says it came to characterize his roughness and uncouthness. Immigrants from Cumberland, England settled in North Carolina and Kentucky, Dunn theorizes, and their descendants brought it into Indiana.

Hubert H. Hawkins, director of the Indiana Historical Society, favors the theory advanced by Dunn. He says it "is the most logical explanation."

He may be right. All that anyone can be sure about is

that the word "Hoosier" was first popularized by John Finley in his poem *The Hoosier Nest,* published January 1, 1833 in the *Indianapolis Journal.* My favorite four lines from it are:

> *Blest Indiana! In whose soil*
> *Men seek the sure rewards of toil*
> *And honest poverty and worth*
> *Find here the best retreat on earth.*

eight

THE KLAN IN INDIANA

I am the law in Indiana.
—D. C. STEPHENSON

TEN MASKED Knights of the Ku Klux Klan quietly filed into the Brightwood Methodist Episcopal Church, 2404 Station Street, Indianapolis, on the hot Sunday evening of July 23, 1922. The large congregation was startled. The Klansmen knelt for a moment of silent prayer, rose and handed the pastor, the Reverend Roy Ragsdale, an envelope in which was enclosed $100.

On the south side of Indianapolis eight miles away, that very same day, the Reverend Charles H. Gunsolus took to the pulpit of the Garfield Christian Church. "Mayor Lewis Shank has proven himself to be more interested in horse races and prizefighting than in the higher and more elevating things in life," he said. The preacher condemned the Mayor's support of the public dance as "immoral" and praised the Ku Klux Klan "because it stands by the Bible, the Constitution and the flag."

The day Ed Jackson was sworn in as Governor on January 12, 1925 the invisible empire of the Klan controlled the State of Indiana. It made the laws and enforced them. Besides Governor Jackson, it had elected legislators, prosecutors, judges and Mayors. Nearly 500,000 Hoosiers, in white robes and hoods, burned their fiery crosses almost nightly to strike fear in the hearts of their neighbors. Masked Klansmen by the thousands paraded through downtown city streets like an avalanche of snow descending.

The Klan preached white supremacy, terrorized Negroes, persecuted Jews, discriminated against Catholics and with a pathological ferocity took unto itself the duties of vice crusading and the punishing of immorality. It swore to uphold the sanctity of women and denounced the curse of alcoholism.

Native-born white Protestants were recruited with advertisements in the *Kourier,* a Klan newspaper widely circulated in church circles:

> Every criminal, every gambler, every thug, every libertine, every girl ruiner, every home wrecker, every wife beater, every dope peddler, every moonshiner, every crooked politician, every pagan priest, every shyster lawyer, every K of C, every white slaver, every brothel madam, every Rome-controlled newspaper, every black spider, is fighting the Klan. Think it over. Which side are you on?

On April 2, 1925, D. C. Stephenson, grand dragon of the Ku Klux Klan in Indiana, which had vowed to uphold virtue and smite immorality, was arrested for the sadistic sexual assault of Madge Oberholtzer. Twelve days later, Madge Oberholtzer died and the charge became first-degree murder.

This was the beginning of the end of Stephenson's dictatorship in Indiana. The Klan dragged on but its power was broken the day the girl's outraged father George Oberholtzer swore out a warrant for the arrest of Stephenson.

Stephenson's sidekick Court Asher, onetime bootlegger, notorious anti-Semite, former editor of the isolationist newspaper published in Muncie, *X-Ray,* told his associates,

> Sometimes we'd leave a wild party, slip into the robes, and go into a church to pray with a bunch of new Klansmen.

Sometimes if the take was real good, we might give them back as much as fifty dollars of their own money.

Stephenson could kneel down and pray as convincingly as any minister. When he was in his cups, no woman was safe from him.

DAVID CURTIS STEPHENSON lived like a king in his palatial home in Irvington, a respectable neighborhood on the east side of Indianapolis, not far from the old Butler College campus. He had a fleet of Cadillacs parked in and around the nearby maple and oak trees. When he wasn't entertaining Senators, Governors and Mayors at home, he wined and dined them on an expensive yacht on Lake Michigan.

He was then about thirty-three, handsome, with blond hair, narrow blue-gray eyes, thin-plucked eyebrows and a thin mouth that broke into a ready smile. He was squat and powerfully built. Wherever he went, his bodyguards went, too. Stephenson dressed conservatively, looked like a banker and had eyes for beautiful women. His friends say he was alert, friendly, ingratiating, well-poised, confident, witty, a tireless worker and with a genius for organization and executive direction. His rise had been spectacular.

Born in Texas in 1891, Stephenson received a grade school education, part of it in a Catholic institution. As soon as he was old enough, he took jobs in printing shops and newspapers in Texas, Oklahoma and Iowa. In Oklahoma, restless and filled with discontent, Stephenson joined the Socialist Party, wrote some articles and made speeches in behalf of its principles and candidates.

He married in 1915. His wife later charged that he had deserted her in the same year, shortly before their only child was born.

In July 1917, Stephenson volunteered for the Iowa National Guard. He was sent to an officers' training camp at Camp Snelling, Minnesota and in November was commissioned a second-lieutenant and assigned to active duty. Years

later, Stephenson and his Klan comrades told and retold
stories of his heroics as a fighting major at Belleau Wood.
The record is clear that he never got closer to France than
Camp Devens, Massachusetts.

Honorably discharged from service in February 1919,
Stephenson says he became interested in the welfare of former
servicemen and started to organize the discharged soldiers
of Indiana with whom he had served in the 36th Infantry
Division.

Evansville was a bustling river-front town in 1920 when
Stephenson sold securities in a coal-mining company. He had
left the Socialist Party and registered as a Democrat. He
entered the Congressional primary and lost. In 1921 he
joined the Klan, taking with him his buddies, the veterans.
He was an eloquent speaker, with a powerful personality and
great magnetism. Hiram Wesley Evans, a Dallas dentist and
Imperial Wizard of the KKK, gave Stephenson the job of
organizing the Klan in Indiana, specifically for the 1922
elections. Before long, Evans added twenty states in the East,
South, and Midwest to Stephenson's responsibility.

Stephenson hit the jackpot when he moved his regional
Klan headquarters to an eight-room office on the third floor
of the new Kresge building in Indianapolis. He also went
into the coal and gravel business.

In 1924 he married again. His second wife divorced him
in less than a year. Stephenson couldn't care less. He moved
in a fast social circle of cocktail parties, and did not adhere
to the Klan's rules of abstemiousness. His Klan activities
were prospering. He had hired professional salesmen to help
him organize it. And politicians in both parties fawned on
him.

Stephenson sold Klan memberships, called *klectokon,*
which were initiation fees or donations, for not less than
ten dollars nor more than twenty-five dollars, out of which he
kept four dollars. The Klan regalia, white robes and peaked
caps, sold at six dollars a set. Stephenson had sets manufac-

tured at a cost to him of $1.75. He kept the difference. His take in eighteen months totaled more than $2 million.

The mumbo-jumbo rituals and secrecy of the Klan fascinated Hoosiers. They joined. They marched. They set up their wooden cross on a hillside, soaked it with kerosene and fired it for all to see. This was the organization Stephenson led into the political campaign of 1924. Ed Jackson campaigned for Governor in Stephenson's Cadillac. Though the Klan principally backed Republicans (because they were generally in control), Stephenson crossed party lines to support some Democrats who would in turn be obligated to the Klan. He made other deals with the political bosses. It is no secret that in the Republican primary, Negro leaders had double-crossed their own race and had thrown support to Klan candidates.

The fight for control of the Klan between Stephenson and Evans was bound to come. Both were bent on absolute, individual power and both were utterly ruthless and unscrupulous.

Stephenson was drunk with power. He boasted he had delivered the Klan vote to Governor Jackson. Utilities, trade organizations and business groups came to him (usually with money) to get their bills passed into laws. He licensed bootleggers and raided those who didn't pay tribute. He dispensed Statehouse jobs to his Klan pals.

Stephenson even got the idea he wanted to buy Valparaiso University and convert it into a Klan Kollege for children of Klansmen. Behind the scenes he grabbed control of the Klan paper, *Fiery Cross,* and started taking potshots at his Imperial boss. Stephenson seceded from the national Klan, but tried to keep the Indiana branch under his own control. He said, "I resigned from the Klan because of repeated disagreement with Dr. Evans and his associates over national policy of the Klan and because of the character of the men with whom Evans had surrounded himself. The national officers of the Klan were planning to use its political influence to protect organized crime throughout the country."

Evans fought back. He began to circulate stories that Stephenson was a not-so-secret lecher and drunkard. Evidence of Stephenson's immoralities was not hard to obtain.

In January 1924 the Evansville klavern formally charged Stephenson with "gross dereliction"—specifically that he had attempted to seduce a virtuous young woman of Evansville and had committed numerous other immoralities in Columbus, Ohio and Columbus, Indiana and in Atlanta, Georgia and on boats and trains. Stephenson was secretly tried, found guilty and banished from the national Klan.

While the Stephenson Klan and the Evans Klan warred on one another, the ex-minister who founded the Klan in 1915 on Stone Mountain, Georgia, William J. Simmons, tried to make a comeback with a third Klan. All three Klans vied for members. All three even had their own women's organizations. Evans called his "The Women of the Klan." "The Queens of the Golden Mask" belonged to Stephenson, and Simmons named his women's group "The Kamelia."

Stephenson was at the height of his power—dictating to the Legislature, police, prosecutors, Mayors, judges and other high-ranking politicians. They would get some of their orders and instructions from Stephenson by telegram. He would sign the wires: "The Old Man."

At Governor Jackson's inaugural banquet in the Indianapolis Athletic Club on January 12, 1925, Stephenson met Madge Oberholtzer. They danced.

MADGE OBERHOLTZER was a nice girl. Everyone in Irvington said so. She had attended Butler College and a business school, taught in a rural school and worked as a secretary before she got a job at the Statehouse. Madge was twenty-eight and unmarried when she first met D. C. Stephenson. She was pretty, but not beautiful. She stood 5 feet 4 and weighed about 140. It was natural, her friends said, that she gravitated to the Statehouse. Madge liked important people. She worked for the Superintendent of Public Instruction.

When they were introduced at the Governor's Inaugural Banquet, Stephenson was an important figure. Having maneuvered Ed Jackson into the Governor's office, he was already strutting around the Statehouse and flitting about the countryside in a Cadillac. Here was a man of wealth, power, influence and, so Madge thought, high moral standing. She was impressed.

Madge Oberholtzer was murdered in April 1925, less than three months after the inaugural banquet. Her dying declaration pinned the murder on Stephenson.

As she lay near death, Asa J. Smith, a respected lawyer who was the family attorney, drafted the document. Also present in the room were Dr. John Kingsbury, family physician, Madge's girl friend Miss Ermina Moore and another attorney, Griffith Dean. Asa Smith read each sentence slowly to Madge. She would either say, "That's right," or pause to correct the words. Then she signed it.

The official court record of Madge's dying declaration is mysteriously missing, along with the historic trial transcript. Alice Whitecotton, former clerk of the Indiana Supreme Court, says she discovered it was missing when someone asked to see it. Indiana Attorney General Edwin K. Steers sent two deputies searching through the vaults of the Statehouse in March 1963 trying to locate the complete Stephenson trial transcript. They reported they could not find it.

Madge Oberholtzer's accusing voice from the grave told the whole brutal story. Here is the full text of her dying declaration:

I, Madge Oberholtzer, being in full possession of my mental faculties and conscious that I am about to die, make as my dying declaration the following statements:

My name is Madge Oberholtzer. I am a resident of

Marion County, State of Indiana, residing at No. 5802 University Avenue, Indianapolis. I first met D. C. Stephenson at the banquet given for the Governor at the Athletic Club early in January, 1925.

After the banquet he asked me for a date several times, but I gave him no definite answer. He later insisted that I take dinner with him at the Washington Hotel and I consented and he came for me at my home in his Cadillac car, and on this occasion we dined together.

After that he called me several times on the phone, and once again I had dinner with him at the Washington Hotel with another party.

Subsequent to this I was once at Stephenson's home at a party with several prominent people when both gentlemen and their ladies were present.

I did not see him again until Sunday, March 15, 1925 when upon returning to my home about ten o'clock in the evening I was informed by my mother, who said to me that there had been parties calling for me on the telephone and saying for me to call Irvington 0492. I called Irvington 0492 and Stephenson answered and said to me to come down if I could to his home, that he wished to see me about something very important to me; that he was leaving for Chicago and had to see me before he left. This was about 10 P.M. Sunday. His home was only two or three blocks from mine. He said further that he was busy and could not leave, but that he would send someone for me. I recognized Stephenson's voice. Soon a Mr. Gentry, whom I had never seen before, came for me and said he was from Stephenson's. I walked with Gentry to Stephenson's home. When we arrived there we went inside. I saw Stephenson and that he had been drinking. His chauffeur, whom he called Shorty, was there also. Shorty is a young man. Later a man whom they called Clenck (sic) came in. Soon as I got inside the house I was very much afraid, as I first learned then there was no other woman about, and that Stephenson's housekeeper was away or at least not in evidence. Immediately upon my arrival they took me into the kitchen and some kind of drinks were produced. It was then Clenck came in the back door. I said I wanted no drink but Stephenson and the others forced me to drink. I was afraid not to do so and I drank three small glasses of the drink. This made me very ill and dazed and I vomited.

Stephenson said to me about this time, "I want you to go with me to Chicago." I remember saying I could not and would not. I was very much terrified and did not know what to do. I said to him that I wanted to go home. He said, "No, you cannot go home. Oh yes! You are going with me to Chicago. I love you more than any woman I have ever known." I tried to call my home on the phone but could get no answer. Later when I tried to get to a phone they would not let me.

These men were all about me. They took me up to Stephenson's room, and he opened a dresser drawer which was filled with revolvers. He told each of the men to take one, and he selected a pearl-handled revolver for himself and had Shorty load it. Stephenson said first to me that we were going to drive through to Chicago. He said for me to go with him, but I said I did not wish to and would not go to Chicago. Later Gentry called the Washington Hotel, at Stephenson's order, and secured reservation in a drawing room for two persons. They all took me to the automobile at the rear of Stephenson's yard and we started the trip. I thought we were bound for Chicago but did not know. I begged of them to drive past my home so I could get my hat, and once inside my home I thought I would be safe from them. They drove me to Union Station in the machine, where they had to get a ticket. I did not get out of the automobile all the way.

Before we left the house I remember Stephenson said to Clenck, "You get in touch with Claude Worley right away and tell him we are going to Chicago on a business deal to make money for all of us." Clenck did not go with us in the car. Stephenson and Gentry sat in the car all the time with me until we got onto the train. We stopped at the Washington Hotel on the way down. Shorty got out and went in the hotel and came back. They would not let me out. I was dazed and terrified that my life would be taken

and did not know what to do. Stephenson would not let me
get out of the car and I was afraid he would kill me. He said
he was the law in Indiana. He also said to Gentry, "I think
I am pretty smart to have gotten her." We got on the train,
and although I cannot distinctly remember, I think only
the colored porter saw us. They took me at once into the
compartment. I cannot remember clearly everything that
happened after that. I know Gentry got into the top berth
of the compartment. Stephenson took hold of the bottom
of my dress and pulled it up over my head. I tried to fight
but was weak and unsteady. Stephenson took hold of my two
hands and held them. I had not the strength to move. What
I had drunk was affecting me. Stephenson took all my clothes
off and pushed me into the lower berth. After the train had
started, Stephenson got in with me and attacked me. He held
me so I could not move. I did not know and do not remember all that happened. He chewed me all over my body, bit
my neck and face, chewing my tongue, chewed my breasts
until they bled, my back, my legs, my ankles and mutilated
me all over my body. I remember I heard a buzz early in the
morning and the porter calling us to get up for Hammond
and Gentry shook me and said it was time to get up, that
we were to get off at Hammond. At this time I was becoming
more conscious and Stephenson was flourishing his revolver.
I said to him to shoot me. He held the revolver against my
side, but I did not flinch. I said to him again to kill me, but
he put the gun in his grip. I had heard no sound from
Gentry during the night. Afterwards Gentry and Stephenson
helped me dress and the two men dressed and they took me
off the train at Hammond. I remember seeing the conductor.
I was able to walk to the Indiana Hotel. I remember begging
Stephenson and saying to him to wire my mother during
the night and he said he had or would, I am not clear about
that. At the Indiana Hotel, Stephenson registered for himself
and wife. I tried to see under what name but failed to do so.
This was about six-thirty in the morning. There were in the
hotel lobby two colored bellboys and two colored girls.
Gentry, Stephenson and myself went to the rooms. I had no
money. I kept begging Stephenson and saying to him to send

my mother a telegram. I said to the bellboy, "Are there any telegraph blanks in the room?" Stephenson made me write the telegram and said to me what to say. Gentry took the telegram and said he would send it right away. Stephenson lay down on the bed and slept. Gentry put hot towels and witch hazel on my head and bathed my body to relieve my suffering. We were in room 416 with Stephenson while Gentry was doing this. Stephenson said he was sorry, and that he was three degrees less than a brute. I said to him, "You are worse than that." Breakfast was served in the room. Shorty came in about this time. He said he had driven up in Stephenson's car. Stephenson ate grapefruit, coffee, sausage and buttered toast for breakfast. I drank some coffee but ate nothing.

I said to Stephenson to give me some money, that I had to buy a hat. Shorty gave me $15 at Stephenson's direction and took me out in the car. Shorty said to Stephenson he had been delayed getting there as he could not find the hotel where we were in Hammond. Shorty waited for me while I went into a store close to the hotel to get a hat. This was a small black silk hat similar to one I have—it cost $12.50. When I came back to the car I said to Shorty to drive me to a drugstore in order I might get some rouge. We drove to a drugstore near the Indiana Hotel and I purchased a box of bichloride of mercury tablets. I put these in my coat pocket. Then we went back to the hotel.

During the morning when we were in the hotel the men got more liquor at Stephenson's direction. Stephenson said we were going to drive on to Chicago. Stephenson made me write the telegram to my mother saying we were going to Chicago. Gentry took it.

When I got back to the hotel with Shorty I went up to the room. Gentry had a room next to Stephenson. His was No. 417. I said to Stephenson to let me go into No. 417 to lie down and rest. He said, "Oh, you are not going there. You are going to lie right down here by me." I waited awhile until I thought he was asleep, then I went into room 417. Gentry stayed in the room with Stephenson. There was no glass in room 417 so I got a glass in 416 and took the mercury tablets. I laid out eighteen of the bichloride of mercury tablets and at once took six of them. I only took six because they burnt me so. This was about 10 A.M. Monday, I think.

Earlier in the morning I had taken Stephenson's revolver, and while Gentry was out sending the telegram I wanted to kill myself then in Stephenson's presence. This was while he was first asleep. Then I decided to try and get poison and take it in order to save my mother from disgrace. I knew it would take longer with the mercury tablets to kill me. Later, after I had taken the mercury tablets, I lay down on the bed and became very ill. I think it was nearly four o'clock in the afternoon before anyone came into the room where I was. Then Shorty came in. He sat down to talk to me.

He said to me what was wrong that I looked so ill. I replied, "Nothing." He said, "Where is your pain?" and I said it was all over. He said I could not have pain without cause. I said to him, "Can you keep a secret?" He said "Yes." I said, "I believe you can," and then I said to him that I had taken poison, and said to him not to tell Stephenson. I was very ill and almost delirious at this time. I had vomited blood all day. When I said to him I had taken poison he turned pale and in a few minutes he said to me he wanted to take a walk. He then went out. In a few minutes Stephenson and Gentry and Shorty came into the room very much excited. Stephenson said, "What have you done?" I said, "I asked Shorty not to tell." Stephenson ordered a quart of milk and made me drink it. I said to Stephenson and the others that I had taken six bichloride of mercury tablets, and I said, "If you don't believe it there is evidence on the floor and in the cuspidor." Stephenson emptied the cuspidor into the bathtub and saw some of the tablets and the cuspidor was half full of clotted blood.

I said to Stephenson, "What are you going to do?" And he said, "We will take you to a hospital here and you can register as my wife. Your stomach will have to be pumped out." He said to me that I could tell them at the hospital I had gotten the mercury tablets through mistake instead of aspirin. I refused to do this as his wife. Stephenson said, "We will take you home." I said I would not go home. Either that I would stay right there, and for them to leave me there and go about their own business, or to let me register at another hotel under my own name. Stephenson said, "We will do nothing of the kind. We will take you home." Stephenson said that the best way out of it was for us to drive to Crown Point and for us to get married. Gentry said he agreed with him. I refused. Stephenson snapped his fingers and said to Shorty, "Pack the grips." Stephenson helped me downstairs. I did not care what happened to me. Just before we left Hammond I said to Shorty to call my mother up. He said, "If I do that she will be right up here." And I said, "What could be sweeter." Stephenson said to me he had called her. I said to him, "What did she say?" And he replied that she said it would be all right if I did not come home that night.

I don't know much about what happened after that. My mind was in a daze. I was in terrible agony. Shorty checked out for all of us, and they put me in the back seat of the machine with Stephenson. We then started for home in the automobile. After we got a piece Stephenson said to Shorty to take the auto license plates off of the car, which he did, and Stephenson said to him to say if questioned that we had parked in the last town we had passed through and auto plates had been stolen. All the way back to Indianapolis I suffered great pain and agony and screamed for a doctor. I said I wanted a hypodermic to ease the pain, but they refused to stop. I begged and said to Stephenson to leave me along the road someplace, that someone would stop and take care of me if he wouldn't. I said to him that I felt he was more cruel to me than he had been the night before. He said he would stop at the next town before we got there but never did. Just before reaching a town he would say to Shorty, "Drive fast but don't get pinched."

I vomited in the car all over the back seat and grips. Stephenson did not try to make me comfortable in any way. He said he thought I was dying, and at one time said to

Gentry, "This takes guts to do this, Gentry. She is dying." I heard him say also that he had been in a worse mess than this before and got out of it. Stephenson and Gentry drank liquor during the entire trip. I remember Stephenson having said that he had power and saying that he had made $250,-000. He said that his word was law. After reaching Indianapolis, we drove straight to his house, cutting across Emerson Avenue or 38th Street some way. When we reached Stephenson's garage he said, "There is someone at the front door of the house." It was sometime during the night when we got to the garage, as I think we left Hammond about five o'clock, and Stephenson said to Shorty to go and see who was at the front door. Shorty came back and said, "It's her mother." I remember Stephenson said to me, "You will stay right here until you marry me."

Stephenson, or someone, carried me up the stairs into a loft above the garage. Stephenson did nothing to relieve my pain. I do not remember anything that happened all night after we reached the garage. I was left in the garage until I was carried home. A big man, the Mr. Clenck mentioned before, took me home. He shook me and awakened me and said, "You have to go home." I asked him where Stephenson was and he said he did not know. I remember Stephenson had told me to tell everyone that I had been in an automobile accident, and he said, "You must forget this, what is done has been done, I am the law and the power." He said to me several times that his word was the law. I was suffering and in such agony I begged and said to Clenck to take me home in the Cadillac car. He said he would order a taxi, but finally said he would take me in Stephenson's car. He put my clothes on me and then carried me down to the car and put me in the back seat and drove the car to my home. I said to him to drive up in the driveway. He did and then carried me into the house and upstairs and into my bed. It was about noon Tuesday when we got into the house.

I, Madge Oberholtzer, am in full possession of all my mental faculties and understand what I am saying. The foregoing statements have been read to me and I have made them as my statements and they are all true. I am sure that

I will not recover from this illness, and I believe that death is very near to me, and I have made all of the foregoing statements as my dying declaration and they are true.

MADGE OBERHOLTZER

AT THE murder trial, which was shifted to Noblesville, a small country town not far from Indianapolis, Stephenson was convicted basically on four points:

1. Madge Oberholtzer's dying declaration was admitted into evidence and other witnesses corroborated her statements.

2. Medical evidence was strong that she died from an infection caused or aggravated by the bites on her breast by Stephenson.

3. Stephenson forcibly took her into his custody after she swallowed poison and restrained her for twenty-four hours from receiving medical aid, which hastened or caused her death.

4. In addition to her respected family doctor John Kingsbury, five of the greatest specialists in the Middle West tried to save Madge and later testified in her behalf. They were Dr. Virgil H. Moon, who occupied the chair of pathology in the Indiana University School of Medicine; Dr. H. O. Mertz, surgeon and specialist in kidneys, ureter and bladder; Dr. J. A. McDonald, diagnostician; Dr. J. H. Warvel, famous pathologist; and R. N. Harger, Ph.D., a practicing biochemist of high standing.

Mrs. Josephine Lowes lived in the house directly behind the Stephenson home. She had testified that on the morning of March 16, 1925 she was awakened by a woman's screams coming from the Stephenson garage followed by the barking of dogs. This corroborated the dying declaration and one of Stephenson's attorneys, Eph Inman, attempted to discredit it on cross-examination:

Q. "Was Butler College in session during that time?"
A. "Think so."

Q. "Students were there in Irvington attending that
college, were they?"

A. "Oh, yes."

Q. "It was a very common thing to hear people at mid-
night out there, young boys and girls, students in automobiles, and parties having good times, and yelling and screaming at the top of their voices?"

A. "They would not be screaming in distress, would
they?"

Perhaps the most damaging testimony against Stephenson came from his own doctor, who was called in an attempt
to show Madge Oberholtzer had committed suicide. The
doctor was brilliantly cross-examined by Charles E. Cox, who
was assisting prosecutor William Remy.

Q. "You told us yesterday, as I recall, that you never
had treated the defendant in his home in Irvington?"

A. "That is what I said, yes, sir."

Q. "But you said you had prescribed for him?"

A. "Yes, sir."

Q. "Where?"

A. "At two or three of the hotels, and then one time, I
have forgotten the address, it was on Meridian Street, some
place."

Q. "Never at any hospital?"

A. "I saw him once at one hospital."

Q. "Which hospital?"

A. "The Methodist Hospital."

Q. "How many different times did you treat him for
delirium tremens or the effect of it?"

(Objection sustained)

Q. "What is the fact as to whether you ever did treat
him for delirium tremens or alcoholism?"

A. "I can't say I ever treated him for delirium tremens."

Q. "Did you ever treat him or prescribe for him for
alcoholism?"

A. "Not alcoholism alone, no."

Q. "For alcoholism, in part?"

A. "Yes, one time he was a little nervous and had been losing a lot of sleep and he might have had a little alcohol, I don't know, I didn't see him take any."

The questioning of Ralph E. Rigdon, a large forceful man from Fountaintown, Indiana, shed little light on Stephenson's innocence, but showed in detail how the Klan was operated. The defense brought Rigdon to testify that he had seen Madge Oberholtzer with Stephenson at times other than those included in her statement. It was an attempt to besmirch her reputation.

Under the skillful cross-examination of Ralph K. Kane, also working with prosecutor Remy, Rigdon began by stating he had solicited funds for the Republican State Committee in 1924.

Q. "Now what was your business before you went with the state committee?"

A. "Salesman."

Q. "What were you selling?"

A. "Stocks and bonds."

Q. "Now you say you met Stephenson three years ago last September?"

A. "Or October, I won't be positive."

Q. "Where did you meet him?"

A. "I met him at what is known as the Schultz Apple Orchard at Laurel."

Q. "Were you down there with him?"

A. "I met him there."

Q. "What was the occasion that took you there?"

A. "I was joining the Knights of the Ku Klux Klan."

Q. "Yes, you were going into the Klan and Stephenson was their organizer, was he, and then did you become an organizer afterwards?"

A. "I did not."

Q. "Well, what was the occasion that took you to Stephenson's place so frequently before the Legislature met?"

A. "We had matters of mutual interest."

Q. "What?"

A. "Politics."

Q. "Anything else?"

A. "No."

Q. "Politics?"

A. "That is all."

Q. "But what were your political schemes you were working at?"

(Objection)

A. "Well, we were trying to elect our friends."

Q. "And who were your friends?"

(To which the defendants object)

Q. "Members of the Legislature?"

(Defendants' objections overruled)

A. "Well, most everyone that was elected."

Q. "Well, did you see members of the Legislature at Stephenson's office on these occasions when you were there?"

A. "Yes."

Q. "How many, about?"

A. "Well, I don't know that I seen all of them there."

Q. "How many?"

A. "Give me a roster and I will name every one that was there."

The trial lasted more than a month. The transcript covers 2,347 pages. Judge Will M. Sparks of Rush County, one of the ablest jurists in Indiana, told the jury that if the defendants, having abducted Madge Oberholtzer forcibly, willfully kept her prisoner in the Stephenson garage and withheld medical attention, they were guilty of murder. The judge defined second-degree murder as unpremeditated homicide committed "purposely and maliciously," and he defined "malice" as not simply ill will but as "any wicked or corrupt motive."

A jury of ten farmers, a businessman and a truckdriver found Stephenson guilty of second-degree murder and he was sentenced to life imprisonment. His two bodyguards Earl Gentry and Earl Klenck were acquitted.

The former Klan dragon never took the stand in his own defense. If he had, prosecutor Remy told reporter Harold Feightner, the prosecution was ready to confront Stephenson with eleven more girls he had savagely ravished.

When Stephenson was led away to prison, he boasted, "Ed Jackson will pardon me." How did Stephenson build up such a powerful political machine in the incredibly short span of three years? What was the Klan like before and after Stephenson went behind bars?

"THE KLAN was a racket, a political and moneymaking racket," says Harold Feightner, who covered some of the activities of the KKK as a reporter in the 1920's.

But this does not explain the amazing growth that in four short years was able to elect a Governor. Nor can it explain the beatings, the boycotts, the hate, the fear.

Indiana was fertile ground for the Klan.

The light that gleamed through the stately sycamores was not from candles but from the blazing new emblem of the Imperial Commonwealth of Indiana—the Fiery Cross. The setting was described by Samuel W. Tait, Jr., a native of Indiana, in the April 1926 *American Mercury*.

> The farmer of the state, for all the advantages of soil and climate, always had hard going up to about the time of the late great moral crusade on Europe. Then, almost over-night, everything became rose-colored, and the dollars began to roll in at a rate for which he was quite unprepared. He spent some of it on flivvers, phonographs, and player pianos —and his evangelism changed fundamentally with his new mode of living. It underwent that evolution which puritan-ism always experiences with an increase in the wealth and security of its devotees. From an inward necessity it changed to an outward compulsion; it dropped all pretense of per-suasion and became undisguisedly militant. It ceased to plead for converts. It began to devote all its resources to forcing its grotesque doctrines upon the indifferent public.

A new spirit of morality—holier than thou—sprang up and was exhibited in the enlarged activity and power of the Anti-Saloon League. It showed itself in the revived National Horse Thief Detective Association, authorized by the Legislature in 1865 in an effort to end horse-stealing. With the increased prosperity of the farmer, the Horse Thief Detective Association got a new lease on life and branched out into a vigilante organization. Instead of hiding behind barns to take potshots at rustlers or someone suspected of swiping a feed bag, the farmers now climbed into their flivvers and started spying on necking parties in country lanes and punishing men (or women) suspected of immorality.

Tait wrote that something was needed to combine the moral forces into an integrated and indomitable union—and it was the Klan that met this need to perfection.

> Here at last was a political weapon calculated to satisfy all the fears and hatreds the evangelical hell-hounds had been instilling in the faithful for so long: fear of the power of Rome; hatred of the wickedness of the cities; fear of the Darwinian heresy; and hatred of the evil individualist who persisted in having a private stock (of liquor).

Intolerance was everywhere. "NIGGER, DON'T LET THE SUN SET ON YOU HERE," was a sign posted in most every small town in Indiana. Through the towns marching men clad all in white paraded pointedly past the home of a Catholic priest. Frightened Jewish merchants made payoffs in silence to ward off boycotts.

Your next-door neighbor might be a Kluxer and you'd never know it. If you got an application, on stationery bearing pen-and-ink sketches of Klansmen on white-shrouded horses, you would be required to answer twenty questions, including: "Are you Jew or Gentile?" "Do you believe in white supremacy?" "What is your religious faith?" "Your politics?"

No Catholic, Jew or Negro could be elected under the

Klan edict that "only 100 percent native-born Protestant Americans should rule this fair land of ours." The Horse Thief Detective Association became the police force of the Klan and made stern reprisals against notorious law violators. In dead of night, prostitutes were taken from their beds and flogged. Drunks were tarred and feathered. Klansmen in hoods and robes entered private homes without search warrants and disciplined errant husbands—or errant wives (and sometimes faithful wives who wouldn't come across to a Kluxer.)

The Klan and the Anti-Saloon League teamed up to pass the Wright Bone Dry Law, which made some prosecutors rich. Under the law, the prosecutor would receive twenty-five dollars for every liquor conviction. Few such prisoners ever escaped a jail sentence.

In Roann, Indiana, in Wabash County, a Catholic grocer was forced to close his shop when no one would buy from him. In Indianapolis, in July 1922, John B. Johnson tried to calm his wife and children in their home at 601 West 28th Street after someone pitched a bomb through their window. The Johnsons were colored.

Down at West Baden, the Indiana Republican Editorial Association was meeting and Klan leader Walter Bossert (a former Indiana University athlete who yearned for a seat in the United States Senate) shook hands with a few GOP leaders, said hello to others and left. A few miles down the road at Tom Taggart's French Lick Springs Hotel, meeting place of the Democrats, white-robed Klansmen entered and blew the weird Klan bugle in the lobby.

Word reached Indiana that the Reverend Oren Van Loon, a minister across the state line in Berkeley, Michigan, had preached sermons against the Klan. His criticism was mild. "The cross should not be used as a symbol of terror," he said. Reverend Van Loon disappeared June 30, 1924 and was found unconscious in another town two weeks later. At the hospital, doctors found he had been drugged and on his back was burned into the flesh the letters KKK.

The Klan paper the *Fiery Cross* carried ads from Indianapolis establishments. Here's one:

When the Sahara Grotto had a parade in Indianapolis, the Klan provided one of the floats. On July 14, 1923, Stephenson organized the first statewide women's meeting at Mooresville. The kiddies of Klan families were not neglected. The Klan had a Junior Citizens Club "for fun and games." The *Klan Kourier* ran an essay contest for Junior Kluxers on Americanism. There was a special page in the *Kourier* called: "Klan Kiddie Korner." In Indianapolis the Klan elected a school board and ran the schools.

IN INDIANA, here and there were Hoosiers who fought the Klan: a doctor in Knox, a lawyer in Lafayette, a railroader in Terre Haute, a minister in Indianapolis, a farmer in Hamilton County. Each had his own personal standard of integrity and decency that was stronger than the pressures of disapproval from neighbors.

There is a great temptation in life always to go along, to conform. In times of stress, history repeats. Most people refuse to stand up to be counted for decency. They are timid. They want acceptance. They want to be "in" with The Establishment.

Yet when the going is roughest, when people are trampled on, and liberty flees, in the face of threats, and hostility, and beatings, at the risk of health, and money, and life itself, there have always been somewhere, somehow, those uncommon men and women with courage to fight the good fight.

Not that the ranks of the Klan weren't filled with good people. Many were victims rather than villains. Klansmen may have been gullible and susceptible to the hocus-pocus secret rituals, and politicians may have played on their fears and emotions and ignorance. But every responsible source, including those who actively fought the Klan, has agreed that the Invisible Empire was made up largely of people of substantial and decent standing, most of them active members of Protestant churches, with definite if somewhat narrow ideals. Many never knew or understood what the Klan was really like. Sworn to uphold womanly virtue, Americanism, law and order, it attracted men and women of all ages, but it projected an image of youth aflame with enthusiasm.

In Indianapolis, the Mayor was Klan-elected. So were the city councilmen. The police chief was a Kluxer. In other areas around the state the sheriffs and prosecutors were Klan members, too.

Who would stand up to them? Who could?

Hiram Iddings Bearss did. He was a Marine whose home was in Peru in north-central Indiana, the old territory of the Miami Indians. Bearss would have been a good catch for the Klan. He was a real war hero, in violent action during the Spanish-American War, in the Philippines and at St. Mihiel in World War I. He was a Methodist, friendly, popular and wanted no part of the Klan when he came limping home to Indiana to recover from physical disabilities. Fellow Marines called him "Hiking Hiram" and the nickname stuck at home.

When the Klan organized Miami County, Hiking Hiram ran for Congress in the Republican primary. He denounced the Klan and lost the election by 300 votes. Up in Peru, politicians say the Klan counted him out.

Just before dusk on Saturday, December 16, 1922, after an initiation ceremony in the woods, the Klan paraded its might down the main street of Peru. The impetuous Bearss jumped into his car and drove straight down the line into the Klan parade. The masked marchers scattered. Klansmen surrounded the car, threw open the door and pummelled the Marine hero as he sat at the wheel. About 200 Klansmen insisted he salute their flag. He got to the running board, grabbed a wrench and shouted, "Salute the flag? You goddam sons of bitches, I salute the flag when it is properly carried. I have followed the flag where you Kluxers would be afraid to look at on a map. Come on, you Kluxers, one and all, I'll take on the lot of you."

Other Peru citizens came rushing to Hiking Hiram's side and the Klan left without further disorder.

Though retired, Colonel Bearss shortly thereafter was promoted to Brigadier-General by Act of Congress. Thirty-three years after he was named in dispatches for extraordinary heroism at Samar in the Philippines in 1901, President Franklin D. Roosevelt pinned the Congressional Medal of

Honor on his civilian suit at the White House. In 1936 he became the Republican nominee for State Senator from Miami County, but was killed in an automobile accident before the election. His brother took his place on the ticket and won. Hiking Hiram Bearss was a gallant Marine who served his country with distinction in war and peace.

NOT ALL the heroes were men of violence. The Reverend Clay Trusty, Sr. was pastor of the Seventh Christian Church of Indianapolis at Udell and Annette streets in 1922. It has since moved to 30th and Kessler.

Reverend Trusty was married and had five children. He was a gentle man and counted among his friends the Catholic Bishop Joseph Chartrand and Rabbi Morris M. Feuerlicht. The church paper the *Christian Visitor* was edited by Reverend Trusty and it contained items of tolerance. The Klan did not appreciate the paper, Reverend Trusty's sermons or the fact that he had the temerity to invite Bishop Chartrand as guest lecturer for a YMCA religion class.

All but four or five families in the Seventh Christian Church congregation at the time were members of the Klan. Clay Trusty, Jr., now assistant managing editor of the *Indianapolis News,* still vividly remembers an incident that occurred in 1923 when he was seven:

> One night Dad came home and told us we were going to eat dinner early. He packed the whole family in the car, all five kids, and we drove to Clifton and 37th Street, where members of his own congregation burned a cross in his honor.

Reverend Trusty was forced to resign, and he died a year and a half later. His congregation had replaced him with a new minister, the Reverend Gerald L. K. Smith, who later distinguished himself as an anti-Semitic pamphleteer and professional rabble-rouser.

STATE COMMANDER Paul V. McNutt of the American Legion called a meeting of top Legionnaires. He said the Legion had to demonstrate it was against the Klan and the best possible way was to elect a Catholic as state commander.

Four Protestant candidates were asked to withdraw. Frank McHale, a Catholic, a Democrat and a political pal of McNutt, got the job. He became the tenth state commander of the Legion in 1927. The Legion regained some of the prestige it had lost, but in its ranks were a number of Kluxers.

One of the more active fighters against the Klan, Mc-Hale says that the principal newspapers in Indiana which condemned the Klan in its heyday were the *Indianapolis Times, Fort Wayne Journal-Gazette, Hammond Times, Gary Post-Tribune, Evansville Courier* and the *Terre Haute Tribune.* And there were others.

In the official history of Indiana, compiled by hundreds of Hoosier writers and authorities under sponsorship of Indiana State Teachers College, it is recorded on pages 74 and 75:

> Early in 1928 the Attorney General of Indiana took the offensive against the Klan in two suits demanding its dissolution. These suits were never tried, but public opinion was beginning to veer; this fact, coupled with a savage campaign waged by the *Indianapolis Times* against the Klan, for which that newspaper was awarded the Pulitzer Prize in 1928, spelled the end of its turbulent growth as a political power.

Before the crusade was over, the *Times* had lost more than 5,000 subscribers. The anti-Klan campaign was directed by editor Boyd Gurley, who seemed immune to threats. Before that, Felix J. Bruner was writing daring editorials for the *Times* against the Klan. The KKK retaliated by saying "the Pope in Rome dictates what the *Times* prints."

Today you find people all over the state who boast how they fought the Klan. If all the people fought the Klan who said they did, then the Klan was the most persecuted minority in history. It is a fact that few Hoosiers dared to stand up to the KKK. There was a civilized minority that quietly opposed the Klan. There were even some few Protestant ministers who risked expulsion from their churches. But not many.

Audacious acts against the KKK were rare in the 1920's. Frank McHale tells how detectives were placed in Klan meetings, and how in Logansport and other places the local Klan meetings were held up at night and lists of names of Kluxers were taken away at the point of a gun. These names were published in anti-Klan papers.

"Is your neighbor a Kluxer?" was the headline in the newspaper *Tolerance,* published in Chicago by Pat O'Donnell, the great criminal lawyer who was born in Carroll County, Indiana.

It is to the credit of the famous Rainbow Division Veterans Association that it stood its ground in a fight with the Klan in 1924. The veterans were holding their national convention in Indianapolis and put on the program the Reverend Father Patrick Duffy, chaplain of the Fighting Sixty-Ninth Regiment, for a speech and memorial service to those who had lost their lives in the battle of Champagne. The Klan called Father Duffy's presence "highly unpatriotic and un-American" and sent a committee to the veterans to protest. One of the veterans replied, "You go to hell! Father Duffy was in the Rainbow and this division knew no question of creed. He is one of our buddies and he is going to speak and if you people don't like it you can get the hell off the stage."

IN 1924, KKK membership rose to 6 million in the United States under Imperial Wizard Hiram Wesley Evans and nearly half a million of them took their marching orders directly from Grand Dragon D. C. Stephenson in Indiana. It was the summit year for the Invisible Empire.

According to some historians, the original Klan was

organized by bored Civil War veterans. Others report it was started to oppose the Reconstruction policies of "the radical Republican Congress and to maintain white supremacy." Still another version is that its sole purpose was to "protect white citizens from Negro outrages and even of insurrection."

Here is the Klan's own official version, taken from the October 1936 issue of the *Kourier:*

> In May 1866 (at Pulaski, Tennessee) a group of young men who had seen action in the Confederate armies formed a social club which they named Ku Klos, after the Greek word for circle. For their amusement they rode about the countryside at night in disguise. Negroes, good and bad, because of their superstitious nature, became alarmed at these terrifying disguised figures. The good ones became better and the bad ones became suddenly good.
>
> The story spread like wildfire. Others organized bands of hooded and robed Klansmen. Leaders of the old Confederacy saw a chance to obtain justice for the white race.

General Nathan Bedford Forrest, famous Confederate cavalry leader from Mississippi, was made Grand Wizard in April 1867. His assistant was General Albert Pike of Arkansas, the philosopher and ritualist of Scottish Rite Masonry. Seemingly under some apprehension as to the abuse of its power, General Forrest ordered the Klan abandoned in 1869 and resigned.

The Klan of the 20th century, founded by Colonel William J. Simmons, an ex-minister and promoter of fraternal orders, owed its names, costumes and customs to the Reconstruction Klan. Stone Mountain, Georgia was the scene of the first meeting called by Colonel Simmons in 1915.

The reborn Klan added to "white supremacy" an intense nativism, anti-Catholicism and anti-Semitism. It did not amount to much until 1920, when two professional promoters, Elizabeth Tyler and Edward Y. Clarke, spread it through the north like a tornado. Colonel Simmons was replaced in 1921 by Evans, Stephenson's mentor and later his implacable enemy.

In the rural counties, from the gently undulating prairies of northeastern Indiana to the impoverished hill farms of southern Indiana, more than half the adult citizens were members of the Klan.

The conviction of D. C. Stephenson for the murder of Madge Oberholtzer disgraced the Klan nationally and opened the eyes of many decent Hoosiers who had been hoodwinked by the KKK's phony appeal to morality. But the Klan did not immediately die out.

It attempted respectability. On December 9, 1927, 300 Klansmen and their ladies, dressed in fine clothes and appearing without masks and robes, attended a public dinner in the Red Lacquer Room of the Palmer House in Chicago. The February 1928 issue of the *Kourier* showed a picture of the guests seated at banquet tables under huge chandeliers in a setting of grandeur. The *Kourier* write-up sounded defensive:

> . . . these ladies and gentlemen are not only among the best, but they are so considered by others—especially by the management of the Palmer House. Otherwise they would not have been able to rent this most attractive dining room and at the busy hour at that. Speaker of the evening: Judge Charles J. Orbison of Indianapolis. Guest of honor: H. Kyle Ramsey of Atlanta.

Said an article in the January 1934 issue of the *Kourier:*

> If you missed the barn dance at the Ford Air Port, in Lansing, on the Indiana-Illinois state line, you missed the time of your life. There were about 1,500 to 2,000 people there and a truly wonderful time was had till the early hours of the night. Klansmen, Let's Ride.

All over the state in early 1936 the word went out:

ANNUAL KLAN CELEBRATION
Klan No. 173, Kokomo, Indiana
July 3, 4, 5, 1936 at
beautiful Melfalfa Park

...

...

The *Kourier* became impatient again in August 1936. In a short message the paper urged: "Klansmen, It Is Time to Ride Again. My Country and My Race, Ahead of My Party."

Governor Paul V. McNutt was in power at the Statehouse. The Democrats were riding high and corruption and scandals among the high and mighty in the Klan had made the KKK political poison in the 1930's.

John Douvall, who was elected Mayor of Indianapolis after a rousing Klan rally in Cadle Tabernacle, was indicted for violating the Corrupt Practices Act and on February 4, 1931 he began serving a thirty-day sentence.

Stephenson for years had collected evidence in two black boxes against the politicians he corrupted. In an effort to spring himself out of prison—"I have been railroaded to protect others"— Stephenson got the black boxes in the hands of the *Indianapolis Times* and later the Marion County Grand Jury. Six members of the Indianapolis City Council, indicted for receiving bribes, resigned and paid fines on minor charges. City Hall was in disgrace and changed hands.

The *Times* produced a $2,500 check paid to Ed Jackson by Stephenson. Former Governor Jackson explained that the check was payment for a riding horse named Senator which had choked to death on a corncob. New evidence was uncovered charging that Jackson, while a candidate, had offered a bribe of money to former Governor Warren McCray, who went to prison on a different charge. (McCray had privately borrowed money from various state banks in Indiana and rewarded some of them with a bigger distribution of state deposits, and he had given out false bank statements.)

Ex-Governor Jackson was indicted. Fred Landis of Logansport, a high-ranking Republican who actively fought the Klan, remarked, "The history of Indiana will record one Governor coming out of the penitentiary passing another going in." Jackson, however, pleaded the statute of limitations and was saved.

By the 1940's, when the Republicans made a strong comeback, the Klan was practically forgotten, if not forgiven. In 1944, Robert W. Lyons, son of a Richmond, Indiana minister, had become a powerful lobbyist in Washington, D.C. for chain stores all over the country. If he was not a millionaire, he lived like one.

His presence in a suite at the Columbia Club, which he had personally redecorated with expensive paintings, caused a stir in Republican politics. He was a lawyer and had been active in the American Legion. Now he was seen in the company of Elmer (Little Doc) Sherwood and Charles (Red) Masten, Legion buddies who were active in the Republican Party. Politicians and reporters who talked with him came away impressed with his sincerity and personality. "He could sell you the moon," one GOP official said.

Earl Richert, now editor of Scripps-Howard News Alliance in Washington, and then Statehouse correspondent for the *Times,* heard rumblings about Lyons on his political beat and arranged for an interview. Lyons told Richert he was interested in government and in helping the Republican Party lick the New Deal.

"Is there any truth," asked Richert, "about your connections in the Klan?"

Lyons thought about this for a moment and then replied,

> When I have a boil on my butt, I sit on it. This (the Klan) has been my boil for years. I don't defend it. I was wrong. But I was a young man at the time and mightily impressed with it. My father was a friend of Senator (James E.) Watson and I went into the Klan to protect Watson. My father thought the Klan might go after him.

The day the GOP State Convention nominated Homer Capehart for U.S. Senator and Ralph Gates for Governor on June 2, 1944, State Chairman John Lauer engineered a power play that raised the Klan issue and almost wrecked the Republican Party. He called a secret meeting in the Columbia Club that night to elect Bob Lyons quietly and quickly as national committeeman.

Some Republicans present protested that by custom and tradition the selection is not made until the day before the Republican national convention. Others objected to the undue haste and secrecy of the meeting. Some didn't want to oust Ernest M. Morris of South Bend from the job. Lauer brushed aside all objections, saying, "This will save time."

Reporter Earl Richert confronted Lauer: "Under what rule did you do this?"

"Under a rule yet to be adopted," Lauer replied.

Lyons had the open support of former Senator Watson and the private behind-the-scenes manipulations of Little Doc Sherwood, then on duty at Fort Harrison as a public-relations major. (For meddling in politics while in service, Sherwood was later transferred to Fort Knox.) Lyons was elected 19 to 6.

One lone anguished voice protested publicly. Congressman Charles LaFollette of Evansville, denounced Lyons as a Klan intriguer and attacked the GOP leadership for rewarding him with a responsible position of prestige and power.

At the time the Allied armies under General Dwight D. Eisenhower were invading Normandy. Yet newspapers around the state kept the Klan issue alive. Walter H. Crim, in his *Salem Republican Leader,* warned about the danger of "Lyonism . . . to the Republican Party" in an editorial which said: "The Republican Party has much to think about in the immediate future, for the former treasurer of the Ku Klux Klan who has catapulted himself into party control has sounded an ominous note in a state that purged itself of this evil influence a decade ago." The Republican *Palladium-Item* of Richmond stated: "This is no time to welcome Fascist-minded men back to public life." The *South Bend Tribune* and the *Michigan City Dispatch* bluntly told the GOP it was inviting defeat. Daily on the front page of the

Indianapolis Star, Maurice Early reported the uproar over Lyons in his column.

Editor Walter Leckrone of the *Indianapolis Times* editorially expressed the fear that was in many Hoosier hearts:

> Lyons' election relighted the fiery cross that once blazed on Indiana hillsides—and the double-cross that flamed beside it in Indiana government. It meant a Stephenson lolling in luxurious office and boasting that he owned Indiana's Legislature and Indiana's Governor and Indiana's courts. It was a symbol of an era of fear and bribery and graft, of intolerance and persecution and cowardly violence.

It was enough to give the most stout-hearted Republican candidate a case of the galloping jitters. The criticism became an uproar. At a cabin behind Johnny Pearson's home in Carmel, the Republican candidates held a secret panic meeting. Most of them showed up, including Ralph Gates, Homer Capehart, Richard T. James, who was running for Lieutenant Governor, A. V. Burch, seeking the State Auditor's post, and Rue J. Alexander, candidate for Secretary of State. At night the worried candidates drove to Carmel and tramped through the woods to the cabin.

"If the papers ever get a picture of this," said Dick James to Gates, "it would look like we're having a konklave."

"My God, that's right," moaned Gates.

The first and only order of business was: What to do about Bob Lyons as National Committeeman?

Everybody quickly agreed it was a big mistake and that if he wasn't deposed, the Republican Party was headed for defeat. It was decided to ask Lyons to resign. They phoned him and said they were en route to his home.

Lyons had a beautiful house in Williams Creek, the most fashionable suburb of Indianapolis. His art collection alone was valued at half a million. The candidates drove from Carmel to Williams Creek, a distance of about five miles.

Bob Lyons was waiting for them. He was gracious and invited them to sit down. Acting as spokesman for the candidates, Gates described the situation and asked Lyons to resign. For eight or nine minutes, Lyons spoke about loyalty and said if they'd stick together they could win. He blamed Gates for not standing by him. Like a teacher with schoolchildren, Lyons made the candidates answer, one by one, if they thought he would cost them the election.

Gates mumbled that all the candidates should resign. Homer Capehart, making his first race in politics, was the last to answer. He had a cigar in his mouth and the ashes were falling over his vest.

"Well, in business, when I'm handed a lemon," said Capehart, "I squeeze it and make lemonade."

Lyons resigned June 13, 1944, eleven days after he was elected.

If the Klan is still operating in Indiana today it is doing so secretly, with few members and no political power. Leaders in both political parties have repudiated it. From time to time there is a cross-burning, but police attribute it to isolated pranks and crackpots.

However, as late as 1946 the *Indianapolis Times* was advised by Daniel Duke, Assistant Attorney General of Georgia, that the Klan was in the process of reorganizing in Indiana. In a letter, Duke reported:

At Klan Post No. 1 on September 9, 1946, Mr. Samuel Green of Georgia and the person who is apparently the leader of the Klan movement in this nation at this time, stated that the Klan had sent out a 10 percent sampling of former members of the 1920's inquiring if they were interested in reorganizing the Klan. He reported that the response to these inquiries was good, especially from Indiana, where he had a 94 percent response. He further told them that they were now in the process of reorganizing a Klavern in Indianapolis and that they would spread from there throughout the state.

There is no indication of any effective Klan activity in Indianapolis or Indiana today. The white sheets are gone. In the old days it may have been more dangerous to locate, expose or fight the Klan, but you could always spot the white sheets.

There is one disturbing thought today. If Klan leader Samuel Green was telling half the truth about the heavy Klan response from Hoosiers, some of the same old KKK sentiment is still riding through the sycamores. And there are no white sheets to identify it.

D. C. STEPHENSON went to prison boasting that Governor Ed Jackson would pardon him, but Jackson refused because Stephenson was too hot. Stephenson has since claimed he had been held a "political prisoner" by the machinations of Bob Lyons.

Over and over, Stephenson protested that he had been framed by Hiram Wesley Evans, Imperial Wizard of the Klan. In defense of Stephenson, Robert A. Butler published a pamphlet in 1940 called *So They Framed Stephenson*. In it, Stephenson is quoted as saying:

> It was the policy of Evans . . . to use women in destroying the reputations of men who opposed him. Edward Young Clarke, Captain William S. Coburn and a number of other men had been framed with Mann Act violations when they were wholly innocent of the charges. I protested to Evans against this policy and he replied, "When you want to get a man, just hang a woman on him."

In the same pamphlet, Stephenson tells how he resigned from the Klan and was "compelled" to again form an organization of former servicemen which was able to "persuade local Klan organizations to surrender their charter and we took them over as a functioning political unit with the qualification that religious and racial questions were taboo." Stephenson added:

Partly through loyalty to me, but chiefly because of the Hoosier will to fairness and decency, a rather formidable political organization was built in the state of Indiana. Its chief function was to prevent Dr. Hiram Wesley Evans from gaining control of Indiana State Government, but it was also used to overcome the campaign of slander which Evans launched against me in his various pamphlets and other anonymous literature, whispering campaigns and occasionally through small newspapers and magazines published in other states and circulated in Indiana.

Was Stephenson framed? Did all these respectable doctors, lawyers and the judge conspire with the Klan to hang a morals charge and a murder rap on him? Stephenson once wrote to an Indianapolis newspaperman: "I should have been put in jail for my political activities but I am not guilty of murder." Did the rival Klan invent the Stephenson sex orgies and drinking parties? Responsible and respectable lawyers and newspapermen say he was a drunkard and a lecher. His own doctor testified he had treated him for alcoholism.

In 1950, Governor Henry F. Schricker, Democrat, paroled Stephenson on the ex-Klan leader's promise he would take a job at Carbondale, Illinois and stay there. When Stephenson turned up mysteriously in Minneapolis instead, the parole was revoked.

Governor George N. Craig, Republican, handed Stephenson a Christmas Eve parole and complete discharge December 20, 1956. The ex-Klan leader settled down in Seymour, where he took a third wife, the former Mrs. Martha Dickinson, who had known him for many years. (Some who knew Stephenson say it was his fourth marriage.)

The onetime Klan leader was arrested when a sixteen-year-old girl identified him November 4, 1961 as the man who tried to force her into his car. She said she broke away.

On November 16, 1961, Magistrate Joseph J. Brady of Independence, Missouri convicted Stephenson of assault.

Indiana's first state capitol building at Corydon.

The Owen laboratory in New Harmony . . . used by David Owen as geological headquarters of the United States.

America's first auto and the man who invented it, Elwood Haynes, at Kokomo, where the car made its initial run.

Stephenson paid a $300 fine on the spot out of his billfold and was paroled from a four-month jail sentence on condition he leave the state.

In court, Stephenson's defense was that he had simply asked the girl for directions and that she had become frightened. Because this latest incident is an important clue to the Stephenson character, I talked by telephone to the judge in the case.

Magistrate Brady had been on the bench for sixteen years. He recalled that Stephenson did not have an attorney. The judge looked up the record. The charge against Stephenson came under a Missouri molestation law.

"Unlawfully and willfully assaulted (the girl)," the arrest slip said. "He grabbed her by the hand and attempted to force her into his auto."

Judge Brady recalled, "The girl told a pretty straight story. She said she broke free and ran back to her house. Other people there said she was emotionally upset. One man went out and got the license of the car."

In court, looking at Stephenson, then in his seventies, the judge said, "It appeared ridiculous that he would do such a thing."

When Stephenson was interrogated and asked what he was doing in the town of Independence, he replied, "I was seeing a man about a family business." (Stephenson has since come back to southern Indiana and disappeared again.)

"Are you positive Stephenson actually grabbed the girl by the arm and tried to force her into the car?" I asked the judge.

"I was convinced of it," he replied. "I wouldn't want to do any man an injustice, no matter what his reputation. I was satisfied he was guilty."

nine

THE AMERICAN LEGION

*For God and Country, we associate ourselves to-
gether . . .*

—PREAMBLE TO THE CONSTITUTION
OF THE AMERICAN LEGION

IN INDIANA, incredible as it seems, the Governor
had been locked out of a state-owned, state-operated and
state-tax-supported building.

Governor Matthew E. Welsh wanted to get into the
World War Memorial auditorium in Indianapolis to make a
speech to the American Civil Liberties Union. The American Legion refused to let the ACLU enter, because the legion
considered it "unpatriotic, leftist" and worse.

Eleven men, all Legionnaires, were members of the
Commission which governed the Memorial. No more determined troops ever manned a barricade.

Roy Amos was the state Legion commander in 1953
when the American Civil Liberties Union formed an Indiana
chapter, applied for and was granted permission to meet in
the War Memorial. When the Legion objected, the commissioners of the War Memorial quickly withdrew their permission. Commander Amos, a farmer who had been active
in Republican politics, declared he would oppose the Ameri-

can Civil Liberties Union meeting "anywhere in Indiana." With no place to meet, the Reverend Father Victor L. Goosens, now a monsignor, agreed to let the ACLU use the family social center operated by his St. Mary's Catholic Church in Indianapolis.

Time after time, in nine years, the War Memorial Commissioners refused to open the building to the ACLU, once even when Republican Paul Hoffman, then president of Studebaker and the man who administered the Marshall Plan for the rehabilitation of Europe, was the guest speaker. Two Governors, both Legionnaires and Republicans—George N. Craig and Harold Handley—declined to intercede in the dispute.

Governor Welsh, a placid, dignified lawyer with a scholarly and philosophic approach to life, also could have remained aloof. He knew, for example, that the great majority of Hoosiers, conservative by nature, were against the ACLU, that leaders in his own Democratic Party would fight him over it, that it was an emotional issue with the shouting patriots on the other side and that his own political career was at stake. He deliberately walked into the raging controversy aware that, politically at least, he had nothing to gain and everything to lose.

The Governor had the authority to fire all eleven members of the World War Memorial Commission by preferring charges against them. This he did not do. Instead he tried persuasion.

Governor Welsh pointed out that Attorney General Robert Kennedy's office had informed him that neither the Indiana chapter nor the national ACLU was or had ever been on the list of subversive organizations.

"There is no greater honor we could pay true patriots," said the Governor, "than that a memorial dedicated to them become a shrine for the freedoms basic to America—the freedom to speak, to think, and to worship as free men in a free land."

The World War Memorial commissioners were unimpressed and again refused to open the building to the ACLU. The man who led the fight against the ACLU and stood up to the Governor was Clarence R. McNabb, a Fort Wayne lawyer, World War I veteran and a continuous member of the War Memorial Commission since he was appointed by Governor Paul V. McNutt in 1933.

McNabb ran on the Democratic ticket with Welsh in 1960 as a candidate for Indiana Supreme Court Justice, but lost. Though he has virtually stopped speaking to newsmen about the War Memorial controversy, McNabb was eloquent when he rejected the ACLU in 1957.

"This is sacred soil," he said pointing to the Memorial, "and it is so dedicated. It is unlike any other public building. They (the ACLU) can meet anywhere they want, except they can't desecrate this sacred soil."

The War Memorial was erected in 1929 at a cost of $3,500,000 to the taxpayers. The project was initiated by the special session of the General Assembly in 1920 on the heels of the Armistice as a memorial to Hoosiers who served in World War I. The state not only built the Memorial, but it also constructed, at the expense of taxpayers, the national Legion headquarters, which is another story we'll come to later in this chapter.

Frank McHale, former state commander of the Legion and political operator for Governor McNutt, says that he was "lobby chairman of the Legion State Legislative Committee when the World War Memorial Bill passed." McHale says, "The Legion had the courage to refuse to accept the state bonus and in lieu of it made an all-out fight for the War Memorial in order to house the national Legion headquarters. In order to get the bill over, I had to write a sister bill enabling each county to likewise build and finance a county War Memorial."

For its part, the ACLU said it should be granted a permit to meet in the War Memorial simply because it had asked for it in good faith, because it is a responsible organization, the War Memorial is a public building and that there should be no other test.

The Legion's position was put on the line publicly by Robert M. Fritz when he was state commander in June 1962. He said:

> The ACLU was conceived in the minds of men who were slackers when America called and draft dodgers when the citizen's first duty was to bear arms in defense of the nation. . . .
>
> When the Indiana fighting men of World War I returned from France, they elected to have the state build a memorial sacred to the supreme sacrifices of so many of their comrades rather than be paid a bonus. So in that respect, the memorial belongs to the veterans of World War I more than it belongs to anyone else. . . .
>
> The founders of the ACLU found their common bond only in their sordid evasion of patriotic responsibilities. Now those who follow in their footsteps here in Indiana, misled by the name of the organization, seek to use the premises of the memorial which is sacred to Indiana loyalty and valor. They do not know of the shameful perfidy to God and Country of the men who founded the ACLU. I am sure they would not knowingly lend their support to those who failed America in the hour of need.

Most of the Legion charges stem from the fact that the founder of the ACLU, Roger Baldwin, declined to bear arms in World War I as a conscientious objector and was sentenced to prison for draft evasion.

When Welsh became Governor in 1961, there developed a constant tug-of-war, with the ACLU keeping pressure on the War Memorial commissioners and the commissioners telling them to go peddle their petitions elsewhere.

In Indiana, the ACLU was not a bunch of beatniks and

wild-eyed zealots. Among its members at this time were
Joseph O'Meara, dean of the law school at the University of
Notre Dame; Rowland Allen, retired personnel manager of
L. S. Ayres & Co., the largest department store in Indiana;
Merle Miller, a partner in one of the most distinguished
(and conservative) law firms in Indiana and Dr. Robert G.
Risk, a dentist with extensive copper-mine holdings. ACLU
members included veterans of both wars from all branches
of service.

Would the Legion dare prevent the Governor from
speaking to the ACLU in the War Memorial? It could—and
did—refuse. This is ridiculous when you consider that the
Governor himself is a Legionnaire, that he personally appointed or reappointed some of the War Memorial commissioners and that he is charged with the responsibility of
maintaining the building.

So long as Governor Welsh has the power of appointment, and the terms of the commissioners continue to expire,
it is probably just a question of time before the ACLU breaks
down the rugged Legion resistance. In 1962, Welsh began
the practice of appointing War Memorial commissioners who
were inclined to open the doors to the ACLU.

Whether the Legion was right, or misguided, it proved
again that it had the power—and effrontery—to defy even the
Governor. Legion influence, nevertheless, has slipped since
World War II. Frank McHale says:

> After World War I, the Legion was much more power-
> ful than the Legion of today in both legislative matters and
> in membership. In each county it was the attitude of the
> Legion to vote for a Legionnaire, regardless of political affili-
> ation, because of the fact there were a lot of slackers who
> stayed home.

Liberals in Indiana never would have dared challenge
the Legion when the boys came marching home from World

War I. By then, social compulsion had become a habit. The small Indiana town, in particular, became a place in which the pressures to conform were strongly felt.

Frederick Lewis Allen described the times:

> The typical American of the old stock had never more than a half-hearted enthusiasm for the rights of the minority. Bred in a pioneer tradition, he had been accustomed to set his community in order by the first means that came to hand —a sumptuary law, a vigilance committee or if necessary a shotgun.

It had become fashionable to legislate and propagandize and intimidate neighbors into what seemed (to the righteous) acceptable conduct. There was a quota for the community chest, the church-building fund, and the hospital-fund drive, as there had been for the Liberty Bond campaign—and woe unto those slackers slow to contribute. In this climate, the Legion flourished.

Soldiers of the victorious American Expeditionary Force, men released from training camps at home and men returned from sailing with the fleet, in 1919, united for power, as veterans have done down through the years—in Caesar's Rome, in Alexander's Greece.

The historical precedent was great. Two of the most famous veterans organizations of all time came from the ranks of the Crusaders: the Knights of the Temple and the Knights Hospitalers of St. John of Jerusalem. The first veterans organization in America was the Society of Cincinnati, holding to high principles of character and citizenship. It was composed of former officers with General George Washington.

The American Legion was born in Paris in March of 1919, weaned in St. Louis in May and permanently housed in Indianapolis near the nation's population center, in the heartland of America, where politics was a game and patriotism a way of life.

Many of the young hotheads wanted the Legion to "get

into politics." They visualized the newborn Legion electing Presidents, Governors, Senators, Congressmen and Mayors.

Older heads cautioned that partisanship could wreck the outfit. They recalled that the Grand Army of the Republic, the great veterans organization created after the Civil War, fell apart when it became aligned with the Grand Old (Republican) Party.

The older heads prevailed. At the first convention in Minneapolis, the Legion wrote into its Constitution:

> While requiring that each of its members perform his full duty as a citizen according to his own conviction and understanding, this organization shall be absolutely non-political and shall not be used for the dissemination of any person seeking public office or preferment; and no candidate for or incumbent of a salaried elective public office shall hold office in the American Legion or in any branch or post thereof.

It is ironic that by keeping out of politics, the Legion became a political powerhouse. It supported no party and endorsed no candidates. But the Legion applied grinding political pressure to both parties, fought and bested the strongest lobby pressure groups, including big business and big labor, and it played (and how it played!) a brutal kind of politics internally.

One Indiana Governor joked publicly that Legion politics was rougher than regular party politics. "In the Legion, you'd be stabbed in the back," he said, "and then they'd have you arrested for carrying a concealed weapon."

In Indiana, at least, the nonpolitical Legion paraded its political might. It elected Governors, Senators, Congressmen, Mayors and came close to nominating and electing a President, Paul V. McNutt. Franklin D. Roosevelt's decision to run for a third term ended McNutt's dreams of marching into the White House behind a Legion drum and bugle corps.

It is a standing joke in Indiana that there are three major

political parties in the state: the Democrats, the Republicans and the Legion.

Two former state Legion commanders became Governor: Republican Ralph Gates and Democrat Paul V. McNutt. One state commander became Lieutenant Governor, Democrat John A. Watkins. Watkins lost the governorship to a national commander of the Legion, Republican George Craig. Two other state commanders became Congressmen, Republicans Forest A. Harness and Raymond Springer. One state commander, Frank McHale, became the Democratic political boss of Indiana for more than twenty years, serving as Democratic National Committeeman.

The Legion was the springboard to political fame. Behind every Legion button in Indiana there very nearly was a politician. Charles Brownson became Eleventh District Legion chairman before he ran for Congress and was elected. Alex Clark was active in Legion affairs before he became Mayor of Indianapolis. There were many, many other politicians who were members of the Legion, but were not overly active, such as former Senators William E. Jenner, Homer E. Capehart, Governor Welsh, ex-Governor Harold Handley and a variety of others. The rough play of Legion politics made it an ideal testing ground for the two political parties.

McNutt brought his entire Legion team into the Democratic Party. Former United States Supreme Court Justice Sherman Minton got his start with McNutt, as did some of the other famous names in the Democratic Party, including Pleas Greenlee, Arthur Ball, Bowman (Bo) Elder, Walter Myers, Sr., Congressman Winfield Denton, former Mayor Al Feeney and Congressman Ray Madden.

When Ralph Gates became State Commander of the Legion, he built up his own political machine along the lines of McNutt, with one important difference. He was a Republican and his lieutenants were Republicans, too—or joined the GOP.

After World War II, there was not the same enthusiasm

among veterans to join the Legion. World War I was a one-front war. It was a more cohesive experience. The veterans came home to find few hospitals and miserable and shoddy treatment for their wounded comrades. There was a solid bond that virtually every veteran deeply felt.

"The GI Bill of Rights was the greatest mistake the Legion ever made," one high-ranking Legionnaire has said privately.

World War II veterans came home to find that a grateful government had spared no expense to help them readjust once again to civilian life. The hospitals were first-class; ex-GI's could go back to college and train themselves for a profession; business, home and farm loans were available at special low rates and veterans were even given preference for government jobs.

"World War II boys accepted all of it as a natural, logical function of government," the Legion executive says bitterly. "They don't realize that Legionnaires fought to get them the benefits that they didn't have when they came home."

Today, despite advanced age, sickness and deaths, World War I veterans remain the backbone of the Legion. More things compete for the younger veterans' time—family, school, job, TV, sports, amusements and friends. Some years ago, one commander of a well-known Indianapolis Legion post complained, "We had to change our meeting night. We couldn't compete with 'I Love Lucy.'"

Dig down to the grass roots, the hometown post, and you'll find the American Legion at its best. Many small towns revolve around the Legion. The post spearheads charity drives, oratorical contests and scholarship funds. It sponsors Boy Scout troops, junior baseball teams and hospital programs. Top Legion officials in recent years have made a determined effort to clean up the relatively few posts which have grown into private drinking and gambling clubs.

In his book *A History of the American Legion,* which

was officially sponsored by the Legion, author Richard Seelye
Jones wrote:

> The Legion exerted plenty of pressure when it chose to
> do so. It did plenty of high-class lobbying in the halls of
> Congress, of state legislatures, of city councils. . . . In plain
> fact, the American Legion lobbied all over the place, and be-
> cause most of its causes were in the public interest and had
> public support, it won more than it lost.

The Legion lobby secured government help for widows
and orphans, for the disabled, for higher army pay, family
allowances, tax exemptions, and civil-rights protection for
servicemen, insurance, maternity care for soldiers' wives, a
bonus for veterans, more hospitals and better care for the
wounded. It also fought to keep the nation's defenses up and
warned repeatedly against Soviet duplicity and trickery.

Perhaps the most successful lobbying effort Indiana Legionnaires participated in came when they put pressure on
the national Legion to bring the headquarters to Indianapolis. Tough as this was, it was just the beginning of a great
lobbying effort. The Hoosier Legionnaires then had to turn
around and lobby the Indiana State Legislature to build the
Legion a national headquarters at taxpayers' expense.

It was a shrewd crew, headed by Dr. T. Victor Keene,
that was dispatched to Minneapolis in 1919. Fortunately, like
most Hoosiers, they were adept at politics.

The Hoosier Legionnaires were armed with a bag of
tricks, determination and a check for $5,000 from Stoughton
Fletcher of the old Fletcher American National Bank to finance their lobbying efforts.

Regular Army men, including Theodore Roosevelt, Jr.
and Franklin D'Olier, wanted the Legion headquarters
housed in Washington, D.C. Minneapolis wanted to keep the
Legion there. The Hoosiers, up against stiff competition,
opened a hospitality room stocked with refreshments and
other goodies for Legion delegates. To make sure everyone

knew where they were, the Indiana Legionnaires gave the hotel's elevator girls boxes of chocolates to steer delegates to the Hoosier hospitality room.

Later, when the committee to select a site split sixteen votes for Minneapolis and fifteen votes for Indianapolis, the Hoosiers took the fight to the rank-and-file delegates. A snowstorm was raging in Minneapolis. The entire Indiana delegation was outfitted with straw hats, identified with huge Indianapolis bands, and dispatched to downtown street corners. While the snow swirled all around them, the Hoosiers in straw hats cussed the Minneapolis weather and won the hearts and support of the Legion convention with their campaign gimmick.

When the issue was put to the entire convention, Washington headed the first roll call. Indianapolis took the lead during the second vote and the Hoosiers spread the word that Indiana would build a splendid veterans memorial (and Legion home) if the Hoosier city became the national home. The opposition collapsed. Indianapolis won.

To keep their word, the Legionnaires went back to Indiana and won a special session of the Legislature in 1920 which authorized construction of the War Memorial Plaza.

The original War Memorial Plaza cost was shared by taxpayers in the state, the county and the city. The State of Indiana paid $4,754,192; Marion County contributed $1,470,000 and Indianapolis $1,247,817. (The Legion later estimated the total bill came to $8.35 for each taxpayer in Indianapolis, $4.93 for each taxpayer in Marion County and $1.44 for each taxpayer in the rest of the state.)

In 1939 other veterans' organizations were casting covetous glances at the Legion headquarters. The Veterans of Foreign Wars asked the State Legislature to build a similar home for it and the Disabled War Veterans and the Spanish-American War Veterans. The bill was later withdrawn.

By 1945 the Legion said it needed larger quarters. Backed by Governor Ralph Gates, a former Legion state commander, the American Legion formally requested the State Legislature to build a new $2,500,000 headquarters or else, it warned, it would move out. The Legislature responded with another Legion building. The old Legion home was presented as a headquarters to the state Legion.

Today the War Memorial Plaza encompasses five square blocks and includes a tree-lined mall, an obelisk square with fountain, University Park, the national Legion headquarters, the state Legion headquarters and the War Memorial.

NOT EVEN its severest critics question that the Legion is patriotically motivated. Why, then, does the Legion become so embroiled in public controversy and why is it so often a target of criticism?

No one person can pretend to have the complete answer, but a few factors stand out clearly. First of all, the Legion took sides on some of the hottest issues of the day and was bound to make some enemies. Then, too, the public became fed up with the pranks of old men parading around town, squirting women and girls with water guns and setting off huge giant firecrackers. The public saw men dressed in Legion caps and blamed the organization itself. Most of the hijinks were perpetrated by members of the Forty & Eight, the so-called fun society of the Legion, which makes up a fraction of the membership.

A deeper and more fundamental reason for the controversy swirling around the Legion was its long-time fight against un-Americanism. Some educators, liberals, lawyers and newspapermen objected to the methods the Legion used to battle subversion. They felt the Legion, in its zeal to protect the United States, went too far in restricting free speech and in pointing the finger of suspicion at individuals and organizations it considered subversive.

Another criticism was the "inconsistency" of the Legion. This argument was simply that the Legion bitterly opposes socialism and the welfare state on the one hand and on the other demands government handouts for itself in the form of bonuses, pensions and even a home.

The Legion got into trouble often when some of the more zealous but misguided members tried to equate liberalism and social welfare with communism or subversion. Some individual Legion posts tried to prevent public speaking by radical orators. Many Legionnaires were ill-advised and served only to publicize the speakers and make them seem martyrs who were denied "freedom of speech." In 1953 the Illinois Legion attracted national attention by charging that the Girl Scout handbook deemphasized Americanism, contained un-American influence and recommended pro-Communist authors. The charges were later dropped.

To understand the Legion's militant fight against un-Americanism it is necessary to examine the history of the organization and the political climate.

Across the nation in the 1920's, and especially in Indiana, the American Legion was troubled by three imports: communism, nazism and fascism. In addition, the home-grown Ku Klux Klan deeply disturbed, and divided, the Legion membership.

Richard Jones, the Legion biographer, tells how the Executive Committee of the Legion discussed the Klan issue behind closed doors in both January and May of 1923, when the members spoke their minds for hours. Jones wrote:

> The available evidence regarding the true purposes of the Klan were reviewed. Its claims to patriotic obligation and Americanism were expressed, and its intolerance and racial and religious doctrines of disruption were presented. None of the committee members admitted membership in the Klan, but some expressed sympathy with its avowed purposes and doubt of the charges against it. Others were vigorously against the white-sheeted organization and wanted it ousted from American life, lock, stock and barrel. . . . The resolution finally adopted was offered by Father William P. O'Connor of Ohio, the national chaplain. It said, "The Na-

tional Executive Committee considers as unfriendly to our nation any group which condemns a comrade because of creed or belief." That was the deliberate and considered opinion of the Committee, a definite anti-Ku Klux Klan position, but something less than a demand that the Legion launch a national crusade against the Klan as some members had proposed.

The Legion declared its violent opposition to Mussolini's fascism, Hitler's nazism and Stalin's communism. Communism alone among the three remained and flourished, giving the Legion one target, which it has blasted spectacularly, if not altogether successfully. It is no secret that there have been times when some Legionnaires were not equal to the task of discriminating between the dangers of trained agents from Russia and liberal college professors.

Yet the Legion, with bulldog tenacity, has performed a valuable watchdog service to the nation. It unerringly pointed to the continuing peril posed by the sinister malignancy of international communism. It also supported with vigor J. Edgar Hoover's Federal Bureau of Investigation, which performed extraordinary feats in protecting the United States from Communist espionage and sabotage, without infringing American civil liberties.

Much opposition to the Legion has been manufactured by left-wingers and even by sincere liberals who label the veterans organization "the war-hero's union" and ridicule its stand for "100 percent Americanism." It is unfortunate that the phrase was lifted by reckless reactionary and screwball hate groups to cover a multitude of their prejudices.

Perhaps the historian, at a safe and confident distance, will be able to say with certainty whether the good overbalanced the bad, whether the good overwhelmed the bad or whether it was a toss-up.

This much it is safe to say now. Never before had so large a group of veterans banded together, without military rank or titles, without distinction as to location, length or circumstance of service, just so long as it was honorable. No other organization had such an influence on the life and character and history and politics of Indiana.

As Richard Jones observed, ". . . the Legion scored many hits and many misses . . . it was always in there, swinging."

ten

WHAT MADE HOOSIERS WRITE

. . . a state where not to be an author is to be distinguished.

—MEREDITH NICHOLSON

No GROUP of writers from a single state ever had such popular success as the Hoosier authors. An average of ten *new* Indiana book authors a year flooded the libraries for 100 consecutive years.

Indiana's claim to literary fame was established, once and for all, in 1947 by a fresh arrival in the state, John H. Moriarity, the new librarian at Purdue University. He wondered if the Hoosier literary reputation was deserved.

Moriarity took the statistical information from Alice Payne Hackett's list of best-sellers and came to the scientific conclusion that Indiana was second only to New York in the United States "and a fighting second at that."

Moriarity reported, "Rather an amazing result in view of the fact that New York's population—and therefore the potential authors of best-sellers—averaged almost four times that of Indiana during the forty-year period analyzed." On artistic merit alone, critics gave Indiana undisputed first place.

"I am well aware that there has been an enormous amount of writing done in Indiana," a lecturer from the East once told a Hoosier audience. "If there are any authors present, I'd like them to come forward and sit on the platform here with me."

According to George Ade, the Hoosier humorist, there was a great commotion as the entire audience arose from their seats and rushed to the platform. Ade later embellished the story by saying that everyone came forward except one old man, whereupon the speaker caustically remarked that he was glad to see that there was one person who didn't consider himself an author.

"He's just deef and didn't hear what you said," someone replied. "He writes, too."

A SMALL Indiana town in the late 1800's had to offer a boy by way of recreation: swimming at the old swimming hole, playing in the open fields, hunting and fishing in the neighboring woods and streams.

There was a charm in the dialect and colloquial expressions and accents and peculiar pronunciation of Hoosiers. There was a hunger for knowledge and a thirst for culture. Libraries and literary clubs sprang up and flourished. Three years after the town of Vevay was founded by a group of Swiss in 1814 on the Ohio River there were eighty-four homes, eight stores, thirty-four shops, three taverns, a courthouse, a church, a school, a jail, a library of more than 300 volumes and also a literary society.

Hoosiers apparently counterbalanced their yearning for learning with a distaste for taxes to maintain schools or libraries. Free public schools were few and far between. In 1850, Indiana had the highest rate of illiteracy in the North. Even this had advantages of sorts.

"In the speech of the illiterate, there is usually something of rhythm and cadence," Meredith Nicholson observed in *The Hoosiers*.

Commenting on this rustic writing, Stephen Leacock says, "It is the work of people who would undoubtedly have been poets if they had had education and academic background."

Was it coincidence that, all of a sudden, made Hoosiers in such great numbers take their pens in hand? Is there really any explanation?

". . . somehow Indiana has been blessed with a large number of imaginative people who have wished to express themselves in written form," says literary historian Arthur Shumaker. He explains that "after the pioneer period, a literary climate developed which inspired new writers, who, in turn, inspired still others, so that a resulting cross-fertilization kept up a lively interest in reading and writing."

There is truth in this, but Shumaker seems on sounder speculation when he says folklore, brought in by the Southerners, was preserved and encouraged. He points out, too, that the Hoosier's fondness for "the tall story" was a social institution in many towns, "where the best tales excited much admiration on the part of the hearers."

My own feeling is that writing was a status symbol for Hoosiers. It was part of the pride of being a particular kind of Hoosier, a reading and writing Hoosier. Being able to write was something special in early Indiana days when schools were scarce. A writer became in time the Hoosier man of distinction. Add to this the natural provincial patriotism of Hoosiers who waxed rhapsodic over Indiana and you might have an even better answer. Some of the writing was splendid. Much of it, the critics say, was deplorable. No one will question that most of it was sentimental, rustic, romantic and readable.

When the Hoosier authors stuck close to home, a picture of Indiana emerged as a pleasant, rather rural place, inhabited by people who were prosperous, generous, neighborly, easy-going. Walter Havighurst painted the Indiana the authors saw in his regional book *The Heartland:* "Nowhere did the moon shine so bright as on the Wabash, nowhere was such contentment as lay over the Indiana fields when the frost was on the pumpkin and the fodder in the shock."

There was, I think, a hunger for expression—a compulsion to write. What made Hoosiers write? You might as well ask: What made fish swim? Or birds fly?

EDWARD EGGLESTON started the great literary ferment in Indiana when he wrote *The Hoosier Schoolmaster,* a vigorous portrait of the illiterate people of southern Indiana in the 1850's. Maurice Thompson wrote *Hoosier Mosaics,* a collection of charming sketches of incidents in the Indiana small-town scene. Meredith Nicholson wrote *The Hoosiers,* a volume of brief historical essays. And Theodore Dreiser, back from New York City for a season in Indiana, wrote *A Hoosier Holiday,* which graphically tells about his life and family in Hoosierland.

But the masterpiece was Booth Tarkington's gently realistic *The Gentleman From Indiana.* It was a romantic and sentimental novel about a promising graduate of an Eastern college who settles down to the community life and politics of a small Indiana town.

"The people in his town live together like a great kind family, who are sufficient unto themselves," is the way Meredith Nicholson describes Tarkington's first novel. "He has thrown into the story the sincerity, affection and loyalty that are their attributes; and he adds, moreover, the atmosphere of the Indiana landscape with a nice appreciation of its loveliness, sometimes hinted and often charmingly expressed."

There is, as Nicholson points out, every reason why Tarkington should know his Indiana well. He was born on July 29, 1869 in Indianapolis into the prosperous Midwestern middle-class environment he wrote about so often. His father John Stevenson Tarkington served as private secretary to Governor Joseph A. Wright, practiced law in Indianapolis, served one term in the State Legislature and, during the Civil War, was captain of a company of the 132d Indiana

Infantry. Later he became a Circuit Court judge and published two books, which would have been better left unprinted. Booth's grandfather, the Reverend Joseph Tarkington, was a Methodist circuit rider during the pioneer period in Indiana.

The eternal sophomore, Booth Tarkington was educated at Shortridge high school, where he frequently played hooky; at Exeter, where he matured somewhat away from home; at Purdue, where he studied and had uproarious weekends at Sigma Chi fraternity with George Ade and John T. McCutcheon; and at Princeton, where he played the banjo, wrote songs for the glee club, went drinking, transformed the dramatic association into the renowned Triangle Club, had a gay time and did not graduate.

A rich uncle carried Booth through lean years of cartooning, amateur theatricals and unsuccessful writing. (The uncle was his mother's brother Newton Booth, a bachelor who made his fortune in California and ultimately became Governor and Senator.) Neighbors, friends and some relatives called Tarkington a bum and a drunk (and worse) who wouldn't work and would come to no good. When he wrote *The Gentleman From Indiana,* publisher S. S. McClure greeted him with, "You are the greatest of a new generation."

Tarkington dressed elegantly, lived high and traveled in fashionable circles in New York, Chicago, London and Paris. He never quite forgot his pranks. Friends tell of the time he and a friend took a drunken companion and put him in the home of two spinster sisters. Once, he introduced a road-show press agent to an Indianapolis country club crowd as Edgar Allan Poe. On another occasion, when driving to Lafayette to attend the opening of a George Ade play, he paused at each village to announce that Senator Albert Beveridge and Vice President Charles Fairbanks were following in another car. When the second car inevitably arrived, Harry Leon Wilson, a writer, and a companion accepted the plaudits of the crowd.

By 1939, when he was seventy, Tarkington was considered the dean of American writers. He had produced thirty-six novels and collections of short stories, nineteen plays, a volume of reminiscences and a flood of awards, including the Pulitzer Prize twice—in 1919 for *The Magnificent Ambersons,* the tragedy of a family on the road downhill, and in 1922 for *Alice Adams,* a study of how greed corrupts.

Tarkington voted the straight Republican ticket, was elected to the State Legislature, but was struck dumb at the thought of making a speech. He opposed the New Deal of Franklin D. Roosevelt and Paul V. McNutt, once writing: "To my old-fashioned mind, the liberty we lose when the government plans our future security is worth more than the benefit this security could possibly give us. Hardship, it seems to me, is a part of life, a test and builder of character."

Tarkington later used his experience in politics as the basis of a book of short stories called *In The Arena.* He pictured the inner workings of the Legislature, describing the dishonesty, the sellout and the crooked politics.

Louise Fletcher of the family prominent in social and financial circles was Tarkington's first wife. He later married Susanah Robinson, who helped him quit drinking in 1912. Tarkington was told by his wife and physician that his alcoholic binges were ruining his work. Almost overnight he became a teetotaler.

Critics have said that the Penrod stories and similar books succeeded because "Tarkington believed that boys should be presented in fiction as they are in life, certainly not as adults think they are nor as adults would like them to be."

In the monumental work about Indiana authors, compiled by R. E. Banta, and published by Wabash College, there is this criticism:

> Of all writers, Booth Tarkington most nearly interpreted the American scene from the beginning of this century through the 1920's as the average American saw it. . . . He was at his best on North Meridian Street (his National Av-

enue) in Indianapolis, or with people who had prospered to a chill eminence above that thoroughfare, or, as in the case of the family of Alice Adams, had slipped below it. . . . There was neither the high romance of George Barr McCutcheon nor the grimy realism of Theodore Dreiser: Tarkington people lived.

Every town in America had its Magnificent Ambersons, and a doting Adams mother, and a frustrated Adams daughter kept up a pretense of gentility in most American towns and cities. Penrod was easily recognizable to any citizen who was a boy in Penrod's day, and to most parents of any age, there were half a dozen prototypes of the Gentleman from Indiana.

O ITS THEN'S the times a feller is a-feelin' at his best,
With the risin' sun to greet him from a night of peaceful rest,
As he leaves the house, bare-headed, and goes out to feed the stock
When the frost is on the pumpkin and the fodder's in the shock.

James Whitcomb Riley heard the wind in the corn, the song of the meadowlarks, the creak of the barn door, the folksy dialect of the Hoosier. He saw sunlit streams, the old swimmin' hole, the green fields and running brooks, the surreys and wagons heaped with harvest.

Riley, a thin, puckish man, was more than Indiana's poet laureate. He was the people's poet. He remembered the pleasures, not the hardships, of country life, though he was a town boy, born in Greenfield, about twenty miles from Indianapolis, in 1854.

As Meredith Nicholson wrote: "The common people caught and held the attention of Mr. Riley and . . . he established himself firmly in public affection. . . . He began to write because he felt the impulse, and not because he breathed a literary atmosphere or looked forward to a literary career."

Riley had little formal education. He studied law, but soon gave it up. His father, a prosecuting attorney and State

Legislator, realized his son had no interest in the law and let him join a traveling patent-medicine and concert wagon. Young Riley wandered about earning his living by painting advertising signs on barns and fences. The journeys, from farm to farm and town to town, gave him an entertaining and exciting glimpse of life and allowed him to begin in his youth the careful observation of the Indiana country folk, their ways and their speech.

Riley's most popular poems are probably *Little Orphan Annie, The Ole Swimmin' Hole, When the Frost Is on the Pumpkin* and *The Raggedy Man.*

His dialect of rural types had cadence. Take this line as a sample: "You don't rickollect her, I reckon? No; you wasn't a year old then!"

Yet Riley was able to write gracefully and musically even when he abandoned dialect, as in "The All Golden":

> *I catch my breath as children do*
> *In woodland swings when life is new*
> *And all the blood is warm as wine*
> *And tingles with a tang divine.*
> *O gracious dream, and gracious time,*
> *And gracious theme, and gracious rhyme—*
> *When buds of Spring begin to blow*
> *In blossoms that we used to know,*
> *And lure us back along the ways*
> *Of time's all-golden yesterdays!*

Many of Riley's poems were first published in the weekly newspapers of Indiana. He came home from his wanderings with the traveling show experienced and with a few literary theories of his own.

One theory was that in order for a poem to be popular and successful it need only be known as coming from the pen of "a genius known to fame." To test his theory, while working for the *Anderson Democrat,* Riley wrote a poem, *Leonainie,* in the manner of Edgar Allan Poe and sent it,

signed with Poe's initials, to the *Kokomo Dispatch,* saying
that it had been found on the flyleaf of an old dictionary.
The *Dispatch* published it and the poem was hailed, even by
literary critics, as an authentic poem of Poe. When Riley
admitted the hoax, he was fired by the horrified editor of the
Anderson Democrat and went on to become the most famous
figure in Indiana literature while working for the *Indianapolis Journal.*

Riley never married. He enjoyed the company of
women, but his verse, his reading, his correspondence and
his conversation with friends filled his life completely, according to his contemporaries.

There are some critics who condemn Riley for his "lack
of penetration of life and reality, for his endless sentimental-
izing over a type of life that never really was." It is, of course,
true that, unlike Tarkington, Riley had no interest in politics. He never voted. Apparently he didn't notice the big
problems around him either. Arthur Shumaker wrote:

> He did not raise his eyes from his books and his papers
> long enough to notice domestic problems, reforms, or reli-
> gious questions and even the drama of the Spanish-American
> War and World War I moved him not. Instead, he lived in
> a sort of sentimental dream, wedded to simple and homely
> joys and ways, a relic of an age that had hardly existed at
> all, and part of an era which he scarcely understood. He was
> obsessed by children and childhood. . . . The blinders that
> he placed on his eyes limited his genius so severely that he
> goes no deeper into the issues of life than the depiction of
> innocent joys and sorrows and the vivid portrayal of simple
> characters. He had no power to discern the soul.

This is all true. But Riley was Indiana. He became a
traveling troubadour, reciting his own poems. No Indiana
schoolchild could forget the performance Riley gave when
he stopped by to deliver with feeling, *Little Orphan Annie*
and *The Raggedy Man.* Many an Eastern audience, attending his recitals to see what sort of rustic character wrote the

backwoodsy verse, was amazed to find that Riley was a dapper little man, immaculately dressed, wearing a white waistcoat and a huge gold watch chain. He could make an audience weep or laugh. He held his audiences spellbound.

The critics have rendered their verdicts. Edgar Lee Masters says: ". . . (Riley's) work (is) of incomparable merit, of unmatched excellence in the field of childhood delineation. He has no equal and no one to be mentioned in the same breath with him. Here he was pure genius." R. E. Banta observed: "In his great talent for the accurate hearing and the true recording of dialect he was unsurpassed in his time. His Hoosier was perfection itself."

In the book *Indiana, A Guide to the Hoosier State,* there is a chapter on literature which points out:

> . . . (Riley) was sunnier, gayer, more genial in temperament, far less conscious of the ethical implications of the faith by which he loved; and perhaps for this reason he was—more than any other American writer—a poet for the people. In popularity only Longfellow, with whom he had much in common, surpassed him; and even Longfellow did not deal with folk themes in so thoroughgoing a fashion.

Meredith Nicholson said Riley was "a preacher of sound optimism and a sincere believer in the final good that comes to all."

At Greenfield, where he gave his first public reading in 1896, the band serenaded him and so many people went to Masonic Hall that the people were warned not to stamp their feet for fear the building would fall.

John Bartlow Martin wrote:

> Despite all honors . . . Riley did remain a people's poet, for they understood him and they framed his poems in their parlors. And he dwelt among them rather than in a poet's tower, performing his act and reading his verses and telling jokes like any carnival clown, drinking with Gene

Debs and other railroaders at Terre Haute or with news-papermen in saloons on the Levee, enjoying good food at Indianapolis' best restaurants.

GEORGE ADE once said in New York City: "Many good men come from Indiana; the better they are the quicker they come."

Frank McKinney Hubbard was as good as they come and he never wanted to leave Indiana. He was the best of the crackerbarrel philosophers.

"I've had a couple of chances to go to New York and make something of myself," he once wrote, "but I'd rather stay here where I can get in the band."

Hubbard had a trenchant style as he showed in his "sayings" of Abe Martin, first published in the *Indianapolis News:*

> Now an' then an innocent man is sent t' th' legislature.
> Of all th' home remedies a good wife is th' best.
> Its th' good loser that finally loses out.
> Ther's some folks standin' behind the President that ought t' get around where he can watch 'em.
> We're all purty much alike when we git out o' town.

Kin Hubbard was an artist who had a touch of the minstrel in him. His great success came when he drew the character Abe Martin. With each cartoon, Hubbard threw in a quip. Almost overnight Hubbard became the Hoosier philosopher. Hoosiers fell in love with his daily drawing, a ludicrous rustic, with baggy pants, ragged coat, shapeless hat and shoes, button eyes, and chin whiskers, placed against the rural background of Brown County. He labeled his locale Brown County because that Indiana county had always been a little on the backwoodsy side—a haven for hillbillies, artists and nonconforming folks.

Will Rogers gave his photograph to Hubbard inscribed:

"To my friend Kin Hubbard. If I was as humorous as Kin, I would be one of the two funniest men in America." Clifton Fadiman, the literary critic, considers Hubbard "a Hoosier Rochefoucauld." Irvin S. Cobb said, "Thank the Lord for Abe Martin."

Kin Hubbard was a newspaperman, a blackface comedian and a keen observer of the passing scene. About Indiana, he wrote: "Everyone in the state is either a politician or a writer. Of course there's a fair sprinkling of tradesmen an' farmers, but only enough t' supply the wants of the writers and politicians."

Like Riley, Hubbard cast his sentences in rustic idiom. Both men could draw and both men educated themselves on the road with traveling wagon shows, and not in the classroom.

All of Hubbard's success was achieved while working for the *News,* though once he was fired by a managing editor described by Hubbard as "like all new managing editors, he raised hell with everyone and everybody." The managing editor wanted Hubbard to draw more than just caricatures.

After knocking around Mansfield (Ohio), Atlanta, Cincinnati, Cleveland and Bellefontaine (Ohio), where he alternately worked on newspapers and organized traveling vaudeville shows, Hubbard came back eventually to Indianapolis where he labored first on the *Indianapolis Sun* and then back on the *News,* where he remained a literary and artistic fixture for life.

This Hoosier created other Hoosier characters for his Abe Martin sayings. You could recognize the types. There was Lafe Bud, a dandy. Miss Fawn Lippincut was the village belle. Mr. and Mrs. Tilford Moots were always having marital troubles. In her manners and dress, Miss Tawny Apple was daring. Hubbard's law-enforcement official was Constable Newt Plum.

Hubbard married Josephine Jackson of Indianapolis on October 12, 1905. "I date all my good luck from that hour," he wrote. "And while my wife doesn't write my stuff, she has all the peculiarities of the genius and is a good manager." With her and their two children, Hubbard was content, preferring his home life (and particularly his garden) to a career of lecturing and making personal appearances, which he shunned.

Kin Hubbard was born in Bellefontaine, Ohio on September 1, 1868 and died a thorough Hoosier on December 26, 1930. His Abe Martin is still being reprinted in the *News* and other daily newspapers. It hasn't lost its flavor. It has, if anything, mellowed with nostalgia.

It was said that Kin Hubbard influenced the thinking of the American people along the lines of plain, homely horse sense far more widely than any serious philosopher of his day. This may be true. But in Indiana he just gladdened the hearts of Hoosiers.

LITERARY hero-worshipers burn no incense at the altar of Lewis (Lew) Wallace, author of *Ben-Hur,* a tale of ancient Judea and Rome which became the biggest best-seller of its generation. He wrote it sitting under a beech tree in the quiet college town of Crawfordsville.

Critics called Wallace an amateur writer, even though he wrote other books, poems and plays. They said his works were the product of his fanciful, dramatic life and his daydreams.

If Wallace were alive today he would be considered a juvenile delinquent. He played hooky from school and ran away from home. Every child has daydreams. With Wallace they were stronger and more persuasive than in most youngsters. He visualized himself as a romantic figure, a bold military hero with a sense of drama and history, a great writer. As a youngster he wrote some poetry, never published, which told of heroic and military tales.

Wallace had little formal education, but his daydreams

carried him to prominence as a soldier (he became a general), a writer, a diplomat, a lawyer, a Governor, as well as a violinist and a painter.

He had an eye for the dramatic and romantic. When he formed a military company called the Montgomery County Guards, it was known popularly as the Zouaves because Captain Wallace dressed his men in the baggy gray pants, blue-and-red jackets and red-visored French caps of Algerian troops.

MAURICE THOMPSON, a Confederate soldier, settled in Crawfordsville and became a law partner and friend of Union General Lew Wallace. Twenty years after Wallace produced *Ben-Hur,* Thompson wrote *Alice of Old Vincennes,* a story of how George Rogers Clark captured the old post on the Wabash. It still thrills the young in heart.

The outpouring of fiction from Hoosier pens was remote and romantic. Charles Major, a Shelbyville lawyer, wrote *When Knighthood Was in Flower,* a royal romance set in England. Critics acclaimed this as his greatest novel, but Frank Edwards, the showman-newsman of radio and television in Indianapolis, has a strong preference for Major's *The Bears of Blue River,* the best-known and most-loved of his books about Indiana. It was a suspenseful, action-packed adventure Hoosier boys loved.

Meredith Nicholson wrote one of the best studies on Indiana culture and history called *The Hoosiers,* but his greatest commercial success came after writing a novel, *The House of a Thousand Candles,* which was a romantic tale set in a big unfinished house on Lake Maxinkuckee, Indiana.

There was no stopping the literary onslaught of Hoosiers. George Barr McCutcheon wrote *Graustark,* high-flown romance about a tiny, mythical Balkan kingdom, enmeshed in intrigue and ruled over by a dazzling beautiful princess with a court full of gorgeous and tempting creatures especially susceptible to the charms of young, dashing American men.

George Ade's racy, rustic *Fables in Slang* captured the fancy of Hoosiers and a great many others. He also wrote in three weeks the play *The College Widow,* based on the rivalry between Wabash and DePauw. It was a hilarious success.

Because of her masculine name, Gene Stratton Porter was often mistaken for a man. Critics panned her books, but people loved to read them. Her novels were called "sugary-sweet." Mostly they were about the great outdoors in Indiana, the Limberlost area not far from Fort Wayne, and dealt with the simple rural life of man, animal and bird. Her best-known books were *A Girl of the Limberlost,* about one who hunts moths in the swamps to finance her education and *Song of the Cardinal,* a biography of a redbird.

Theodore Dreiser wrote about the seamy side of life in a manner few others dared at the time. When he wrote *Sister Carrie* it was withheld from circulation because of its supposed immorality. When he wrote *An American Tragedy* it created another sensation. In the East he was hailed for his realism. In Indiana, it was said he could find a rotten spot in every apple.

IF YOU want to know more about Indiana's greatest poets, dramatists, humorists and authors, with critical commentary on their style and informed interpretation of what they mean, you must look elsewhere. This is not a textbook.

For those interested in scholarly research, I recommend *A History of Indiana Literature* by Professor Arthur Shumaker. Here you will find that William Vaughan Moody, who wrote *The Faith Healer* and *The Great Divide,* was Indiana's best dramatist and poet and that George Ade was the state's best humorist.

Ernie Pyle wrote simply and eloquently about *Brave*

Men and brought the sights and sounds and smells of World War II into the homes of millions through his column in Scripps-Howard newspapers. A sensitive, shy man from Dana, Indiana, Pyle overnight became a celebrity, which he deplored. The public came to love Ernie. He told them what it was really like over there, with the boys, not the brass. There has never been another war correspondent clutched in so many hearts.

Ross Lockridge, Jr. wrote a masterpiece, *Raintree County,* which was as Hoosier as corn. *The Desperate Hours,* a novel and play, came from the gifted pen of Joseph Arnold Hayes. Elmer Davis, the journalist, belongs in a special class for his interpretive dispatches and books.

John Bartlow Martin wrote *Indiana: An Interpretation, Break Down The Walls, The South Says Never* and many, many others. In 1961 he was appointed Ambassador to the Dominican Republic.

Today's Indiana authors are realistic. They are writing about things as they are, not as they dream them to be.

The Golden Age authors were sentimentalists and their stuff was full of nostalgia and romance. Their books excited and entertained. In those days, Indiana was unique. When Hoosier authors wrote about local customs and folkways they created a Hoosier tradition.

The Indiana that was is no more. Is it any wonder the Hoosier literary tradition is different?

The Memorial Day race at the Indianapolis Speedway.

Lake Michigan washing up on the picturesque sand dunes.
Brown County State Park.

eleven

ABE LINCOLN OF INDIANA

*All politicians talk about Lincoln but none of
them follow him.*

—WILL ROGERS

ABRAHAM LINCOLN, who doesn't need one, has
a press agent by the name of Roy T. Combs.

Press agent Combs is affectionately called the chaplain
of the Republican Party, because he is connected with a multitude of religious organizations and is active in the GOP.

"Combs tries so hard to imitate Lincoln," says Frank
Edwards, Indianapolis showman-newsman, "that he'd appreciate being assassinated."

A politician with his eyes on the Governor's chair,
Combs is the front man for the Indiana Lincoln Foundation.
It has influential support. Eli Lilly of the Lilly drug firm
and Kurt Pantzer, Indianapolis' best-known lawyer, are its
principal backers. At present the Lincoln Foundation is engaged in a mammoth program. It wants every schoolchild in
Hoosierland to help establish a national shrine at Lincoln
City in Spencer County, Indiana, where Lincoln spent fourteen formative years of his life.

When Lincoln came from Kentucky to Indiana in 1816,
he was a lad of seven. When he left the Hoosier state for

Illinois in 1830, he was a grown man, 6-foot-4 and weighing more than 200 pounds.

The Lincolns crossed the Ohio River in as historically significant a movement as when George Washington crossed the Delaware. The Ohio River was a boundary line between slavery and freedom. If Lincoln had grown up in the state of Kentucky, where slavery was tolerated, the North would have been without his leadership and inspiration in the great struggle between the states.

It was in Indiana, historians say, where Lincoln's political philosophy was molded, where he learned the value of honesty, integrity, hard work and self-discipline.

To many it is ludicrous for the wealthy Eli Lilly to ask schoolchildren to earn a dollar and contribute it to his favorite project. It is true Eli Lilly would not miss the money if he wrote a check and built an even bigger memorial. But then it would be his memorial, his gift.

The Lincoln Memorial, in the eyes of its founders, must belong to the schoolchildren of Indiana. The only way it can is for them to work for it.

Neither Roy Combs, nor Kurt Pantzer, nor Eli Lilly know if in the process some Hoosier youngsters—a child here and a child there—can absorb or appreciate, can learn or be inspired by the Lincoln legend. They are operating on the theory that "it is better to light one candle than to curse the darkness."

MUCH ABOUT Lincoln is legend and folklore. This much is fact: The Lincoln family came to an area known as Little Pigeon Creek, Indiana in a covered wagon and settled in a homemade cabin in the wilderness. They brought four horses, two cows, ten chickens and one small black dog. Abe cut the undergrowth and his father felled the trees. At night, while his father worked, Abe held a blazing pine knot for light.

As a boy, Abe rode a horse hitched to a plow, planted potatoes, onion, beans, pumpkin seed and picked wild berries for his mother, gathered bags of hazelnuts and walnuts, carried water, shelled corn, ground corn into cornmeal between stones and helped his father build a raft and a three-sided cabin.

Abe's mother was busy all day sewing, spinning, weaving, washing and cooking. Sometimes at night she sat in the firelight and read from her big Bible.

One book that young Abe read over and over was *Aesop's Fables*. Other books which he read were: The Bible, *Robinson Crusoe, Pilgrim's Progress, Autobiography of Benjamin Franklin* and *Weem's life of Washington*. He once borrowed a book from a lawyer called *Revised Laws of Indiana*. Included in it were the Declaration of Independence and the Constitution of the United States.

As Lincoln grew to manhood he attended trials in Booneville, Indiana and visited with lawyers in two other Hoosier towns, Rockport and Princeton.

IN THE fall of 1818, milk sickness swept southern Indiana and ravaged the area near the Lincoln homesite. Abe's mother, Nancy Hanks Lincoln, who had nursed and comforted others, fell ill.

Dennis Hanks, a relative of Mrs. Lincoln, related the pathetic scene many years later: "She knew she was going to die and called up the children to her dying side and told them to be good and kind to their father—to one another and to the world, expressing a hope that they might live as they had been taught to live . . . love—reverence and worship God."

Mrs. Lincoln impressed on her twelve-year-old daughter Sarah the responsibility that would fall on her shoulders and the care and attention she should give to her young brother. Her final words to Abe were: "I am going away from you,

Abraham, and I shall not return. I know that you will be a good boy and that you will be kind to Sarah and to your father. I want you to live as I have taught you, and to love your heavenly Father."

Mrs. Lincoln was 5-foot-5, a slender, pale, sad and sensitive woman who shrank from some of the rude, rustic life around her but overcame it with heroic determination. They laid her to rest under a cluster of oak, maple and walnut trees on a crest 1,500 feet south of the cabin. Sitting on her grave, ten-year-old Abe wept. Years later, Lincoln, with tears in his eyes, said to a friend, "All that I am or hope to be I owe to my angel mother—blessings on her memory."

IF ALL the days that Abe Lincoln attended school were added together, they would not make a single school year. It was necessary for him to work most of the time on the farm or in the shop, or hire out as a common laborer to help support the family.

His first class was in a log schoolhouse a mile and a half from the Lincoln cabin. The school had holes for windows, and they were covered over with greased paper to admit light. The roof was just high enough for a man to stand erect. On especially cold days, the children put hot rocks in their pockets to keep warm. Hazel Dorsey was the teacher.

In the same rustic school cabin, Andrew Crawford came as the teacher. He taught readin', writin', cipherin' and spellin'. Abe was a superior student and the best speller in the class. Once the teacher threatened to keep the whole class all day and night, if necessary, until someone correctly spelled the word "defied." When Ann Roby's turn came, she started out hesitantly, "d-e-f" and looked at Lincoln. Abe had one finger pointing to his eye for "i." Ann took the hint. She spelled the word correctly and class was dismissed.

Abe was good at writing compositions. One of his first

was against cruelty to animals. He was especially annoyed and disturbed that his friends were in the habit of catching terrapins and putting coals of fire on their backs. Nathaniel Grigsby, one of Lincoln's school chums, said, "Abe would tell us it was wrong and would write against it."

By this time Abe was growing at an enormous rate. He was fifteen and was nearly 6 feet tall. To school Abe wore buckskin breeches, which were too short and too tight, and a linsey-woolsey shirt and low shoes. Tall and awkward, Abe was a sight in class, especially when the pupils were learning about "good manners." They would, under the teacher's patient prodding, take turns introducing each other to the class.

The third and last school Lincoln attended was four and a half miles away. The distance was so great and his work chores so many that he did not attend for long. The teacher was twenty-one and there are historians who say young Lincoln was as well-versed as the teacher.

ABRAHAM LINCOLN had a reputation as a bashful young man when he was growing up in Indiana, and it is said that all the young girls made fun of him because he was tall and gawky. Abe's stepbrother John D. Johnston commented that "Abe didn't take much truck with girls . . . he was too busy studying at the time."

While no one is making young Abe out to be a Casanova, it is a fact that he had romantic notions about some girls. He himself told about his first romance with "the covered wagon girl."

One day, so the story goes, a pioneer's wagon broke down near the home of the Lincolns, and while it was being repaired, the family was invited to cook its meals in the Lincoln cabin. There were two girls in the family and Abe took a fancy to one of them. After they were gone he had a number of dreams about eloping with her. He recalled this many years later, saying, "I think that was the beginning of love with me."

Polly Richardson, daughter of John and Nancy Richardson, claimed, "I was Abe's first sweetheart." She said Abe took her to church and spelling bees and that he wanted to marry her, but she refused. There is considerable doubt about this, since Polly married someone else when Abe was about twelve years old.

Other Indiana girls said they were courted by Abe, went to church with him, or took strolls down the river with him, or were his schoolchums. Elizabeth Tully said she kept company with him for several months. Abe was supposed to have given a pair of earrings to Elizabeth Ray. When Abe was working as a ferryman on the Ohio River, he is said to have crossed over to the Kentucky side quite often to call on Caroline Meeker. Everyone said that Abe had only a brotherly feeling for his stepsister Matilda Johnston. Although he did visit with Elizabeth Wood, some said she declined his company because of his awkwardness and large feet. Hannah Gentry, whose father was rich, was helped out by Abe in a spelling bee and Lincoln was understood to have a crush on her. Sarah Lukins told neighbors Lincoln once took her home from church, adding, "I could a'been Abe Lincoln's wife, if I'd wanted to, yes sirree."

In Princeton, Indiana, Abe told a friend he fell in love at first sight with a beautiful girl, Julia Evans, who was the village belle and reportedly bowed to him on the street. The real romance of Lincoln's Indiana youth, so the legend goes, was with Ann Roby, who had attended school with Abe and later moved to Rockport, where he was engaged in building a flatboat. Ann described sitting on the bank of the river with Abe and "watching the moon come over the hills."

Possibly, Abe Lincoln was just a normal, restless, growing boy interested in young ladies for their companionship and not their affections. Historian Louis A. Warren throws cold water on all the Lincoln romance in Indiana. "It is doubtful," says Warren, "that he seriously considered matrimony while living in Indiana."

IN INDIANA there was one woman Abe Lincoln loved as much as his mother. It was his stepmother.

Thirteen months after the death of his first wife, Thomas Lincoln, unable to stand the loneliness of the dreary cabin any longer, returned to Kentucky seeking a wife and a mother for his children. His choice was Sally Bush Johnston, a widow with three children.

When the new Mrs. Lincoln and her children arrived at her new home in Indiana, she was horrified at the contrast between the glowing representations which her husband had made to her before leaving Kentucky and the real poverty and wilderness. She went to work immediately to make the place more comfortable and respectable.

Under her orders, Abe's father put down a floor, fixed windows and doors and used his considerable carpentry skills to make other improvements in the cabin. For the first time, historians say, Abe and his sister Sarah slept in warm beds, ate with knives and forks and had warm and clean clothes to wear.

The new Mrs. Lincoln had a great affection for Abe. She encouraged him in his studies and the time he spent at school was due to her. How Lincoln reacted to this affection can best be shown when he became a lawyer many years later in Springfield, Illinois. He had just won an important court case and was rewarded with a $500 fee. Lincoln told his friend, a judge, that he was going to take the money and purchase a quarter section of land and "settle it upon my old stepmother."

His friend then advised him, "Your stepmother is getting old and will probably not live many years. I would settle the property upon her for her use during her lifetime, to revert to you upon her death."

With much feeling, Lincoln replied, "I shall do no such thing. It is a poor return at best for all the good woman's devotion and fidelity to me, and there is not going to be any halfway business about it."

What did Abe's stepmother think of him? By today's standards, Abe Lincoln was almost too good to be true. She described his behavior this way: "He never drank whiskey or other strong drink, was temperate in all things. . . . He never told a lie. . . . He never swore or used profane language. . . . Abe was the best boy I ever saw or expect to see."

EVERY schoolboy has read that Abe Lincoln borrowed law books and heard outstanding lawyers plead their cases in court. (In those days it was considered excellent entertainment to go to court to hear legal oratory.)

There is no positive evidence that Lincoln made up his mind to be a lawyer while in Indiana. Abe did practice his oratory on members of the family and was involved in one court episode, "The Old Gray Goose Case."

Two of Lincoln's neighbors each had a flock of geese, the story goes, and one accused the other of swiping a goose. The dispute wound up in the local court. The lawyer for the defendant was unable to attend and Abe was asked to substitute. According to one version, he won the case. Another account is that the entire neighborhood packed the courtroom to hear the case. While waiting for the justice of the peace to arrive, Abe reportedly rose and made such an eloquent appeal that plaintiff and defendant were shaking hands before the justice of the peace arrived.

IT IS impossible, of course, to say what incident in Indiana made the most important contribution to the character of Lincoln. There is no question that Lincoln was molded by the hardship he had to endure, the books he read, the talks about politics at home in the evening by the fireside, the affection he had for his family and neighbors.

There is no question, either, that Lincoln gained much insight, knowledge and perspective because of a trip he made by flatboat down the Mississippi River to the gay and exciting city of New Orleans, Louisiana. James Gentry, owner of Gentry's Store, decided to send a flatboat to New Orleans and asked Abe, then twenty years old, to accompany Gentry's son Allen. Abe's salary was eight dollars a month plus his passage back by steamboat.

The two young men (Allen was a year or two older than Abe) loaded the boat with produce (corn, pork, hams, corn meal, chickens and oats). They took turns sleeping in the tiny cabin and manning the rudder. They drifted slowly on the placid Ohio River and later on the Mississippi River, swept along by strong currents. The distance from the cliffs of Rockport, Indiana, their starting point, to New Orleans by water, was 1,222 miles.

It was an exciting trip. They passed steamboats, saw flocks of wild turkeys along the shore and were impressed by the sunsets and the long stretches of forest. They looked at cotton crops and tobacco fields and sugar plantations and the city of Natchez, Mississippi.

One of the adventures the two boys were supposed to have encountered took place below Baton Rouge (Louisiana) as they were trying to trade much of their cargo for cotton, tobacco and sugar. They tied up their boat for the night near a plantation where they had been trading in the afternoon. Seven Negroes planned to overpower the two young men and rob the boat. According to the legend, both Abe and Allen were on guard, gave the would-be robbers a warm reception and drove them off the boat. Both boys were reported hurt and bore marks from the fight.

In New Orleans, Abe and Allen found themselves in an exotic city of 40,000 people, most of whom spoke only

French. They saw narrow streets, picturesque houses with projecting roofs, painted sides and windows and fancy iron grillwork. They also saw and felt mosquitoes.

This was the New Orleans of the public ball, which featured dances three or four times a week with beautiful girls known as quadroons. Their blood was a mixture of Indian, African and French.

It was here, too, that Abe Lincoln saw his first slave market and where Virginia slaves and North Carolina slaves were auctioned. The *New Orleans Argus* for December 17, 1828, advertised:

S L A V E S

29 young Virginia slaves of both sexes to
be sold cheap for cash

43 Virginia slaves, women, men, girls and
boys may be bartered for sugar or sold
on a liberal credit say for one or two
years on undoubted paper.

New Orleans was a flourishing town of commerce. Allen and Abe disposed of their cargo, sold their boat, which was no longer useful to them for the trip back, and went sightseeing.

It is possible they sampled some of the strange foods and went shopping in some of the stores. Years later, Allen recalled,

"We stood and watched the slaves sold in New Orleans and Abraham was very angry. . . ."

IT HAS been said that the spark of genius that enlightened Abraham Lincoln was within him during these impressionable years in Indiana, and that his mother nourished it, that his father cultivated it and that his stepmother encouraged it.

Louis A. Warren says Lincoln was Indiana's finest contribution to civilization and that it was in the near wilderness of Indiana that Lincoln first became "everywhere a favorite, always simple, genial, truthful and unpretending."

The Indiana of Abe Lincoln is still present. The people of southern Indiana now have TV, radio, electricity, farm-to-market roads and improved schools, but they still have the ancient customs, rich folklore and a hard-shell religion to discourage pessimism.

Readin', writin' and tellin' stories still are among the more appreciated ways of entertaining. There remains a rustic simplicity about many Hoosier areas. Even today it is possible for a youngster to motivate himself by hard work and sacrifice, by reading and dreaming. There are, perhaps, other places to learn self-reliance, but the opportunities peculiar to Indiana that Abraham Lincoln found are still there.

twelve

THE DREAMERS

Robert Owen had a theory that if you took a man away from the pressures of commercial competition and surrounded him with books, science, philosophy and flowers, you could eradicate selfishness, crime and evil from the earth.

—ROBERT C. RUARK

KARL MARX was a seven-year-old school boy in Germany in 1825 when Robert Owen tried his experiment in communism on the banks of the Wabash River at New Harmony, Indiana.

In Owen's utopia, everyone was equal. He dreamed of a heaven on earth, a paradise where life was all milk and honey, where there was no poverty, and no bills, and no anxieties over class distinction or riches, where the sick and the aged were cared for, where music and drama and literature enriched lives, where education and science changed a wicked world.

Before Marx even said it, Robert Owen practiced it. Each would give according to his abilities and each would take according to his needs. It was pure, unadulterated communism.

Members of Owen's New Harmony settlement shared

work, clothes, food, culture and education. The community was more important than the individual. Men labored in the fields or in the factories that manufactured soap and candles and clothes. Some women milked cows. Others worked in the laundry or the communal kitchen. Jobs were assigned not by preference, but by a committee which supervised the settlement. To keep everyone happy, there was planned activity at least three nights a week: concerts, dances, balls, dramatic presentations and general discussions.

Today in Indiana, labor unions are still viewed with suspicion, social welfare is labeled un-American and federal aid is considered degrading. But in the 1800's, Hoosiers considered the Owenites respectable. Hoosiers did not regard their communist neighbors as immoral or wicked. There was not the emotional hostility toward communism then, as has developed since totalitarian communism ruled the Soviet Union with an iron fist and exported it around the world.

The New Harmony experiment failed. How and why it failed are significant. What New Harmony gave Indiana, the United States and the world is precious and important. This is why today, even the most conservative elements in Indiana society, including the Colonial Dames, are active in trying to keep alive the New Harmony story.

ROBERT OWEN believed that if society were uncorrupted by the profit motive and other evils, man would become honorable and happy. He believed in the innate goodness of man. He was a restless, impatient and daring do-gooder who wanted to change the world.

When he was twelve years old in May 1781, he left home in Newton, Wales. His father, Robert Owen, a saddler, and his mother, Ann, pleaded with him to stay.

"But don't you see that I have to go," he replied. "I am finished here. . . ." With a total of forty shillings in his pocket, the boy, confident about the future, got a job in a retail store. He got board, lodging and laundry the first year, but no pay. The second year he received an annual salary of eight pounds, and the third year it was raised to ten pounds. What made it all seem worthwhile to Owen was a nearby library to which he had access.

When his three years were up, the employer was anxious for Robert Owen to remain, but he declined. He moved on to retail stores in London and Manchester. This was the extent of his training when he heard that a large cotton-spinning plant in England was in need of a superintendent. Owen had never before been inside such a plant. Nevertheless he applied for the job and convinced management to hire him. For the first six weeks he spent his time looking and developing the techniques which he was to use in improving the process for his employer and also in amassing the beginning of his own fortune.

In a matter of months the inexperienced Owen had become so valuable to the plant that the owner, a Mr. Drinkwater, took him into partnership. In the pamphlet *The New Harmony Story,* Don Blair gives this account of a momentous occasion in the life of the future philanthropist:

> Robert Owen was soon spending considerable time on the road in the interest of the firm. These trips often took him to Scotland and on one he meets Caroline Dale. With his usual ego, he said that Miss Dale fell in love with him at once, however, it was some time before he fell for her.
>
> Miss Dale confided to her friend, Miss Spear, that she was going to marry Owen, if anyone, this in spite of Robert Owen's not being a handsome man. Miss Spear plays Cupid and tells Owen of Caroline's confession. With this bit of information to encourage him, he asks Miss Dale to marry him. She agrees, but says she doubts that her father will share her enthusiasm.
>
> To overcome the idea that he might be marrying her for money and position, he raises capital in Manchester and buys the Dale Mills from Caroline's father. Now, having se-

cured the promise of the young lady, he lays siege to her father. Eventually, he convinces Mr. Dale that he is a good risk and receives his consent to the wedding.

As the owner of the mills, Robert Owen overnight became a controversial figure in New Lanark, Scotland. His business associates condemned him. The clergy preached against him. His own workers were suspicious. All because he raised wages, shortened hours, corrected abuses and elevated the living standard of the working man. He improved the lot of the children in the mills. He treated employees as human beings. He encouraged cleanliness of workers—in the plant and in their homes. He set up a system of gradually diminishing the work load of older workers, instead of pushing them to the limit and discarding them when worn out. He set up a drunk patrol to keep men sober. He had "silent monitors" to encourage workers to good conduct. He sought out the natural leaders of the workers (there were no unions in those days) and spent time with them to have things as pleasant as possible.

All employee suspicion and resistance to him vanished when the plant was forced to close because an American embargo cut off raw materials. In his most radical humanitarian effort, Owen paid the employees not for work, but to keep them from suffering because of the lack of money. When the workers realized Owen's generosity was not with an ulterior motive, he became extremely popular. He continued his philanthropy. He established an infant school, free to families of the employees.

Not only did he improve conditions of the workers, but as a reflection of this new spirit of harmony between management and labor, profits from his mills were greater than ever.

Owen's partners were not such humanitarians. They could not see that the greater profit flowed from the pleasant employer-employee relation. They believed that money which could have been theirs was being spent needlessly to improve the conditions of the working man. Secretly, they planned to take over the management themselves.

Owen was more than equal to the occasion. He had connections and sources of information. He had obtained enough money from interests in London who were excited about his humanitarian work as well as his providing good returns for money invested. He walked into the supposedly secret meeting and offered to buy out all of their interests. They gave in, stunned.

In complete control of the mills, Owen leased a twenty-four-room home called Braxfield House, where his seven children were born and grew up. The boys were educated at Hofoyl, Switzerland in the famous school of Pestalozzi. The Owen family lived happy, useful lives, helping others in New Lanark.

Into their lives came Richard Flower with glowing stories of America, the new land of freedom and a community then called Harmonie, a settlement of 20,000 acres of first-rate land in the wilderness of Indiana. Flower, who came from Albion, Illinois, had been commissioned to sell Harmonie, which had farmland, orchards, warehouses, granaries, brick homes and log homes, factories and barns.

It would be an ideal place, thought Robert Owen, to start a new society, based on community ownership and equality of work and profit. He decided almost immediately to go to America with his son William to see for himself what Harmonie was, how it started and what could be done there to start changing the world.

The promised land was bought ready-made by Robert Owen from the followers of George Rapp. It cost Owen $200,000 of his fortune of $250,000, a not-inconsiderable sum in those days. Included in the purchase price were nineteen farms, eighteen acres of bearing vines, the village of Harmonie with its great church, its brick, frame and log houses, its factories, with almost all of the machinery.

On dormitory No. 2, which was built for unmarried men

and was later used as a community center, this message was chalked: "In the 24th of May 1824, we have departed. Lord, with Thy great help and goodness, in body and soul protect us."

The Rappites were leaving because they couldn't stand prosperity. In their ten years at Harmonie, they turned a wilderness into a civilized community. They came to America from Württemberg, Germany to be free to worship God as they saw fit. They wanted a place where they could practice their religious beliefs unmolested by the established churches.

The group's every action was dictated by the religion founded by Father George Rapp, a 6-foot German with a flowing beard. The Rappites believed in the imminent second coming of Christ and made all preparations for it. They expected the end of the world and made preparations for it. Father Rapp encouraged his followers to practice celibacy, since it would be folly to bear children with the end of the world at hand. The Rappites were led from the Lutheran Church in Germany because Father Rapp and others felt the church had lost sight of the significance of the religious ceremonies and that too much importance was placed on the act rather than on the meaning. It disturbed Father Rapp particularly that children thought more of the clothes they wore at confirmation than they did of the meaning of the ceremony.

Accustomed to hard work, privation and rigid discipline, the Rappites thrived in America. It seemed, to them, a haven to have Father Rapp take the responsibility to provide food and clothing and lodging in return for their work. The Rappites had no worries or anxieties, because Father Rapp took care of everything.

When their colony flourished, and some of the work slackened, they grew restless. Father Rapp worried. Life was getting to be easy and quiet, with leisure for thought. Father Rapp found it difficult to keep his people in order, except during the intense sunup to sundown hard work of starting a new settlement. He feared idleness would bring discord. He decided to sell the successful community and move to Pennsylvania, where the Rappites could busy themselves building a new settlement.

KARL MARX and Frederich Engels were impressed with the social-welfare achievements of Robert Owen. "Every social movement, every real advance in England on behalf of the workers, links itself on to the name of Robert Owen," Engels once wrote. Twenty-three years before Marx and Engels published their *Communist Manifesto,* Robert Owen began his experiment in communism at New Harmony. Marx and Engels studied what he did there and what he said. Upon arriving in America, Robert Owen declared:

> My purpose is to commence a new empire of peace and good will to men. I am come to this country to introduce a new state of society, to change it from an ignorant, selfish system to an enlightened social system which shall gradually unite all interests into one, and remove all causes for contests between individuals.

In the rude wilderness, on the Indiana side of the Wabash River, in the deserted Rappite settlement, Robert Owen brought his dream, a community of equality. He saw his experiment as an adventure in happiness, a lesson in human harmony for all the world, where there would be no more weeping over poverty and no more pride over wealth. It was to be a sort of Garden of Eden.

One other dreamer joined Owen—William Maclure, a wealthy and brilliant Scottish scientist with a passionate desire to educate the world. Maclure believed educational excellence was the key to changing the world. His avowed intention was to make New Harmony the center of American education and scientific exploration, and for a time he did.

With the assistance of Robert Owen, he brought to New

Harmony the most distinguished coterie of scientists, educators, artists and musicians in America. Among them were Thomas Say, father of American Zoology; Charles Alexander Lesueur, the first to explore and publish an account of the mounds found in Indiana; Constantine Samuel Raffinesque, first teacher of natural history in the West; Dr. Gerard Troost, a Holland geologist; John Chappelsmith, a wealthy English artist and engraver; and a flock of teachers from Europe, including Professor Joseph Neef, Madame Marie D. Frotageot and Phiquepal d'Arusmont.

The party of forty-three educators, scientists, musicians, writers and artists embarked for New Harmony from Pittsburgh in a keel boat. It became famous as "The Boatload of Knowledge." With such talent, could such a noble project fail?

New Harmony became the rendezvous of enlightened and progressive people from all over the United States and northern Europe. Sprinkled among them, however, were the cranks, the crackpots, the curiosity seekers and the drifters and those attracted by the prospect of life without work.

In old age, in sickness, or when an accident occurred, a member was cared for "with kindness." Each member could draw a fixed amount of clothing from the general store. Women, for the first time treated as equals with men, formed their own women's club. A dramatic club and a band were organized.

Robert Owen turned his community over to a committee to run. The committee decided which people would work at which jobs. Some men worked in the fields, some in factories. Women were also assigned "equal" duties. The family must give way to the community, Owen declared, and children were placed in boarding school away from their parents to be indoctrinated in the new philosophy. Evening school was started for adults. Before long, the dances, balls, concerts and dramatic presentations were taking place. Members ate, not at home, but in a communal dining room served by a communal kitchen.

Life was exciting, gay and interesting—for a time.

THOMAS PEARS, a naturalist, was a resident of Pittsburgh, Pennsylvania when he decided to join in the social experiment of Robert Owen. His wife was Sarah Palmer, daughter of a Birmingham, England minister.

Their letters to friends and relatives gave a realistic picture of the life and times of the New Harmony colony.

"We arrived at New Harmony after a most fatiguing and disagreeable journey from Mount Vernon (Indiana)," Mrs. Pears wrote to a friend. "The roads were terrible, and though the distance is but sixteen miles, it was many days before we recovered from the effects of our ride."

Discord at New Harmony was first recorded as early as September 3, 1825 in a letter from Thomas Pears to a friend in Pittsburgh: "The idle and the industrious are neither of them satisfied. The one contending that they do enough for their allowance, and the other thinking themselves entitled to more."

There was despair mingled with hope in another Thomas Pears letter later the same month: ". . . we have not yet done with scandal, calumny, nor self-interest, nor the love of power or distinction; and tho' I expect we shall ultimately succeed, yet the time will be longer than I wish."

Hopes of betterment at New Harmony with Robert Owen's expected return were expressed in the fall of 1825 in letters both to and from that place. Owen had gone to England to bring back members of his family and additional settlers, and to make more speeches along the way about the new social order.

Mrs. Pears was unimpressed with events at New Harmony even after Owen returned with the brilliant array of educators, scientists, artists and musicians on the Boatload of Knowledge.

"Oh, if you could see some of the rough, uncouth creatures here, I think you would find it rather hard to look upon them exactly in the light of brothers and sisters," she wrote to a relative.

The depths of Mrs. Pears' unhappiness, however, did not come through until March 10, 1826, when she wrote:

> . . . all our elder children, those whom we expected to be comfort and consolation and support in our old age, are to be taken away from us at an age, too, when they so peculiarly require the guardian care of their parents; and are to be placed in boarding houses. The single males and females above the age of fourteen are to live together in one house, over which there is to be one married woman to superintend.
>
> Instead of our own dear children each housekeeper is to receive two more families, one of which will have a child under two years old. The rest will be at boarding school. These three families are each to live in community and take the cooking by turns. . . .
>
> . . . Instead of four or five hours' labor being sufficient for one's maintenance, as people were led to imagine by Mr. Owen's representations, the bell is now rung at half-past five to get up; at six to go to work; at seven for breakfast; at eight for work again; at twelve for dinner; at one to go to work; at six in the evening to return home. If those who are regularly employed are not punctual, they are liable to be reported at the nightly meeting of the intendants. If they are sick, they must have a certificate from a physician. If this is not slavery I know not what is.

As a communist colony, New Harmony lasted only four years. It failed for a variety of reasons, but principally because human nature had not yet advanced to the unselfish ideals of Robert Owen, if ever it could. There were other reasons. Skilled men were needed and the unskilled came.

There was a theory, too, that if a woman worked in the fields all day she would feel strong, vibrant, resolute, alive, significant and happy working side-by-side with her menfolk, singing with them, and eating bread and cheese under the hedge with them. It did not turn out that way at New Harmony. The women wanted to stay home and care for their children. They wanted to be mothers and wives, not workers.

Too many of the settlers who came were cultivated ladies and gentlemen, scholars and artists and musicians, perhaps, but unsuited to the rigors of the wilderness. Another problem was that Robert Owen himself did not stay around long enough to make New Harmony work. Then, too, far too many had come for a free ride.

Owen saw his experiment as an adventure in happiness, but it lacked a precious ingredient—the family. Under the spartan system of education set up by Maclure, the infant was surrendered to the community as soon as he could be safely taken from the arms of the mother who bore him. Maclure wanted the government to be mother and father to the child, as if a bureaucracy could replace flesh and blood and tender, loving care.

With all of its faults, with all of its hardships, with all of its failures, and as inconsistent as it sounds, New Harmony was a spectacular success. Free public schools became a tradition there, as well as free public libraries. The first infant school, the first kindergarten and the first trade school in America were established there, as well as the first night school for adults. Whether they wanted to or not, women were treated—and educated—as equals. America's first dramatic club was located there.

Out of all proportion to its size, New Harmony had a significant cultural and educational influence on the state, the nation and the world. Owen's followers and his own children were in the forefront of the fight for social progress. They were reformers, liberty-lovers, humanitarians. His sons became statesmen, diplomats, educators, philosophers, scientists.

One son, Robert Dale Owen, more than anyone else, influenced President Abraham Lincoln to free the slaves. He had sent Lincoln a letter urging the President to issue a proclamation emancipating slaves of the South. Lincoln said of the letter, "Its perusal stirred me like a trumpet call." Secretary of the Treasury Salmon P. Chase said Owen's letter had "more influence upon Lincoln than any other document . . . than all others put together." Five days later, Lincoln freed the slaves.

There is a statue of Robert Dale Owen on a pedestal about thirty feet from the south entrance of the Statehouse in Indianapolis. It was put there, not for his antislavery work, but for his tremendous and ceaseless activity to emancipate the American woman.

thirteen

INDIANA, THE BEAUTIFUL

*I am a native Hoosier, and the lakes and streams
and hills of Indiana early brought to the boy I
used to be, courage to carry on through all the
years.*

—SAMUEL A. HARPER

ON DECEMBER 3, 1962 in the late sports and
stocks edition of the *Indianapolis Times* this headline story
splashed across eight columns of the front page:

BETHLEHEM STEEL WILL BUILD
$250 MILLION PLANT AT DUNES

By John V. Wilson

Bethlehem Steel Co. will spend $250 million to build a
new steel plant in Porter County, making Indiana the largest
steel-producing center in the world, Governor Matthew
Welsh announced this afternoon.

Welsh said the huge project will insure Indiana's plans
to construct a deep-water harbor on Lake Michigan at Burns
Ditch.

This industrialization—so eagerly coveted by huge steel
companies, utilities, industries and railroads, and so fanati-
cally promoted by powerful politicians—is the beginning of

280

the end for the last four miles of Indiana's irreplaceable scientific and recreational treasure, the sun-seared sand slopes shimmering along the south rim of Lake Michigan.

This paradise is called The Dunes. There sun-bleached beaches rise in sloping deserts, their sandy sweeps broken only by clumps of bright green marram grass. Wind currents and waves erode shores far to the north, grind this into sand and eventually cast it up on the Indiana shore. It is one of the unique formations in America, an area of startling beauty, majestic serenity and spectacular resources.

Richard Lewis described it so:

> The inland slopes, where sand devils swirl on a summer afternoon in a wind as hot as the breath of a blast furnace, are studded with prickly pear cactus of the American Southwest. These fall to a brief tundra, covered with the sub-Arctic Bearberry.
>
> Then the land rises to become a piney woods where the air is cool and scented. The pineland merges into an oak forest. The forest becomes a prairie. And the prairie dips to a moist, quaking bog of paleozoic ferns, wild grape and dogwood.
>
> The wildly varied scene is the product of a thousand summers. It is a landscape constantly in motion, for the dunes move under the pressure of the winds blowing down the bore of the lake. From one decade to the next, the dunescape is never quite the same.

As a city boy, on my first visit to the dunes, I was struck by the brilliance of the sky. It was so light the white sand shone at night. Part of it, of course, was the absence of any other light. But the biggest element was the fact that the air was clean—the eternal blanket of airborne filth that hovers over all of our cities was not there, and heaven itself seemed to be celebrating.

Over the outraged protests of conservationists, there has been a relentless erosion of the dunes, which originally had stretched twenty-five miles between Gary and Michigan City. Less than four miles of undeveloped frontage remains today, in addition to the state-owned Indiana Dunes State Park, which covers about two and a half miles of lakefront.

Between the dune ridges, bodies of water have been trapped, forming ponds, lakes and swamps. Directly in the migratory path of many birds, bobwhite and chickadee, warblers and white-throated sparrows, scarlet tanagers and herring gulls and a hundred others find a retreat among the old pines and oaks and maples. More than a thousand species of plants and trees thrive in dunelands. The wild flowers include twenty-six members of the orchid family. In the fertile forests, foxes, deer, coons, beavers, skunks, squirrels, chipmunks, dragonflies, fireflies and turtles find sanctuary, even as humans do.

This is a land worshiped by nature-lovers and cherished by botanists, zoologists, geologists and ornithologists.

Phillip Kingsley captured the spirit and historical significance of the dunes in this article:

It is a place unspoiled. The trail winds by a great swamp where cattails abound, and along the Indian portage, where the Iroquois once marched to attack the Wisconsin Foxes. It passes the big pines and the so-called big blowout, where the sand has formed a great amphitheater, the graveyard of trees that flourished centuries ago, and comes at last to Paradise valley.

There one may hear the weeping of the Indian maiden Taheta, whose lover was lost on a buffalo hunt, and hear the march of the feet of the soldiers of the American revolution, who came this way to hold the Little Fort by the sandhill against the British in 1780. There the song of the French fur traders was heard, and the more important voices of the pioneers who came to establish the frontier of the new Northwest Territory, out of which our present liberties sprang.

There is a "Save the Dunes" movement, which bravely fights against overwhelming odds to conserve every acre of precious duneland. But it is a losing fight. An imposing array of powerful politicians in both parties have conspired to industrialize the area and plant a port there.

Among the Democrats were Governor Matthew Welsh and his administrative assistant Clinton Green, who spent virtually all of his time promoting the port. Aiding and assisting was Frank McKinney, a powerful financial figure and director of the New York Central Railroad, which sought to lease and operate railroads and warehouses within the port area.

In the Republican Party, the port promoters were ex-Governor George N. Craig, who now represents a contractor interested in bidding on the project; former Governor Harold Handley, who is on especially friendly terms with steel companies in the area, and who threw the full weight of his administration behind the port; John Van Ness, former State Senator of Valparaiso, a prime mover in the Legislature on the port. The latter became chairman of the State Public Service Commission and resigned to become assistant to the president of Midwest Steel, which has a plant in the port-project area.

Former Senator William E. Jenner organized the St. Lawrence Seaway Corporation to speculate in land areas influenced by the completion of the St. Lawrence Seaway, which he bitterly opposed on the floor of the United States Senate. The prospectus of the Jenner company specifically mentioned the proposed Indiana port, and its directors included Robert W. Matthews, then GOP chairman; Ivan H. (Jack) Morgan, then Ninth District GOP chairman, and George W. Stark, treasurer of the GOP state committee at the time.

There are also hundreds of thousands of Hoosiers—some unknowingly and some unwillingly—helping to build the port and industrialize the dunes area. They are the taxpayers of Indiana. In the dying hours of the 1957 session of the State Legislature, the lawmakers appropriated $2 million from the state's general fund for the purchase of a site for a public port. At the time, State Representative John F. Shawley (R., Michi-

gan City) raised a voice of protest. He said the public aspect
of the harbor was dubious because the site was entirely surrounded by land owned by Bethlehem, Midwest Steel and
the New York Central system.

The "Save the Dunes" Council said it was shocked that
public funds were used for a harbor of principal benefit to a
few private interests.

Every Governor since George Craig has stressed that the
port would be an economic boon to the state, that prosperity
would filter down from Lake Michigan to the Ohio River.
Others interested in the industrialization of the dunes have
been inclined to dismiss the "Save the Dunes" people as a
bunch of bird-watching dodos and the sand dunes as a gritty
wasteland.

Carl Sandburg was on the other side. About the sand
dunes, he wrote: "They represent the signature of time and
eternity. Their loss would be irrevocable." Senator Paul
Douglas of Illinois, the only major politician publicly opposing the port, wants to make a national park of the area.

In his book *A Hoosier Tramp,* Samuel A. Harper tells
how he felt when he first sighted the dunes:

> Standing on the beach, with the great waters stretching
> far to the north, the long shoreline curving away in the mid-
> distance, and the sandhills tumbling up against the southern
> sky, one feels an emancipation of spirit which suddenly and
> involuntarily expands his chest, straightens his shoulders
> and raises his forehead to the sky. It is an untouched, un-
> spoiled and solitary place where the tired heart may find
> peace.

But probably not for long.

ON MAY 1, 1816, when James Madison, fourth President of
the United States, issued a proclamation announcing that
"certain lands in the Indiana territory" would be offered for
sale to the highest bidder, Hoosierland was the frontier.

Pioneering was a life of few comforts, rare pleasure, great drudgery, much sickness. Hard as it was, the pioneer welcomed winter, for it meant the Indians would hole up. Roads were few—choked with dust in summer, impassable in winter.

The settlers came from the East and the South, over the mountains, or down the rivers, across forests and prairies covered with head-high grass. Who could blame them if they didn't take time to appreciate the deep woods of Brown County, the charm of the "singing sand dunes," the beauty of the Ohio River?

They were too busy cutting trees, clearing brush, building cabins, uprooting stumps, plowing the earth and gathering their crops. In time, they noticed the brooks, the sun-splashed streams, the green meadows, the banks of the Wabash, the sandy beaches, the hills covered with a riot of wild flowers. Perhaps they didn't begin fully to appreciate them until the great industrial cities started to overshadow everything and unspoiled vacant land vanished at an alarming rate.

THERE is something about Brown County, that wilderness in the hills of southern Indiana, that makes it exceedingly difficult to concentrate on the rest of the world.

There is always the gurgle of Gnaw Bone Creek, always the gentle rustle in the trees, always the birds to flit and whistle, always a log cabin in sight, some still lighted by coal lamps and with wood-burning stoves to cook on, always the peace and quiet of this rustic range of rugged, wooded hills, where life's tempo is slow and easy. Even the hamlets of Bean Blossom, Greasy Creek and Stone Head divert you from serious meditation.

Deep in wooded hills it is still possible to find deer, coyotes, badgers, opossums, owls, hawks, ferrets, foxes and even bears.

One of the most famous art colonies in the United States is situated in Nashville, Indiana in the heart of Brown

County, surrounded by authentic sights and sounds and smells of a bygone era. Because some of the loveliest scenery is here, the town is a mecca for painters, photographers and tourists. Along the street you can buy bittersweet, sassafras root, berries and nuts, pails of maple syrup and wild flowers.

By auto and by bus, thousands of people weary of the hustle and bustle of the cities come to Brown County to relax, escape the tension and recharge their spiritual batteries. They find slopes too steep for cultivation and a wilderness of hills and valleys, jumbled and heavily foliaged.

The natural beauty of Brown County is said to have inspired Bill Herschell, with a touch of James Whitcomb Riley in his pen, to write this poem:

> *Ain't God good to Indiana?*
> *Folks, a feller never knows*
> *Just how close he is to Eden*
> *Till, sometimes, he ups and goes*
> *Seekin' fairer, greener pastures*
> *Than he has right here at home*
> *Where there's sunshine in the clover*
> *An' there's honey in the comb:*
> *Where th' ripples on th' river*
> *Kind o' chuckle as they flow;*
> *Ain't God good to Indiana?*
> *Ain't He, fellers? Ain't He, though?*

Natives of Brown County say it is lovely in the springtime, cool in summer, gorgeous in autumn and cozy in winter.

Here you will find one of the few old covered bridges (just below Bean Blossom Overlook, three miles north of Nashville on a county road), an old log jail, and a "liar's bench" on the old courthouse lawn and, here and there, a primitive log cabin that survived modern improvements.

The spirit and atmosphere deliberately have been preserved by the people of Brown County, although modern and expensive ranch-style homes are being built all over the area.

Nowhere is the spectacular beauty of the area more apparent than in Brown County State Park, a retreat for city folks who can, in rustic simplicity, fish, swim, ride horses, and hike along foot trails used years ago by the Indians.

Margaret Wyatt, editor and owner of the *Brown County Democrat,* published a paragraph about the surroundings by an unknown writer who wrote:

> As you enjoy the scenic splendor, you may, unconscious of the fact, be led along some valley road of enchantment, near the close of day. Suddenly you glimpse a silvery crescent in the western sky, symbolic of what is in store for you—the beginning of a glorious life that is to be well filled.

Certainly Brown County is a place for artists and writers and poets. Who among us is not one—at least in heart?

SOUTH of Brown County, along quiet, scenic Indiana State Highway 135, you pass Salem, Palmyra and the old state capital at Corydon, and then Mauckport, where for generations people crossed the Ohio River by ferry.

Further west on the winding Ohio River, opposite the mouth of the Anderson River, Abraham Lincoln's family crossed from Kentucky into Indiana near Troy. Although they had only sixteen more miles to go, the most difficult part of the journey still faced the Lincoln family to reach Hurricane Township of Perry County.

(In 1818, the General Assembly voted to divide the counties of Perry and Warwick and create a new county to be called Spencer after Spier Spencer, who had lost his life at the Battle of Tippecanoe. The county seat was established at Rockport on the Ohio River. The Lincoln farm now lay within the bounds of Spencer County, in Carter Township.)

There are paved roads now, but then Abe Lincoln's father had to "cut his way to his farm with an ax, felling the trees as he went." Then the area was a dense thicket covered with heavy timber. It was described as having oaks, beeches, ash, three kinds of nut trees, gum trees, hackberry, sycamore, persimmons, wild cherries, apples, plums and wild-grape vines.

This is Lincolnland.

Abe's mother is buried there in the Lincoln State Park and there is Lincoln memorabilia from which one can gather eyewitness impressions as to how this poverty-burdened family lived. Here is where Abe went to school, went to church, tramped in the woods, piloted a ferry across the Ohio.

Fourteen years later, when the Lincolns eventually moved to Illinois, they went by what was then a well-traveled log road—The Old Buffalo Trail—through Vincennes, crossing the Wabash River there. (The Old Buffalo Trail is now U.S. 50, a well-known East-West route.)

Charles W. White, a Hoosier writer, describes some of the charm of Southern Indiana:

> Corydon has its famous old State Capitol building where one can see the legislative chamber and many of the articles our pioneer legislators used. Over at Vincennes, one can go even further back in Hoosier history than that, visiting "Grouseland," the fascinating home of William Henry Harrison, the ex-Virginian who was Indiana's first territorial governor. (You'll enjoy examining a hole in the window, where angry Indians tried to shoot the Governor, or looking at the secret staircase built to escape possible Indian raids.) And Vincennes, of course, is the site of a famous Revolutionary War event, the storming of Fort Sackville by George Rogers Clark and his men, commemorated, now, by a beautiful Federal Memorial and Museum.

YOU CAN still see virgin forests, river valleys and lakes in Indiana. There is marvelous hill country in the southeastern Whitewater Valley. Every lover of rural scenery should visit

Owen County, west of Bloomington, called "Sweet Owen" by its residents. Indiana has some of the most beautiful state parks in the country, especially Spring Mill, Turkey Run and Clifty Falls.

The real wealth of Indiana's countryside, though, is in its fine farms, with their cattle, and (in central Indiana) some of the best cornland in the world. Big barns, well-painted houses and thriving livestock tell their own story.

In the early days of Indiana, you had a fine cabin if you could build a fine cabin. You had a well-stocked farm if you were a good farmer and industrious. You were not chased off your land by Indians if you organized with your neighbors into a militia.

It was more than a survival of the fittest in a constant battle against hardship and privation. It was rugged individualism, plus just enough cooperation when the elements (or the Indians) proved too formidable. The doctor would go by horseback to visit the sick and return home to his plow. The teacher would go straight from his class to the fields. The minister, the lawyer and the judge knew the meaning of hard, common labor. There were no hired hands. It was every man for himself.

R. Carlyle Buley, Pulitzer Prize-winning historian of Indiana University, had the mood of the times when he wrote about those big, dark woods of Indiana:

> Equality was not a theory or a creed; it was merely a natural circumstance. Nature is a great leveler and no respecter of persons. Before her the individual pioneer was just as good as his right arm, keen-sighting eye, and constitutional resistance to her vapors and pests.

Down through the years, men have referred to the forests and fields of Indiana as "the fields of enterprise, the cradle of freedom, the land of rest to the weary, the place of refuge to the oppressed."

With some unrestrained, but perhaps typical Hoosier pride, Sarah T. Bolton wrote:

> *The winds of heaven never fanned*
> *The circling sunlight never spanned*
> *The borders of a better land*
> *Than our own Indiana.*

◆══◆ *fourteen* *◆══◆*

A FINAL WORD

Discontent is the first step in the progress of a man or a nation.

—OSCAR WILDE

INDIANA is more than a state. It's a state of mind, a sense of belonging, a pride in being part of something permanent and substantial. There's elbow room, where you can move around, breathe and relax. It's a place where you can fight City Hall—and win. It's a feeling of independence.

Indiana is many things: the deep woods of Brown County; the lush, undulating farmland of Carroll County; the oval racetrack at Indianapolis, with Rodger Ward roaring by, and a farmboy in Milan throwing a basketball at a hoop attached to the side of a barn; the factories at Anderson and Muncie, and the thousands of autos belonging to workers in the plant parking lots; the banks of the Wabash and the beautiful Ohio River.

Even the people are different in Indiana. They may look and talk like rustics from the backwoods, but this is a glorious fake. They are country smart and their kids are university educated. They go places and do things—and can't wait to get back home in Indiana. A Hoosier likes to be one of the folks, and when he and his neighbors get together late at night, there is a much better chance you will hear "barber shop harmony" than the latest song hits. There is little pretense among Hoosiers and comparatively little of the intense, second-by-second financial sharpshooting for business advantage. And less than you might expect of the sophisticated struggle in the society jungle. By New York, Chicago, Los Angeles, Detroit and Boston standards, Hoosiers have an ambition deficiency. They save their competitive fire for sports, which is fun, and politics, which to them is also a game. Dennis Hanks, cousin of Abraham Lincoln, said, "We lived the same as the Indians, 'ceptin' we took an interest in politics and religion."

Generally speaking, Hoosiers have learned the value of the simple things in life. They are in no great rush and are not overawed by wealth, position or prestige. Hoosiers may live in the present and plan for the future, but they jealously guard the past. They are born with memories. They care. They have a provincial sense of history and it matters to them, for example, that the capital city of Indiana was patterned after Washington, D.C. by surveyor Alexander Ralston and named Indianapolis by Jeremiah Sullivan of Madison. (It looked for a while as if the city would be called Tecumseh in honor of the great Indian leader who fought the advancement of the white people into Indiana until defeated in the battle of Tippecanoe.)

Indianapolis is like a museum, or a fair, exhibiting samples of the Hoosier culture. It belongs to the housewife in Dana, the farmer in Benton County, the lawyer in Paoli and the factory worker in Kokomo. So do the State Fair, and the Governor's Mansion and, more than anything else, Indiana University and Purdue. The farmer in Floyd County has as much pride in state-owned Purdue as the youngster who attends. Ever since he became a father, the Fort Wayne grocer has been pointing his son toward Indiana University. Hoosiers who never have set foot in Purdue or Indiana feel instinctively that the schools belong to them.

Whereas many states are nothing but a conglomeration of cities and towns and rural areas loosely tied together by state officials for administrative purposes, Indiana has an entity. It is almost as if Indiana had a fence around it and different customs and traditions than the rest of the country.

Some Hoosiers, perhaps, are still pushovers for peddlers of hate like the Ku Klux Klan and other extremist groups. In their naïve simplicity, many simply cannot accept the fact that the world was not made exclusively by or for Hoosiers. They are too ready to suspect the enemy is in Washington, D.C. and not in Moscow. They have a tendency to blame their leaders because of their own discontents—high taxes, the draft, the United Nations, and organized labor.

Understandably enough, many Hoosiers don't want to live in the world as it is, but in a world of their own, perhaps as James Whitcomb Riley and Booth Tarkington had pictured it—isolated from war, threats of war, Hell Bombs, strangers and foreigners. But the old confident basis of isolationism—"We don't care what you do as long as you don't bother us"—is passing with each drift of atomic dust over Indiana skies.

There is a new breed of Hoosier today. He is the descendant of an old poineer family, perhaps, like industrialist J. Irwin Miller of Columbus (Indiana), president of the National Council of Churches, or a minister like the Reverend James Armstrong of Broadway Methodist Church in Indianapolis. He might be the editor of a Catholic newspaper, the *Criterion,* like Father Raymond T. Bosler, or it might be Johnny-Come-Latelys like Robert Gamble of WFBM-TV and Editor Thomas L. Boardman of the *Indianapolis Times* and Publisher John A. Scott of the *Lafayette Journal & Courier.* It might even be an articulate and enlightened politician like Governor Matthew Welsh. Each, in his own way, and with hundreds of college professors and clergymen of all faiths, is bringing, as they say, Indiana back into the union.

The jet, the train, the auto and the motor truck have

diminished distance, but it remains for the new breed of Hoosier (with an assist from newspapers and television) to flatten out regional differences and replace the rural folkways.

FOR A boy who was one of the faceless millions on the sidewalks of New York City, living in Indiana has made me somebody. I'm a Hoosier. I belong. No matter what happens now, no matter where I roam, I can take pride in being a Hoosier and sharing with other Hoosiers the folklore of Indiana and crying in my beer about the new-mown hay and the candlelights gleaming through the sycamores.

Whether I really belong or not, whether I am really a Hoosier is beside the point. I think I am. I feel it. Not everyone shares this feeling, however.

When former Governor George N. Craig became impatient with me (and my column of political items), he said, "This is the first time a transient ever came to Indiana and tried to kick out a native son."

Thomas McNulty, an old-time Indiana lawyer and politician, once told me the story of a Boston bank. Stockholders of the bank were voting for a new director. There were 150 Irish stockholders and only three Jewish stockholders. An Irishman was nominated and a Jew was nominated. The Irishman won by 150 to 3. As they went out the door, Pat turned to Mike and said, "And did ye notice how those damn Jews stick together?"

I have tried to write the story of Indiana the way I saw it. I did not aim to glorify or criticize it, only to interpret and try to understand it. Nor did I attempt a complete work on Indiana or even a short, informal history. This book is not history, but one man's interpretive (and prejudiced) look at Indiana.

This is my Indiana—the good men and the wicked men, the good places and the bad places. It is, with good and bad, the heartland of America, with its pride, its prejudices and its passions.

Here are proud people with the fire of protest in their hearts. And pleasant, easy-going, confident people who are simple and shrewd—full of noisy provincial patriotism, perhaps—but ruggedly independent.

This is where the livin' is easy. I love it. I never had it so good.

A NOTE ABOUT SOURCES

MUCH of this book is either direct evidence picked up by my own eyes or ears, or from trusted friends by word-of-mouth.

Yet it was necessary for me to read a good deal of history and commentary.

This book never could have been written without the help and advice of Hubert Hawkins of the Indiana Historical Society and James Farmer of the Indiana State Chamber of Commerce. Or without the inspiration of my friend James Francis Rourke and the patience of my wife Plum. I never would have attempted it at all were it not for the three editors of the *Indianapolis Times* in my time: Walter Leckrone, Richard D. Peters (now editor of the *New York World Telegram & Sun*) and Thomas L. Boardman. They guided me, elevated my sights and, good or bad, made me what I am today.

The book I found most useful in research was *Indiana: An Interpretation* (Knopf) by John Bartlow Martin, one of America's great reporters.

Source of material used in preparation of this book included the following books: *The Cross-Examination of Witnesses* (Bobbs-Merrill) by Asher L. Cornelius; *500 Miles to Go* (Coward-McCann) by Al Bloemker; *A Hoosier Holiday* (Little & Ives) by Theodore Dreiser; *Dateline: Indiana* (Indianapolis Press Club); *Cross-Currents* (Doubleday) by Arnold Forster and Benjamin R. Epstein; *The Heartland: Ohio, Indiana, Illinois* (Harper & Row) by Walter Havighurst; *A History of Indiana Literature* (Indiana Historical Society) by Arthur W. Shumaker; *Indiana Authors and Their Books* (Wabash College) by R. E. Banta; *New Harmony Papers of Thomas and Sarah Pears* (Indiana Historical Society) edited by Thomas Clinton Pears, Jr.; *The New Harmony Movement* (Appleton) by George B. Lockwood; *The Hoosiers* (Macmillan) by Meredith Nicholson; *A Hoosier Tramp* (The Prairie Club) by Samuel A. Harper; *Lincoln's Youth: Indiana Years* (Indiana Historical Society) by Louis A. Warren; *A History of the American Legion* (Bobbs-Merrill) by Richard Seelye Jones; *Indiana: A Guide to the Hoosier State* (Oxford University Press) by WPA writers; and *Hoosier Caravan* (Indiana University Press) by R. E. Banta.

Many people encouraged and helped me in the preparation of this book, including John V. Wilson, Ted Knap, Olive Hoffman and Robert Bloem. I interviewed and talked for hours with William E. Jenner, Frank McHale, Lisle Wallace, Carl Dortch, Asa J. Smith, Harold C. Feightner and Jack Cejnar. Hundreds of other generous people helped me, including Earl Hoff of Indiana University and the staffs of Notre Dame and Purdue.

I want to thank them all and, at the same time, point out that nobody but me is responsible for the mistakes, faulty judgments, factual errors, prejudices and lopsided opinions.

INDEX